Privateer Press Presents

PRIMAL

CREDITS

The Creators of the Iron Kingdoms
Brian Snoddy
Matt Wilson

Creative Director
Matt Wilson

Managing Editor
Bryan Cutler

Game Creation and Design
Matt Wilson

Lead Developer
Jason Soles

Art Direction
James Davis

Rules Development
Rob Stoddard ¤

Fiction
Doug Seacat †

Painting Guide
Mike McVey

Continuity
Jason Soles ¤

Editors
Kevin Clark † ¤
Lauren Cutler
Andrew Daniels

Cover Art
Matt Wilson

Illustrations
Andrew Arconti
Daren Bader
Matt Dixon
Mark Gibbons
Daryl Mandryk
Karl Richardson
Brian Snoddy
Mattias Snygg
Keith Thompson
Eva Widermann
Matt Wilson

Lead Concept Artist
Matt Wilson

Additional Concept Art
Brian Snoddy
Keith Thompson
Sam Wood

Cartographer
Pierre-Alexandre Xavier

Graphic Design
James Davis
Josh Manderville

Layout
Bryan Cutler
James Davis
Josh Manderville

HORDES Logo
Brian Despain
Matt Wilson

Miniatures Direction
Mike McVey

Sculpting
Adam Clarke
Gregory Clavilier
Jason Hendricks
Bobby Jackson
Werner Klocke
Victor Martins
Mike McVey
Jerzy Montwill
Paul Muller
Felix Paniagua
Edgar Ramos
Jose Roig
Steve Saunders
Ben Seins
Dominique Seyes
Jason Weibe
Kev White
Jeff Wilhelm

Miniature Painting
Ron Kruzie
Alison McVey
Mike McVey

Terrain
Alfonso Falco

Photography
Bryan Cutler
James Davis
Mike McVey

President
Sherry Yeary

Office Administrator
Marky Erhardt †

Convention/Front Office Manager
Erik Breidenstein †

Customer Service
Erik Fleuter †

NQM EIC/Marketing Manager
Duncan Huffman † ¤

Press Gang Quartermaster
Dan Brandt †

Production Manager
Mark Christensen †

Administrative Assistant
James Kerr

Technical Director
Kelly Yeager

Mold Making
Alex Badion † ¤
Ben Tracy
Tom Williamson
Allen Wright †

Casting Manager
Doug Colton

Casting
Nick Berk-Sohn †
Brandon Burton
Alex Chobot ¤
Tony Crawford
Steve Kanick
Bradford Lannon ¤
Nym Penga
Jon Rodriguez
Scott Sollars ¤
Seth Taylor ¤
Jeff Thomas ¤

Shipping and Packing Manager
Kevin Clark † ¤

Shipping Lead
Christopher Bodan †

Shipping/Receiving
Aaron Gaponoff †

Packing
Ryan Gatterman
Craig Lowry
Casey Orr
James Spangler
Marc Verebely † ¤

Webmaster/RPG Line Director
Nathan Letsinger †

Web and Forum Support
Peter Gaublomme
Adam Johnson
Eric Lakin
David Ray

Technical Advisor
Nicole Vega

Playtesters
Amanda Adams
Robert Baxter
Trisha Bluhm
David Carl
Jessica Carl
Earl Chandler Clay III
David Cordy
Andy Daniels
Keiron Duncan
Jefferson L. Dunlap
Jeff Faulkner
Curt Goble
Vince Hoogendoorn
Matthew J. Hoskins
Chad Huffman
Adam Johnson
Anthony Jones
Chris Keimig
Eric Lakin
Brian Martin
Iain A. McGregor
Isaiah Mitchell
Eric Morgan
Chris Oakley
Dave Perotta
David Ray
Karl Reinders
Geoff Roscoe
Tim Simpson
Dan Smith
Bryan Steele
Mark Thomas
Ben Tracy
Brent Walder
Sam Wood
Juan Zapata

† Privateer playtesters and additional development
¤ Proofreaders

We at Privateer Press would like to give our special thanks to everyone who came together to make this book a reality. From the playtesters devoting so much time testing and retesting new abilities to the illustrators and artists who really came through on some tight deadlines, we recognize your exceptional effort and appreciate every moment of it. In addition, we would be remiss if we did not thank all our spouses, significant others, families, and friends for putting up with us during our long hours and stressful deadlines. We could not have done it without your continued support.

TABLE OF CONTENTS

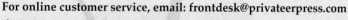

Visit: www.privateerpress.com

Privateer Press, Inc. 2601 NW Market St. • Seattle, WA 98107
Tel (206) 783-9500 • Fax (206) 783-9502

For online customer service, email: frontdesk@privateerpress.com

First printing: February 2006. Printed in China.

HORDES: Primal . . . . ISBN: 1-933362-05-7 . . . . . PIP 1005
HORDES: Primal Hardcover . . . . ISBN: 1-933362-06-5 . . . . . PIP 1006

FOREWORD

A New Genesis

It was 1991. From my seat in the back of a California state university classroom in the middle of a Psych 101 lecture, I turned to my friend and wargaming buddy and said, "I want to make a game called HORDES." That little nugget of inspiration so long ago has continued to germinate on the edge of my subconscious ever since that moment.

Ten years later I found myself plunging into the epic world of western Immoren as creative director of Privateer Press. Development on WARMACHINE was chugging along at full steam, and the game world continued to grow and evolve every day. I hadn't forgotten about HORDES, but warjacks and warcasters demanded a great deal of attention. HORDES would have to wait.

Over the next couple of years, we socked away ideas, shelved concepts, and tabled proposals as we tried to look ahead at what HORDES would become. As far back as the first expansion for WARMACHINE, we began integrating rules specific to HORDES. We knew the conflict between machine and beast would be a spectacle that could not be missed, but then however, we did not know if the armies of the Trollbloods, Circle, Skorne, and Legion would be merely ad-ons to WARMACHINE or find their own life in a completely different product.

The decision to make HORDES its own game, and not simply an expansion, emerged less from strategic marketing than it did from the fact that the game, though utilizing the same basic mechanics of its predecessor, is so dynamically different. It simply demanded to stand on its own. The creatures, characters, and stories tying them together are every bit as rich as anything done in the Iron Kingdoms to date, and these creations could not stand by in the shadow of any precursors, no matter their origins. HORDES is a game in and unto itself that offers a completely original experience while still maintaining the ability to be played against its steam-powered counterpart.

This book is just the beginning. The creatures and cultures living in the shadows of the Iron Kingdoms have stories to tell, and over the coming years we will do our best to expand and explore the tales set in motion in the following pages. We will watch the characters develop and events unfold in both epic glory and tragedy in the tradition of Privateer Press products. Prepare to be swept into a continuing saga where the soul of a dragon wages conquest upon a continent, and a dying race of monstrous trolls may be the last best chance for all of civilization. Though the stories of HORDES are exclusive, the impact of their outcomes will reverberate throughout the rest of the Iron Kingdoms, echoing change and altering the future of the human nations. Machine and beast indeed will clash in a monumental explosion of metal and flesh.

Although it bears little resemblance to the concept that hit me back in that Pysch lecture hall so many years ago, HORDES is more than I ever thought it would be. The game builds on everything that makes WARMACHINE so fun, and it ushers in a whole new level of conflict in our world. With two different games, you have a bounty of options before you for how to partake in this world at war, but no matter who you choose to follow, make your decision quickly. Brace yourself; these creations have waited a long time to see the light of day. They're hungry, and I hope you are too. It's time to unleash the HORDES!

Matt Wilson
Creative Director

Animal Style

For those who have experienced Privateer's games before, what follows will feel like a warm and cozy familiar blanket. For the uninitiated, this is the moment where we open up your bloodshot and beady little eyes to the cold, hard reality of truth—the truth that what you hold in your hands is nothing like you have ever seen. This is going to change how you play games, and the difficult truth is that right now, most likely, you can't handle it.

But don't despair. There is a legion of die-hard, stone-cold, tabletop killers waiting to beat your ass until you can.

At Privateer Press, we inject our games with a special blend of testosterone-laden aggression and grade-A, cold filtered reality. We treat the tabletop like the battleground it is—a place to prove your might is right. We don't suffer whiners, sissies, momma's boys, daddy's little princesses, or punk-mouthed pukes with more excuses than moves. We come for the beat down—deliver it with gusto or take it like a trooper. There is glory in both as long as you've got the rocks.

Don't be deceived. HORDES is simple on the surface. You roll some dice, you add some numbers, and you mark some dots on cards. It's the deep strategy that is going to turn your brain into a pretzel. Whether you're a seasoned veteran of tabletop conquest or some doe-eyed rookie who accidentally wandered into this den of ruthless vipers, the mental gymnastics you're going to have to master are not going to come without some severe bruising along the way. Keep your head and hands inside the window, face forward, and pay attention because you only get to hear this for the first time once, and if you don't get it then, you're going to look like 200 lbs. of ground beef praying for the sweet release of death.

Punch first, hit hard, show no mercy, and expect none in return.

The beasts we've bred for HORDES are fury-fueled monsters, and the only way to handle them is with the same disregard they have for each other. HORDES is powered by unchecked brutality. It's not survival of the fittest, meathead. It's survival of the most badass, and the winner takes all. If you can't hang with the animals, you best get out of the jungle now before something mistakes you for a snack.

Privateer Press is building upon a tradition of untarnished honesty, unwavering respect, and unrelenting gratitude for the people who play our games, blazing away a new era where the quality of game, experience, and inspiration are worth the hard earned coin you just traded. We are freed from the shackles of corporate mediocrity and have charged ourselves with delivering unto you only the most visceral episodes you can encounter in adventure gaming. We throw our blood, sweat, and souls into these creations, and we back it with a simple creed.

This is primal. This is savage. This is HORDES.

Play like you've got a pair!

CUTTING THE STRINGS

Autumn of 606 AR, east of the Glimmerwood

The albino chieftain wrenched his axe free and let his foe collapse at his feet. He did not pause to catch his breath but instead turned immediately to face the next enemy. He blinked as he realized there was no foe within striking distance. In fact, there were no foes in sight. The tenor of battle had changed, mellowed. There was the groaning of pain around him and the occasional hacking of a blade into flesh, but this had slowed. He shook off the mind-numbing haze of battle lust and pulled his consciousness from the full-blood trolls he was goading to battle.

The fight was over.

The surviving trolls were feasting so their hardy tissues could regenerate their grievous wounds. There were corpses enough to glut and keep them torpid. Despite their remarkable endurance, several were slain including his best spear-throwing impaler Vok—a troll who had been in his service for almost twenty years. Madrak did not grieve for trolls but regretted any reduction in their strength, particularly the loss of such a well-trained asset.

Madrak Ironhide felt no triumph in victory; its cost was too high. The blood-saturated ground was churned to mud by the boots of clashing warriors. Corpses and dismembered limbs littered the scrub plain along with tattered scraps of banners, splintered standards, broken and bloodied weapons, and other detritus of war.

He looked down at his most recent kill. The strange armored invaders from across the eastern sands were tall but slender. He no longer inspected them with the same curiosity as a few weeks earlier when the novelty had yet to wear thin. Now they were nothing but another threat to his people and his family, his kith. This last attack had been brutal. He hoped making it costly to take this ground would deter them, but it had only prompted them to regroup and come again harder.

One of his steadfast allies saw him, approached, and nodded respectfully. This was Horthol, a powerfully muscled trollkin of the northern Thornwood bearing the ornamented armguard identifying him as chief of his own kriel. He deferred to Ironhide and had fought alongside him in many fights, accepting orders without complaint. "The day is ours, Chieftain."

The two of them walked among the bodies helping any trollkin who showed some semblance of life. Madrak gave a skin of water to a badly mangled shaman whose ribs pierced through the skin of her crushed side. Any still alive now would recover. Missing limbs, gouged eyes, or maiming which would permanently cripple a human were all recoverable with time and food. It was the trolls' blood flowing in all their veins—Dhunia's gift.

Too many would not rise. It pained Madrak to see familiar faces as lifeless meat with the animating spark stripped away. They had not the people to waste in this scrubland on the fringes of the Bloodstone Marches a hundred miles east of their forest birthplace. This was their adopted home, and they would defend it.

Pokrul, another chief who fought alongside Madrak now as a champion, also joined them. Earlier in the fight the rampaging charge of a four-armed beast had separated them. Pokrul was examining this latest horror from the skorne. "Even in the darkest Thornwood there is nothing as strange as this."

Madrak was in no mood to speculate. "Have your people scavenge whatever weapons and armor they can, but do not linger. We must get back to the villages. There is metal here we can use. Load up the trolls with as much as they can carry."

One of the great brutes looked up. The massive ten-foot axer used his weighty cleaver to carve off a haunch of the four-armed creature and gnawed the meat with enthusiasm. He held the chunk toward Madrak with a fanged grin as if showing a treasure. The display lightened Madrak's mood. The troll named Bron was not smart, but he was fierce and loyal in battle.

Madrak spoke to Pokrul who seemed reluctant to make haste. "We must regroup. If they attack again we will not survive."

Pokrul did not take graciously to commands, but he passed this down to one of his subordinates. He seemed eager to stay near Madrak who suspected he wanted to argue. Pokrul was a seasoned fighter and a chief of a kriel closer to Corvis, but he was prone to sulking when Madrak ignored his advice. Today Madrak was weary and eager to return to his mate who was even now working to reinforce the stonework bulwarks shielding the eastern approach to their villages. He would argue with Pokrul another time.

Scattered along a lengthy line, the trollkin made the march west toward the trees loaded with spoils. Madrak noted with approval the watchtowers erected here on the fringes by his industrious kin.

Their new villages were in the Glimmerwood and the Widower's Wood northeast of Corvis, outside Cygnar's borders. There was a large stretch of territory with difficult soil between Cygnar, Ios, and Llael unclaimed by any of those nations, but it was not as barren as the Marches to the east. It served as a refuge from the warring humans and rapacious Cryxians who had recently invaded the Thornwood tearing apart many kiths.

No one had anticipated the eastern invaders. Their incursions cast a dark shadow on Ironhide's status, and his people had begun to grumble about his arrangements with King Leto Raelthorne. Madrak too felt bitter and ill used, having recently returned from a tense meeting with Cygnar's king who would not honor earlier promises. His uprooted kin were in the path of the skorne who were more numerous every week. It would not be the first time Cygnar had proven content to use trollkin sacrifices to delay an intruding army.

There was another large community of trollkin just to the east, settled around Scarleforth Lake, but they had no land to spare and troubles of their own. Ironhide had recently made efforts to unite their chieftains and convince them to move west to combine their strength. They too battled the skorne who sought any gap from their blasted lands into the fertile west.

As Madrak crossed a brook and approached the Glimmerwood, a band of trollkin approached from the trees. They were stout and well armed, but Madrak scowled that they had arrived too late to join the battle. Ironhide's people were scattered behind him. Many had lingered for salvage, and his trolls had finished eating and were slowly catching up. Ironhide was accompanied by Horthol and Pokrul, his best champions, and a few scattered groups of other trollkin within shouting distance.

He felt a hint of misgiving as he saw the *quitari* patterns of these trollkin. It was unfamiliar, and he knew the patterns of all the Thornwood kiths. Accompanying them was a smaller figure in black garb leaning on a great iron-shod staff. The face below the cowl was pinkish brown—no elder trollkin sorcerer, but a human. This had to be one of the human druids whose council had recently been scarce. Ironhide had no fondness for the secretive forest masters and their cult, but traditionally the trollkin greeted them with respect.

He stopped and waited with his muscled arms folded. Horthol and Pokrul took up positions on either side of him slightly behind. A number of the battle weary trollkin stopped to watch the unusual meeting, but they remained at a respectful distance. Not inclined to get close, they did not want to intrude on elder affairs.

The presence of the druid did not worry Madrak, but the posture of the stranger trollkin put him on edge. They were young and eyeing him in the disrespectful fashion for outsiders. He wondered if they comprised an unaffiliated *shen* fallen under the sway of the druids. The quitari patterns looked like those worn in the Gnarls.

The druid stepped forward and pulled back his hood to reveal a familiar lined and weathered face. "Ergonus." Madrak greeted him, keeping his tone neutral. His disquiet increased—this was one of

three so-called omnipotents, the leaders of their dark cult. Ergonus and Madrak had spoken recently, but it was not amiable.

"Chief Ironhide. Perhaps you now regret refusing my offer." Ergonus spoke their language with smooth fluency.

"Unless you are here to help, your words are hollow. Nothing has changed." Madrak was aware of the druid's considerable power and intended to be polite, but he felt no patience.

"You wound me." The druid leaned on his staff, but his aggrieved expression was an affectation. "You ask for my help yet do not offer assistance in exchange? We could have supported one another in these difficult times, but you are too sure of your own importance."

"As I told you when last we met, we have worries enough without shouldering your burdens."

Ergonus shook his head, and a small smile formed on his lips. "The time has come for you to step down, Madrak."

The words were so unexpected Madrak almost could not believe them.

"You have led the Thornwood kriels astray. It was a mistake to move here. You were naïve to heed the promises of Cygnar's king. Let a younger leader guide the kriels. Step down and retire to a place of respect among your elders. There will be no loss of status."

Horthol snorted derisively, but Madrak noticed Pokrul stepping away, axes in hand. His expression was strangely smug and Madrak realized how many of that champion's kith gathered nearby, approaching while Ergonus spoke. "Pokrul, you turn *kulshenk*?" It was a Molgur term meaning "blood traitor" and a strong epithet applied to one who turned his back on his chief and kriel for his own gain.

This trollkin spit to the side and held his head up proudly. "A true chieftain does not ask kin to die over worthless ground. I will take us north to Scarsfell."

"*You* will unite the kriels? This druid feeds you lies. Following him will not bring prosperity. He will use our people as fodder in his wars." Looking them over, he saw that Pokrul's kin seemed reluctant for violence. They wanted Madrak to surrender, but he had no doubt they would fight if prompted. The strangers from the Gnarls were more eager and clearly hoping for a brawl.

A shout went up from the trollkin near enough to see two huge towering creatures striding from the Glimmerwood. Madrak saw them with the first

sensation of true fear. Dire trolls! Horrible enough if there was one, it was rare to see two in the same place except when mating. He could not fathom what their presence signified other than death. They stood easily twice the height of a trollkin and three times the mass of a regular troll, bulged with thick corded muscle and sinew, and boasted gigantic clawed hands. Whereas trollkin had developed a bond with full-blood trolls, no one could control dire trolls. They were too powerful, their minds were flooded with uncontrollable rage, and they had no interest in cooperating with lesser creatures. They had refused to enter pacts with their smaller cousins, and they only tolerated the pygmies they were prone to devour when food was scarce.

Madrak reached back instinctively to the minds of his own axers and impalers recruited to carry pillaged supplies. They were not far, and they heard his call. Meanwhile he heard the distinctive bellow of one of his village's fell callers announcing danger was near. Help would come too late.

He became aware of a wizened form standing calmly between the dire trolls. Though stooped over by age, this trollkin had broad shoulders and was still fit. He wore the garments of a revered elder shaman with sacred scroll-tubes tied in netting on his back. Madrak realized why the Gnarls quitari patterns were familiar: those trollkin standing near Ergonus were the kin of Hoarluk Doomshaper, the mightiest shaman of that western forest. At this, Madrak knew his death had arrived. He and Doomshaper had argued bitterly on many occasions.

The Dhunian priest had somehow enlisted the dire trolls! It was an unprecedented feat, and now they would slay him. So be it. He could not stand against Ergonus, Doomshaper, Pokrul, and the gathered young warriors, let alone the dire trolls. He would not surrender. They would have to spill his blood and show those gathered what master they served.

He turned to Horthol and saw dread in his eyes. "Go! Live to lead your people. This is my doom, not yours."

Horthol scowled. "I stand by you, Chieftain."

Madrak nodded and felt pride. He turned back to the shaman. "Doomshaper. My death must be a powerful lure to bring you from your forest. I am honored."

The elder shaman sighed and shook his head as if Madrak's words were wearisome. There was a strange fire in his eyes. Ironhide had never been able to read that ancient face.

The druid Ergonus glanced at Doomshaper with narrowed eyes. "Ironhide refuses to step down. Kill him."

Pokrul raised his weapons and took a cautious step toward Madrak. Ironhide raised his ancient and sacred axe, feeling its heavy grip in his hands. The Molgur name of this axe was Rathrok, meaning World Ender. It was the only legacy of Horfar Grimmr, the last great trollkin chief to fall to Priest-King Golivant almost three thousand years ago. It was a relic of tremendous potency and dire significance now only wielded reluctantly. Its use in battle was reputed to signify the end-times. Madrak had sworn to carry it in the defense of his people, but now he felt the temptation to use it to strike down Pokrul for his treachery.

Before he could hurl the axe, one of the dire trolls bellowed and charged. Madrak sensed the command from Doomshaper like a chord of dissonance in the air, yet its timbre confused him. Instead of coming for Madrak, the gigantic troll grasped Pokrul in its claws and tore him in half. The air was filled with a bloody mist as the dire troll let loose a roar and turned to Pokrul's gathered kin. It spread its claws wide in anticipation. Several fled immediately while others backed away, weapons held feebly. Ironhide's people gathered, but the sight of the dire trolls gave them pause. Several shouted questions at Ironhide, but he could not spare the attention to answer.

Ergonus whirled on Doomshaper with indignant fury burning in his eyes. "What are you doing?"

Hoarluk gripped his staff and snarled with withering disdain. "Too long you have manipulated my people. We will not be your assassins, druid." He spit the word as if it were an insult. The Gnarls trollkin looked nervously between the druid and their shaman. Doomshaper spoke to them, "You are fools! This druid is not our ally. He seeks to pit us against our blood to start a war between us! Defend Chief Ironhide or suffer the same fate as the traitor." He pointed a long finger at the bloody remains of Pokrul.

Ergonus was suddenly alone.

The druid was not fearful or diminished. He stood glowering in a wide stance with his staff in hand. A nimbus of power shimmered around him like gathered storm clouds. He spat, "I have no further use for either of you." There was a blinding flash and a thunderous explosion.

Potent Krueger of the Circle Orboros observed from the trees. He considered the omnipotent's eagerness to confront Ironhide as foolhardy hubris. He argued against this plan at the conclave and was tasked to accompany Ergonus as a rebuke.

Krueger saw his signal to act. Omnipotent Ergonus unleashed a powerful thunderclap while Krueger strode from concealment. Creatures obedient to his bidding poured from the forest, sounding bloodthirsty howls and war cries. Dozens of Tharn ravagers led the charge with loping strides and features transformed into bestial mockeries of humanity. On either extreme of the advancing wing advanced enormous warpwolves with muscular lupine bodies covered in thick matted fur and an assortment of fang-like spikes. Nearer to Krueger walked two stone and wood constructs—one smaller, the other tall and massive—with glowing runes along their limbs.

The thunderclap instilled chaos across a large area. All trollkin who had seen the flash staggered and clutched their eyes, and many were knocked prone. Even the dire trolls howled and shook their heads against the deafening peal of thunder. When they recovered their wits, the Gnarls trollkin backed away from Ergonus toward Doomshaper. Krueger smiled like a predator and summoned wind and storm to his fingertips.

Madrak felt a searing pain in his shoulder. His legs did not obey him and he felt disconnected from the ground, but he did not fall. He backed away while shaking his head to clear it. His ringing ears made the tableau dreamlike, and he blinked away a haze just in time to see dark forms loping from the trees. His lips pulled back in a snarl as he recognized the Tharn—a reminder from his youth when he had nearly died at their hands. Tharn were carnivorous savages twisted by Devourer worship and cannibalistic feasting. Madrak felt rage building as he saw them mauling Doomshaper's trollkin, heedless that they had been enemies just moments before.

More trollkin joined the fray. The flash blinded those nearest, but those further away were unaffected. Several of Madrak's trolls were close, including Bron. His nearest warriors were shaking off the blindness but had gathered to confront the dire trolls, believing them to be the threat. Ironhide yelled at them and pointed to the Tharn. His command became clear when the dire trolls turned away and ignored the trollkin to charge the oncoming druidic reinforcements.

Ironhide saw Doomshaper almost overrun when his defenders fell rapidly before the Tharn. Madrak rushed forward and grabbed the Dhunian priest's arm to pull him out of harm's way. He hurled Rathrok in a powerful throw. The weighty blade severed clean through one Tharn's neck and ricocheted at an unnatural angle to sink into the chest of a second. He held out his hand to draw on the ancient power of the weapon. Its craft was never to find rest except in the hand of its wielder, and the dissonance of separation became a strain increasing with distance like an unseen tether. The axe blurred through the air and returned to his palm.

Doomshaper pulled out of Madrak's grasp with surprising strength, but there was grim amusement in his ancient eyes. The shaman planted his staff in the ground and seemed almost to swell as he drew on the power and ferocity of the dire trolls linked to him. He chanted a blessing of Dhunia and let it instill holy strength in his minions. Both dire trolls engaged. One knocked several Tharn aside to hurl itself on a slathering warpwolf. Tharn surrounded the other dire troll while the large woldwarden moved to engage. The ground around it erupted in a thorny growth that grasped at the legs of any who came near.

The battle fell into familiar chaos.

Ironhide sensed the great axer Bron charge past him like a locomotive as he barreled into the Tharn line. Madrak was reassured to notice the champion Horthol had regained his feet and was now moving to intercept anything which tried to flank. A second troll named Jor charged up from behind, raising a spear the thickness of a small tree to hurl it across the battlefield. It sank with a satisfying

crunch deep into the exposed side of a warpwolf that had been circling toward Doomshaper. The beast howled in pain and whirled to face its new foe while its form shimmered as tendons and muscles shifted and bony spikes erupted to protect its vitals.

As the trolls let loose their inner rage, Madrak drew on the fury and gathered it to him with a surge of strength like a flood of adrenaline as if there were three hearts in his breast. The power flowed into every portion of his body, giving a godlike rush and nearly pushing him to sympathetic battle frenzy. His mind merged with Bron and Jor, and he felt each troll's weapons as if they were in his hands and their bodies were extensions of his will.

Madrak forced their bestial impulses aside for a moment to focus his thoughts. Taking some of the power he siphoned from them, he knitted his wounds. His flesh mended instantly to erase all traces of the lightning burn from the battle's outset.

Ironhide knew time was precious. The concentrated druid forces were pressing through the line and were barely held in check by the might of Hoarluk's dire trolls. There were too many adversaries, and in moments he would be flanked. Madrak could not hold them with just one axer and one impaler. He sensed other trolls nearby outside his reach; the dire troll scent had them wary to approach closer.

Doomshaper leaned toward him, "There is another druid…" He pointed with his staff, and Ironhide saw a slender black form

near the tree line. Even as Madrak saw him, more Tharn rushed from the woods joined by the tall and muscled profile of an enraged gorax. Hoarluk added, "Both druids are very powerful. We cannot hold."

A wind picked up and the skies darkened with racing black clouds gathering with supernatural swiftness. Lightning flashed nearby, and another peel of thunder rocked the air. The wind began to howl. Madrak saw a trollkin on the right flank die screaming under the assault of the smaller rope-knotted construct where the bloodied ground erupted and trees shot forth through his body to lift his corpse high into the air.

Madrak bent his will to Bron, the troll axer, and willed him to pull away from the Tharn and intercept the approaching gorax on his flank. Madrak pushed the troll to its limits. His sight tinted red as he tapped into its most primal instincts and ferocity, and it began swinging its axe in a blur. Madrak reached out and wrenched that rage into himself again with his teeth clenched and his eyes mad with a killing lust as new vitality flowed to his arms. His axe flew once more to deal a horrendous gash in the gorax's side. Still, the wound only enraged the beast and gave strength to its frenzy. It lifted Bron and hurled the troll into a nearby tree. As the troll recovered, the bleeding gorax moved in flanked by more Tharn. Nearby, the impaler Jor was quickly losing its battle with the warpwolf.

Ironhide clenched his teeth in anger. "We must kill Ergonus! We cannot win beast to beast."

The shaman agreed, and both turned to this task. Ironhide and Horthol circled to the left toward the omnipotent, but they kept the bulk of a dire troll between to block the druid's sight. A great swirling wind surrounded the druid, and a similar vortex peeled from Krueger the Stormwrath to tear through a nearby formation and send one trollkin flying back with a bone-shattering crunch.

Ergonus spoke a word of power that prompted lightning to pierce down from the clouds and explode into Doomshaper, lighting the tableau in a moment of clarity before heavy rain began to fall. The shaman raised his staff and drew on his parasitic link to a nearby dire troll, letting the wound pass instead to the beast. The dire troll howled in agony as his skin blackened, split, and smoked as if the lightning had struck him instead. It went berserk in a frenzy of destruction against anything in reach, tearing apart Tharn and stuffing them into its fanged maw. Its wounds closed with every bite.

The smaller elemental construct had seen movement and lumbered to intercept Ironhide. His axe spun into the woldwatcher as Horthol brought his own weapons to bear against its toughened rope-knotted sinews. It shimmered to solid stone, yet their mighty blows made quick work of it, shattering it to rubble at their feet.

The second dire troll—pushed by Doomshaper's relentless urging—gave forth a tremendous burst of strength and speed and pressed the warpwolf back with a blow that would have torn its head from its shoulders. Its efforts opened a wedge in the line.

Madrak Ironhide gave the great battle cry of his ancestors. This ancient Molgur phrase had no translation, nor did his kinfolk need to ken its meaning to feel their hearts lifted to heroic effort. They had heard that cry in other battles and knew it meant the final press.

Doomshaper's voice filled the air as Madrak's faded. The chant of the greatest Dhunian war-priest walking Caen caused all hearing it to tremble. The warpwolves and gorax howled in pain as suddenly their muscles clenched with a spasm and tore apart while arteries burst, insufficient to the pressure of the blood coursing through.

The line stretched wide from the peerless strength of the dire trolls, and the path to Ergonus lay open. Ironhide charged as Doomshaper's prayer chants rang in his ears. Holy power gripped the omnipotent who found his limbs wracked by pain. So paralyzed, the secret words of power stuttered on his lips. Ironhide advanced and barely evaded the lightning strike smiting the ground near him.

Krueger the Stormwrath observed the sudden reversal with disbelief. Their attack had been flawless. Ironhide and Doomshaper should be dead, yet they had rallied to break the line. Troll endurance was inexhaustible. The initiative was lost.

Krueger could see the next few minutes with perfect clarity in his mind's eye. Trollkin would surround and slaughter them. There was nothing he could do now except distract the trollkin from Ergonus to buy a short reprieve and doom himself, but he stopped short of doing so. Far better that he should live to carry on the work and bring warning to the council. Krueger felt no sympathy for Ergonus, only anger at a squandered opportunity. He stepped back from the fight and became one with the wind and storm, letting it sweep him from the field like a bird caught in a hurricane.

Ironhide's axe struck Ergonus in the chest with fatal finality, exploded the druid's rib cage under the impact, and sliced his heart in half. The light in the druid's eyes died as an anguished expression froze onto his face. The wind around him released as a great outward burst of freezing air that hurled Madrak tumbling backward. Several Tharn came for him, but Horthol was there killing one and engaging the other until Madrak gained his feet. The rest were fleeing with howling laments into the forest. The gorax and one warpwolf were dead, and the other limped away bent down to all fours. Madrak and Hoarluk reigned in their trolls to prevent them from giving chase. It was time to return to their villages and see to the wounded.

Madrak rejoined the elder shaman who stood over the corpse of Ergonus with a satisfied expression. The two clasped hands and then bowed to touch their foreheads together. They engaged in the *Tohmaak Mahkeiri* for the first time, standing still for several minutes as an unspoken oath sealed in bloodshed shaped between their joined minds.

"We will never trust the druids again," Ironhide said loud enough for others to hear. "Word must spread of their treachery."

Doomshaper agreed. "We must fight as one people. We must be hard and cruel, and kill or be extinguished. You must promise not to reserve mercy… even for the humans

of Cygnar." His old eyes were fierce. Madrak thought of his last audience with King Leto and nodded resolutely. The time for compromises and peaceful dealings had ended. They had much to discuss and plan.

Unknown to the participants, there was a rapt audience of one watching the struggle. Atop a tall hill northeast of their position, a lithe figure crouched with bow in hand. She was a peerless hunter far from her domain. She had stalked the one called Ergonus cautiously trying to gain the measure of this adversary. Her cruel lips betrayed sated satisfaction as she witnessed him slain, and she examined those who had accomplished the task. There was much to learn here of interest to her draconic master. She could feel that rustling presence in her mind, folding and unfolding to the beating of her pierced heart. It was a vast overpowering dark presence so much greater and stronger than her own. She rode on the surface of these ruminations like sliding on ice. She crept down from her perch and watched with distraction as a small dragonspawn chewed on a nearby carcass, ravenously adding to its bulk. She touched its scaled hide, peered to the north, and listened to a voice only she could hear. She could feel a far-away response as a tendril of the Legion broke free. Its blighted soldiers and spawn marched at her bidding, and they would come quickly to tear apart any barriers standing in their path.

Shadow Histories of Western Immoren

Winter 606 AR

We've been stuck in our corner of Caen for so many centuries that we forget there is anything beyond the edges of our maps. Western Immoren is small, but it's our home, and we are proud of what our ancestors have accomplished. Our kingdoms arose on the backs of scattered fiefdoms and feuding warlords. Rock-by-rock and home-by-home through a tide of blood, massacre, famine, disease, warfare, and the occasional bright moments of clarify and self-awareness, we have carved a place for ourselves and created a rich, though war-torn, history.

I have fought in countless wars, seen the rise and fall of kings, and walked the scope of this land. Believe me when I say we have the barest perception of the dark and powerful forces shaping our histories from the shadows. We are on a strange, foggy precipice about to tumble off. My description of our situation will not prevent it, for momentum has been building for centuries, yet if we are to survive the fall, we must keep our eyes open.

I can smell change, and I have always had a sense for disaster. We are entering a new era, and such transitions never occur without weeping widows and mothers grieving their slain sons. The specter of death is our constant companion, and fire burns away what we know to make room for something new.

Dwelling on the ancient past is not my habit, but we must look back to the Orgoth to understand what rests ahead of us. That was the last time we experienced such a violent period of change. The Orgoth were a brutal empire of foreigners from across the western ocean that conquered the region twelve hundred years ago. We know little of the land that spawned these black-hearted warriors. They crossed the Meredius—a feat no one born of our shores has repeated. Their longships arrived in an unending procession pouring forth Orgoth soldiers to reinforce those lost as they attacked town after town sacking and conquering any who resisted them.

The Orgoth found our ancestors divided and unready for a threat like this. We were only starting to emerge from a long era when any warlord with a few soldiers and a strong arm could crown himself king. The Orgoth set upon the scattered city-states and devoured them one by one. It was a difficult conquest requiring nearly two centuries, but the Orgoth were patient and relentless.

The Orgoth changed everything. They enslaved the region using strange dark magic from warwitches and overlords. They stripped away our will to resist with inventive torments, and for four centuries they dominated us completely. It took this long before at last a spark ignited to begin an ongoing rebellion. This was not one battle or even a series of wars. The Rebellion encompassed two brutal centuries of organized resistances and uprisings. Each time a rebel group gained some slight victory, the Orgoth slaughtered them while survivors scattered to plot again. The Rebellion was a perilous enterprise stretching ten generations.

You'll find no shortage of groups to take credit for the Rebellion and the defeat of the Orgoth. Maybe there is truth in each of these wild tales and boasts. This victory might have in fact required the combined efforts of several religions, secret cabals, dark cults, and dire pacts as well as the sweat and blood of ten generations of courageous Immorese.

By the end we had learned to master arcane power and combine ingenuity and invention as mechanika. We crafted potent weapons never before seen: alchemical blasting powder giving rise to the firearm, battle wizards and sorcerers who would in time become warcasters, and the great animated mechanisms of war called colossals. With the Orgoth driven away at last, the leaders of the surviving Rebellion formed the Council of Ten and signed the Corvis Treaties. This document outlined the borders for the nations we would call the Iron Kingdoms as a tribute to the Iron Alliance of the rebels who won ultimate victory against the oppressors. Our ancestors felt they had entered an age that would prove the end of strife, discord, and bloody conquest.

We can understand their naïve hopes at the end of so dark a period; most were dead and buried before they could witness how little had changed in the heart of man. Removed from fellowship against a shared foe, our kingdoms reverted quickly to the natural state of war. This is as inevitable to the human condition as the drawing of breath. Even more intrinsic—we have seen lifeless corpses of the dead march to battle and been told by priests that the afterlife is an extension of fighting by the bidding of the gods. Peace has always been intransient, a time of reprieve when nations lick their wounds and sharpen their blades before leaping back into the fray with lustful abandon.

The Iron Kingdoms

Nowhere is man's love of battle truer than in the north among the sprawling kingdom called Khador—the inheritors of the ancient Khardic Empire. A hot-blooded but cold-hearted people, the Khadorans enjoy national rhetoric, but they are not a single tribe. They are descended from dozens of tribes that once haunted the north from horseback or stalked the wilderness of their lands. Brought together under a single name, they share a thirst for empire. Their ruler, once Queen Ayn Vanar, tired of her title and recently crowned herself empress. She knows how to keep her people happy by providing an endless list of enemies to hurl themselves against and immortalizing their patriotic sacrifices with monuments and honors.

I do admire the Khadorans. In another time they were my sworn enemies, but I have fought beside them and walked the streets of their capital. I have earned their coin and spoken to the lowest of their soldiers freshly recruited from the cold farms north of Korsk. I feel I understand them. Historically Khador was once termed a primitive kingdom; their inhospitable lands are spread across such a vast expanse that it was difficult for them to exploit their resources. In recent decades they have made great strides modernizing, freeing their serfs, investing in industry, inventing powerful tools of war, and putting aside old superstitions. They are a people of strong spiritual beliefs, whether Morrowans or Menites, and have embraced both faiths without stirring up civil war unlike another nation I'll discuss.

South of Khador is the lonely kingdom of Ord—lonely because it rests between the two great powers of our age and is unwilling to ally with either. It is fortunate to have avoided the vortex of warfare consuming the Thornwood Forest just east of their border. Ord is a kingdom of proud and rugged people known for skilled sailors and indomitable soldiers as well as smugglers, ruffians, pirates, and shrewd merchants plying the ocean trade. Ord has much to recommend it as long as you are not born in the gutter or out on the peat marsh. I have spent many fine evenings laying low in Ordic cities like Five Fingers—a haven for soldiers of the coin removed from the so-called civility that makes many towns and large cities stifling. The kingdom lacks the resources to contend with its larger neighbors on equal footing, yet it has managed to survive the last few

centuries. I expect it will endure the coming storm, at least for a while.

Even strong kingdoms need a place to hire mercenaries and exchange goods. I have spent considerable time in Ord in recent years, and I appreciate its unexpected charms. King Baird Cathor II is called the "Bandit King," for he taxes his wealthy castellans and thereby has earned the adoring support of the masses. He's a cunning old man, and I expect he has a few tricks up his sleeves before he lets his eldest son replace him. I will miss him when he's gone and feel no shame in raising a glass to his health. I hope he continues to keep his nose unbloodied in current wars despite considerable pressure to join the fight. His people would become pawns or victims were they to enter the maelstrom, and King Baird is too clever to become either.

Llael was once a small but storied kingdom northeast of Ord, but it has changed dramatically since Khador invaded and occupied the majority of its cities a year ago. They were the first to enjoy a taste of Khador's new imperialism. Despite a strong alliance with its southern ally Cygnar, Llael could not stand against Khador's might. There is considerable belief that their Prime Minister aided this invasion. I have no trouble believing it since he was a reprehensible and spineless wretch. Like a snake, Prime Minister Glabryn was able to slither into the cracks and survive. He serves Empress Ayn Vanar now and retains nominal control over the region. Its citizens are still proud Llaelese, but that nation is more a memory than a reality.

Some cling to hope in the southeast of its territories where impotent rebels gather to commiserate and drink wine. Llael has always been the smallest and least influential of the Iron Kingdoms, but it once earned its way as a center of trade and a hotbed for intrigues. Their inevitable fall was rooted in the failure to replace their king after his death. A nation without a king is a ship without a rudder; regardless of able crew, stout design, and ample supplies, a storm will come and end its travails. The ultimate fate of Llael is to become a territory under the Khadoran flag and perhaps be absorbed into their empire as a protectorate. I feel little sympathy for them.

The last of the original Iron Kingdoms is Cygnar, Khador's southern rival. It is not easy to describe so complex a nation. Cygnar is a land with every advantage: a large population, varied geography, fertile farmland, powerful cities, and capable citizens. Their arcane and technical prowess is second to none, they boast a strong economy, and their military is both well equipped and highly trained. Still, they suffer from a lack of resolve. Cygnar's rule has always been irregular with brief tenures by brilliant and potent kings followed by wastrels or soft-hearted muttonheads too indecisive to accomplish significant goals. Whenever Cygnar has been on the brink of true greatness, a pathetic king has pulled them back.

Rather than crushing their foes and pressing the advantage, Cygnar has too often been content to return to the status quo of the Corvis Treaties. This policy is ridiculous given no other kingdom has held to these treaties—the borders defined in that document were the product of the Orgoth's arbitrary provinces. Cygnar has never made any attempts to expand its borders or to cripple its enemies, and it has come back to haunt them. Had their kings been more aggressive and decisive, the region might already have been united, the Cryxians annihilated, and the Protectorate of Menoth a historical footnote.

The headquarters of the Morrowan Church—the faith of most people of this region—is the Sancteum within Cygnar's capital of Caspia. Accuse me of blasphemy, but the church is one of Cygnar's greatest weaknesses. Their primarch has sat by the side of most Cygnaran kings whispering homilies. I hold no hatred for the church. They accomplish worthy goals, but their priests have no place in the halls of power. Khador is more pragmatic in this regard; Cygnar confuses affairs of state with the lofty province of the soul. Religious philosophy and statesmanship can never stand hand in hand.

In 594 we witnessed the ultimate example of the church meddling in politics. In that year the rightful king, Vinter Raelthorne IV, suffered a coup by his ambitious brother Leto. The coup would have failed without the intervention of the Church of Morrow and their politically savvy primarch. This was an unfortunate turn of events, for the Raelthorne dynasty had been achieving great strides and had positioned the kingdom to grasp its destiny. Vinter IV had isolated himself from church influence but did not notice his brother had become their pawn. Unable to endure removal from the halls of power, the primarch seduced prince Leto to turn on his brother. I'll grant that King Leto has been a shrewd politician and a passable king in times of peace. He managed to strengthen the nation's economy, but he did so at the expense of military readiness. Since the eruption of war, King Leto has squandered his opportunities, and now enemies beset Cygnar on all sides. Unless something drastic happens soon, the kingdom will fall. Leto is prone to the same weak policies that allowed trollkin rebels to prosper in

Cygnaran forests even after the Trollkin Wars of the 3rd century and granted leniency to the Menites at the end of the Cygnaran Civil War.

That brings me to the Protectorate of Menoth—for all practical purposes the fifth and newest Iron Kingdom. As much as I may rail against the meddling of the Morrowan Church in politics, they are nothing compared to this nation of zealots and fanatics. The Cygnaran Civil War began in 482 AR in Caspia. Let us be very clear on what happened here. A Menite religious leader named Sulon gathered together almost a million Menites in eastern Caspia—the capital of Cygnar—armed them, and then urged them to take over the city and reclaim the government for their faith. There are terms for this type of activity: sedition, treason, insurrection, or rebellion. Do not let the Menites tell you differently. The Cygnaran soldiers' attempt to disperse these armed and violent fanatics prompted an eruption of open warfare that consumed the capital.

In typical Cygnaran fashion, when Sulon died in battle and the uprising began to wane, the king sued for peace. The king granted these treasonous fanatics their own government and territories! The mind boggles at the logic of this peace negotiation; it is no coincidence that the Church of Morrow was heavily involved in the process. Cygnar gave the eastern section of the capital, renamed Sul, and all lands east of the Black River to the fanatics. This became the Protectorate of Menoth. Though nominally still part of Cygnar, they have acted as an independent nation since their founding. Their current ruler is Hierarch Garrick Voyle. Under his pragmatic leadership, this nation has created a modern army, openly defied Cygnaran law, and began a bloody crusade to restore their once-waning religion to prominence. Where the Morrowan religion is often too forgiving, the Menites are hard and brutal. If they were to have their way, we would see an uncompromising tyranny such as would make the Orgoth seem lax in comparison. Their numbers seem too few to represent a major threat, but recent events have elevated them to a true power. In particular, the manifestation of a divine prophet called the Harbinger has brought many converts among a large number of Khadorans.

Beyond the Nations of Man

It is easy to forget that the nations of mankind only represent a section of a single continent on our uncharted oceans. There are races other than humanity that have carved territories and may one day wage war. Even within our borders there are those who dwell in the shadows and act to undermine the foundations of

our nations. Too often we dismiss these outsiders, and we will soon face the consequences of that disregard.

East of Khador is the mountain kingdom of Rhul, home to the dwarves. They are a race not too dissimilar from humanity, and in recent years they have increasingly been drawn into our struggles. Where once they stood aloof and isolated, the dwarves are now a common sight. They assisted in the creation of the colossals that fought the Orgoth, and their mastery of mechanika and warfare is similar to ours, albeit based on different traditions. The dwarves are a conservative people politically. Despite their increased contact with the human kingdoms, this will not change. They have avoided destruction by sidestepping open war with man. They are willing to trade, and certain clans have sent mercenary bands to profit from southern wars, but I don't expect to see more in coming years. If any nations can endure the coming storm, it will be those who stay out of the fight—Ord and Rhul being the most likely candidates.

South of Rhul and northeast of Cygnar rests the small kingdom of Ios, home to the mysterious elves. I will not pretend to be an expert on these people, but they are one of several unpredictable forces that could

change the balance in the west if they make a move. I do not think we can count them out or ignore them, for they boast weapons and secrets unique to their people. Ios has been quiet—too quiet—for decades, having withdrawn entirely from contact with other nations. This is dangerous. They worry me more than the Rhulfolk who have a vested interest in friendly relations. Violent elves have been creeping from Ios in recent years, working in secretive cells and lurking on the fringes of our wars. Without more information, there is little we can do about them.

The last kingdom of this region is the Cryxian island empire. Nothing shows the insignificance of humanity more than this malignancy lurking off Cygnar's southwestern shores. The Dragonfather known as Lord Toruk is very real. There is no mightier being walking Caen than Toruk, and the Cryxian Empire exists to serve His will. These people are more than the reaver pirates we see raiding coastal villages and towns. In Cryx the dead walk, and necromancy is openly encouraged by Toruk and His twelve lich lords—each immortal, vastly powerful, and patient beyond human conception.

The dragon is so pervasive a force of darkness that He has blighted the land and people for a hundred miles around Him. Only the dead can endure the dragon's immediate presence. Members of His own priesthood—yes He is their god as well as their tyrant—are hideously deformed. Dealing with Cryxians is not something I enjoy, but war can prompt strange alliances of convenience. Through mutual mistrust, cautious negotiations are possible. In truth I've had some measure of success and even on occasion enjoyed my visits to Blackwater, as strange a city as ever you'll discover. There is a liberating freedom there where no man is a criminal if he can stay alive, and the dead walk the streets next to the living. Not a place I'd like to live, but spending time there has opened my mind to the way the Cryxians see our cloistered lives.

Cygnar could have eliminated Cryx long ago had they the will. Cygnaran kings have not had the stomach to endure the horrible losses required to launch a serious attack on those islands. It would have required a similar effort as casting off the Orgoth, but it would have left a safer legacy for the future. I wonder if the loss of so many great heroes during the Rebellion has permanently diluted all courage from our blood. Cryx was allowed to fester, grow, and build an unliving army of tremendous potency. When Khador invaded Llael at the end of 604 AR, the long anticipated war between Khador and Cygnar began in full force. From this battle, both nations became vulnerable to weaker forces that have beset them to slice open their soft bellies.

Time after time we have seen that the ignored menace will grow in the shadows. In the years ahead I expect many of these groups to emerge. Complacency and a belief that we can enjoy the luxuries of peace and prosperity have led to this. Peace is an illusion—a pause in a fight when a man lowers his guard and is surprised to feel a killing thrust open up his bowels.

The shrewd combatant watches for these openings. They do not walk up to face a foe when his armor is on, sword in hand, and standing rested and ready. Only idiot nobles and theater actors fight this way. Far better to wait until your enemy is tired, overextended in the mud, and perhaps blinded by rain and fog. Wait until he is already bleeding from other wounds and his eyes are watching the distant hill, and strike unseen from the shadowed forest. That is true warfare. There is no one to claim foul play or decry a victory as ignoble when you stand alone on the field with your enemy dead underfoot. Who is more noble, the man whose allies return safely home or those who must bury their dead?

Consider the trollkin who have endured hardship by the human kingdoms, continually forced into the wilderness and away from farmlands. We have forgotten them as we have forgotten many other groups in our thirst for conquest and territory. What do we care if they take over our most inhospitable mountains and densest forests or eke a frugal living at the desert fringes? I have visited these tribes and spent time recovering from wounds at their hospitality. I know they are more than this. They are not primitive savages content to occupy ever-smaller territories and be trod upon by our wars. They are organized, well trained, courageous, and capable of enduring hardship and tragedy which would crush a man's spirit. They are as smart and adaptable as you or I, and they are angry. Though once they were reluctant to challenge kingdom armies, it is another thing to strike while we are distracted fighting one another and require steady supply lines to maintain the fight. In a time of war, a "minor uprising" can change the outcome. We will see this soon.

It's the same with certain religious cults relegated to the fringes that watch kingdom politics with a hungry eye. I am not a religious man, but I do not discount those who take these things to heart. Any time spent among the Protectorate will teach the folly of underestimating faith and unquestioning conviction. Despite the dominance of the Morrowan and Menite faiths, there are other religions thriving like fungus in the darkness. Some of these groups wield surprising influence.

It is not paranoia to see a web of plots connecting seemingly disparate and perplexing events. The most common scapegoats are the Thamarites, those who worship Morrow's dark sister. The common man credits them with depravities beyond their reach. More disquieting are the worshipers of the enigmatic goddess Cyriss, the Maiden of Gears. Her cult has infiltrated the educated among many large cities, and they are capable of unified action and long term planning. In the end all these cults have a vested interest in the supremacy of mankind and ultimately prefer to stay out of our wars.

Those who follow the ancient primal gods worry me. A Dhunian shaman protecting his tribe is like an enraged bear whose cubs are threatened. They are the true leaders of their communities, not the chieftains, and it is the shamans who influence the hearts and wills of the warriors. More dangerous are the cannibalistic followers of the Devourer Wurm—a god of rampant destruction and natural chaos. We thought we'd seen the end of these berserkers in 305 AR after the siege at Midfast where an Ordic soldier named Markus fought off the northern tribes, but they have never truly vanished. Like the trollkin we pushed them into the isolated wilderness where they have recouped their losses. They dream of annihilating the cities of mankind and sending us back to a dark age.

Heed the infamous reputation of the men and women calling themselves druids who are sometimes called blackclads. Their Circle is an ancient cabal, and after recent events I have gained an awareness of this group. The druids draw on the powers of natural chaos and revere an untamable god, but their membership follows a rigid hierarchy. We have seen druids stepping from the shadows in recent years, for the cover of open warfare has allowed them to become active as never before, and the berserker Devourer cults follow their lead. I do not understand their motives or their agenda, but do not underestimate them. We must watch them closely in coming months.

Among both druids and trollkin I have seen something I did not expect—a breed of warrior-mages called warlocks who feed on the fury and strength of beasts through a familiar synergy. I believe this power can stand against modern innovations, and our own warcasters are an echo of this ability like a new manifestation of something far older. This occurred to me as I watched a druid send his beasts to battle. The druids have been secretly harvesting those with this talent, called the *wilding*, since the rise of the Menite priest-kings. How many of these masters of beast, storm, and stone do they boast? How much destruction can they unleash?

Besides these cults, monstrous beings stir from slumber. We forgot there are other dragons than Lord Toruk, each descended from Him. In a long forgotten era, Toruk divided His athanc—the impervious heartstone containing His essence—and birthed a group of godlike progeny. Rather than serve their father, the dragons turned on Him and each other and scattered into the world. The dragons have been quiet in recent centuries, but three are reputed to lurk somewhere in the frozen north. There are reports of turmoil in Khador's northern mountains where a splinter group of non-Iosan elves have become refugees fleeing a terror they cannot name. This terror has descended like a disease on northern Khador. Though the new "Khadoran Empire" has adopted a stoic face, their war efforts have stalled as their empress has recalled soldiers from the front. I have personally witnessed these troop movements. There is nothing in northern Khador that would warrant such activity other than the rise of one of Toruk's spawn.

With these forgotten forces tearing at the fringes of our kingdoms, one may wonder if there is a hope of survival. How can we endure and persevere? I insist this is the natural way of things. We grow stronger and more powerful with each century of warfare and violence. This is a time for us to rise and confront our enemies. We must have a strong leader to rally us, a man who is willing to pay the cost to bring order and unite us despite our worst instincts. A period of strife is necessary to allow for change; change is neither easy nor bloodless.

From the east an army marches toward our war-torn region. This is an army as has never been seen in the west crossing through the Stormlands and across the Bloodstone Marches. This is the gathered might of a people who have endured far worse than we can imagine and who know the meaning of strength forged by survival against horrible adversity. They are the skorne, and they will fall on western Immoren as a hammer strikes clay. They are a catalyst for change.

Leading them is the greatest man born of my generation. He is a true king descended from the proudest of Cygnar's royalty. I speak of Vinter Raelthorne IV who was great even before his treacherous brother usurped his throne. The last twelve years have forged him into something new—an unstoppable avatar of conquest.

I have no illusions about what comes. Vinter the Exile brings a nightmare army of inhuman and relentless warriors. They come to enslave my race and take our lands. Still I welcome them. Their cruel might is our only hope of ultimate survival. It is only by their chains that we will find the inner strength to grasp our destiny. They will inspire in us the old strength as when the Orgoth walked among us.

I pray I have chosen the right side, the winning side. The victors in these battles will be empowered to shape our future. They call me a traitor, but by my sword and the blood of my foes, I will leave an immortal legacy. Bring on the storm. I am ready.

RULES BASICS

General Knowledge for Combat in Hordes

GAME OVERVIEW

Take control of a powerful warlock and wreak havoc on your foes with a horde of hulking warbeasts fueled by unbridled rage. In HORDES, only the strongest, fastest, and most cunning will survive while the rest are a feast served up for your warbeasts.

HORDES is a new fast-paced and aggressive 30mm fantasy tabletop miniatures combat game set in the wilds of the Iron Kingdoms. Players jump into the action controlling powerful warrior-sorcerers or battle-shamans known as warlocks. While warlocks are formidable combatants in their own right, their true strength is drawn from their parasitic synergy with packs of savage warbeasts—large and monstrous creatures of flesh, blood, muscle, and bone—that allow the warlocks to contend on equal footing with the greatest modern armies of the Iron Kingdoms. Players collect, assemble, and paint fantastically detailed models representing the varied beasts, minions, and warriors in their horde. This book provides rules for using those models in brutal and visceral combat. This is monstrous miniatures combat, and your tabletop will never be the same!

A horde is built around a warlock and his warbeasts. Squads of soldiers and support teams may be fielded to bolster a horde's combat capabilities further. Sometimes huge hordes with multiple warlocks and legions of soldiers take the field to crush their enemies with the combined might of spears, spells, and claws.

What you need for HORDES

IN ADDITION TO THIS BOOK AND YOUR ARMY OF HORDES MODELS, YOU WILL ALSO NEED A FEW BASIC ITEMS TO PLAY:

• A TABLE OR PLAYING SURFACE WHERE YOU CAN CONDUCT YOUR BATTLES (TYPICALLY 4' X 4').

• A TAPE MEASURE OR RULER MARKED IN INCHES AND FRACTIONS THEREOF TO MEASURE MOVEMENT AND ATTACK DISTANCES.

• A FEW SIX-SIDED DICE. FOUR OR MORE WILL BE PLENTY.

• A HANDFUL OF TOKENS TO INDICATE FURY POINTS, SPELL EFFECTS, ETC.

• THE APPROPRIATE STAT CARDS INCLUDED WITH EACH MODEL. WE SUGGEST YOU USE PHOTOCOPIES OR PUT THEM IN CARD SLEEVES AND USE A DRY ERASE MARKER TO MARK DAMAGE.

• THE MARKERS AND TEMPLATES FOUND ON PAGE 208 AT THE BACK OF THIS BOOK. YOU MAY PHOTOCOPY THEM FOR PERSONAL USE.

Warbeasts are mighty creatures born or trained to fight and drawn from the wilds of the continent of Immoren: deep in the forests, mountains, frozen tundra, or across the desert wastes. All are chosen for their ability to fight and work themselves into a frenzied rage at the command of their warlocks. Most rely on claw and fang but boast other supernatural powers, and some wield massive weapons, both melee and ranged.

A warlock is in constant telepathic contact with the allied warbeasts in his vicinity, and he can force them to attack with greater accuracy, perform exceptional feats of strength, or launch difficult special attacks, all of which generate fury. During the course of a confrontation the warlock can leach this fury from his warbeasts and use it to boost his combat abilities, heal himself or his beasts, transfer his own injuries onto warbeasts, or cast formidable spells. In addition to his own spells, a warlock can tap the dormant innate power (called animus) of the warbeasts brought to battle.

The warlock is both the tie that binds the horde together and its weakest link. If all warlocks fall, the warbeasts lose interest in the fight and head home.

The outcome of battle depends on your ability to think quickly, use sound tactics, and decisively employ your forces. A crucial component of strategy is the management of warbeasts' fury to enhance their own attacks and fuel a warlock's powers. Properly managed, the use of fury can turn a warpack into an unstoppable horde of destruction! However, generating too much fury can backfire, causing warbeasts to frenzy uncontrollably and attack the nearest friend or foe.

In these conflicts it's survival of the fittest, so bring the hurt or head for the hills!

SUMMARY OF PLAY

Before a battle begins, players agree on an encounter level and a scenario to be played, and then they create their hordes based on those guidelines. Next, determine the turn order. It will not change throughout the game. Players then deploy their forces and prepare for the battle to begin.

Battles are conducted in a series of *game rounds*. Each game round, every player receives one turn to command his own horde. During his turn, a player may activate all the models in his force, one after the other.

When activated, a model may move and then perform one of a variety of actions such as attacking, healing a *warbeast*, or casting spells. Once all players have taken their turns, the current game round ends and a new one begins starting again with the first player. Game rounds continue until one side wins either by destroying all opposition, meeting scenario objectives, or accepting its opponent's surrender.

Dice and Rounding

HORDES uses six-sided dice, abbreviated d6, to determine the success of attacks and other actions. Most events, such as attacks, require rolling two dice. Other events typically require rolling from one to four dice.

Some events call for rolling a d3. To do so, roll a d6, divide the result by two, and round up.

Some instances call for a model's stat or a die roll to be divided in half. With the exception of distances, always round a fractional result to the next highest whole number.

General Guidelines

This section covers how HORDES handles game terms, the relationship between standard and special rules, sportsmanship between players, and the procedures for resolving rules disputes.

Game Terms

When these rules introduce a game term in a definitive fashion, its name appears in bold. If the rules reference a term from another section, its first appearance in that section will be in italics. For ease of reference, game terms are defined in the Glossary.

Rule Priority

Though HORDES is a complex game providing a multitude of options, the rules are actually intuitive and easy to learn. The standard rules lay the foundation upon which the game is built and provide all the typical mechanics used in play. Additional special rules apply to specific models and modify the standard rules in certain circumstances. When they apply, these special rules take precedence.

Sportsmanship & Sharing Information

Although HORDES simulates violent battles between mammoth forces, you should still strive to be a good sportsman in all aspects of the game. Remember, this is a game meant to provide entertainment and friendly competition. Whether winning or losing, you should still be having lots of fun.

From time to time, your opponent may wish to see your records to verify a model's stats or see how much damage a particular warbeast has taken. Always represent this information honestly and share your records and information without hesitation.

Resolving Rules Issues

These rules have been carefully designed to provide as much guidance as possible in all aspects of play. However, you may encounter situations where the proper course of action is not immediately obvious. For instance, players may disagree on whether or not a model has *line of sight* to its intended target.

> ## What's a d6? How about a d3?
>
> A SIX-SIDED DIE IS REFERRED TO AS A D6. TWO SIX-SIDED DICE ARE ABBREVIATED AS 2D6, THREE DICE AS 3D6, AND SO ON.
>
> A D3 IS A QUICK WAY TO SAY, "ROLL A D6, DIVIDE BY 2, AND ROUND UP." QUITE A MOUTHFUL! HERE'S HOW TO READ THE RESULTS OF A D3 ROLL QUICKLY:
>
> 1 OR 2 = 1
> 3 OR 4 = 2
> 5 OR 6 = 3

During a game, try to resolve the issue quickly in the interest of keeping the game flowing. After the game you will have plenty of time to decide the best answer, and it can then be incorporated into future games.

If a situation arises in which all players cannot agree on a solution, quickly discuss the matter and reference this rulebook for an answer, but do not spend so much time doing so that you slow the game. In striving to resolve an issue, common sense and the precedents set by the rules should be your guides.

If the dispute cannot be solved quickly, have one player from each side roll a d6—the highest roller gets to decide the outcome. Reroll any ties. In the interest of fairness, once a ruling has been made for a specific issue, it applies for all similar circumstances for the rest of the game. After the game ends, you can take the time to reference the rules and thoroughly discuss the issue to decide how best to handle that same situation in the future.

MODELS–THE DOGS OF WAR

Model Types, Stats, and Damage Capacity

Each HORDES combatant is represented on the tabletop by a highly detailed and dramatically posed miniature figurine referred to as a **model**. There are several basic model types: *warlocks, warbeasts, troopers, and solos*. Warlocks, troopers, and solos are collectively referred to as **warriors**. Models are living models unless otherwise noted.

INDEPENDENT MODELS

Independent models are those that activate individually. Warlocks, warbeasts, and solos are independent models.

Warlocks

A **warlock** is a tremendously powerful shaman, druid, or elementalist with the ability to control a group of warbeasts telepathically. A warlock is a deadly opponent, for he is highly skilled in both physical combat and spell casting.

During battle a warlock commands the warbeasts of his horde in an effort to complete his objectives. A warlock may use his *fury points* drawn from friendly *warbeasts* to enhance his combat abilities and cast spells. Throughout a battle, the warlock *forces* warbeasts to excel in combat.

Warlocks are *independent models*.

Warbeasts

Warbeasts are creatures noted for formidable battle prowess and an affinity or conditioned ability to be controlled by warlocks. Warbeasts come in a variety of shapes and sizes and are drawn from diverse geographies and ecologies. They are smarter than an animal but more primitive and savage than the cultured races leading the battles across the face of Immoren. Each of the armies in HORDES brings distinct types of warbeasts to their battles with individual techniques for recruiting and controlling them. Once brought to fight, the fury of their attacks strengthens their warlocks, and together they form an almost unstoppable synergy.

Warbeasts would be termed the most terrible of monsters by civilized nations, for each is capable of ripping a dozen armed men limb from limb. Many have had their considerable natural abilities enhanced by being outfitted with heavy armor and the best-made weapons their warlocks can find. Most have endured considerable training to capitalize on their abilities and fight ably alongside both warriors and warlocks. Though warbeasts are capable of acting on their own, a warlock's dominating will overrides their individuality except in cases of frenzy.

Warbeasts are classified according to base size: Generally speaking, a **lesser warbeast** has a small base (30 mm), a **light warbeast** has a medium base (40 mm), and a **heavy warbeast** has a large base (50 mm). Warbeasts are *independent models*.

Solos

Solos are individuals such as monster hunters and champions that operate alone. Solos are *independent models*.

UNITS

A **unit** is a group of similarly trained and equipped trooper models operating together as a single force. A unit usually contains one leader and two or more additional troopers.

Troopers

Troopers are models such as swordsmen, archers, and scattergunners that operate together in groups called **units**. A unit always operates as a single coherent force. Troopers in a unit share identical attributes and carry the same weapons.

Some special rules and spells affect entire units. When any trooper in a unit is affected by a special rule such as terror or a unit-affecting spell, every member of that unit is affected. Special rules and spells that affect units are noted in their descriptions.

Leaders

Usually one trooper in a unit is trained as a **leader** and can give its unit *orders*. It is represented by a model with a different stat profile and possibly different weaponry. A leader generally has a higher Command (CMD) stat than the other troopers in his unit, and a unit uses its leader's CMD stat for all command checks while its leader is in play.

MODEL PROFILES

Every model and unit has a unique profile that translates its combat abilities into game terms. HORDES uses a series of *stats* to quantify and scale the attributes fundamental to game play. In addition, a model may have *special rules* that further enhance its performance. The faction section provides all the game information required for your horde to battle across the tabletop.

A model or unit's **stat card** provides a quick in-game reference for its profile and special rules. The card's front has model and weapon stats, a special rules list, and a damage track or life spiral if applicable. Field allowance, point cost, unit composition, victory points, and summarized special rule descriptions appear on the card's back. Warlocks have an additional stat card used to explain their spells and feats. Refer to this book for the complete text of a special rule or spell; it takes precedence over the abridged version on the stat cards.

MODEL STATISTICS

Model **statistics**, or **stats**, provide a numerical representation of a model's basic combat qualities—the higher the number, the better the stat. These stats are used for various die rolls throughout the game. The **stat bar** presents the model statistics in an easy-to-reference format.

IRONHIDE				CMD 9	
SPD	STR	MAT	RAT	DEF	ARM
6	8	7	5	14	16

Chieftain Madrak Ironhide

The model statistics and their definitions follow:

Speed (SPD) — A model's normal movement rate. A model moves its SPD in inches when *advancing*.

Strength (STR) — A model's physical strength. Add a model's STR to the *damage roll* of its melee weapons.

Melee Attack (MAT) — A model's skill with melee weapons such as swords and hammers or natural weapons like fists and teeth. Add a model's MAT to its *melee attack* rolls.

Ranged Attack (RAT) — A model's accuracy with ranged weapons such as guns and crossbows or thrown items like spears and knives. Add a model's RAT to its *ranged attack* rolls.

Defense (DEF) — A model's ability to avoid being hit by an attack. A model's size, quickness, skill, and even magical protection can all contribute to its DEF.

An *attack roll* must be equal to or greater than the target model's DEF to score a hit against it.

Armor (ARM) — A model's ability to resist being damaged. This resistance may come from natural resilience, worn armor, or even magical benefits. A model takes one *damage point* for every point that a *damage roll* exceeds its ARM.

Command (CMD) — A model's willpower, leadership, and self-discipline. To pass a *command check*, a model must roll equal to or less than its CMD on 2d6. Command also determines the *command range* of a model with the *Commander* ability, such as a warlock.

Fury (FURY) — When warbeasts are *forced* to perform certain actions, they generate *fury*. Warlocks draw on that fury to enhance their own abilities. A warlock's FURY stat represents the maximum amount of fury that he can normally have at one time. It also determines a warlock's *control area*. A warbeast's FURY is a measure of how much the warbeast can be *forced*. Only warlocks and warbeasts have a FURY stat.

Threshold (THR) — A measure of the difficulty of controlling a warbeast. To pass a *threshold check*, a warbeast must roll equal to or less than its THR on 2d6, adding one to the die roll for each *fury point* it has. Only warbeasts have a THR stat.

Some special rules change a model's **base stat** to a specific value. Apply this change before applying any other modifiers to the stat. For example, stationary targets have a base DEF of 5 against ranged and magic attacks, so a stationary model behind cover has a net DEF of 9 (base DEF 5 + 4 DEF for cover).

WEAPON STATISTICS

Each of a model's weapons has its own stat bar. A sword icon denotes a melee weapon, and a pistol icon denotes a ranged weapon. A weapon's stat bar only lists the stats that apply to its use.

THROWN AXE			
RNG	ROF	AOE	POW
8	1	—	7

sample ranged weapon stat bar

RATHROK		
SPECIAL	POW	P+S
Multi	7	15

sample melee weapon stat bar

Power (POW) — The base amount of damage a weapon inflicts. Add the weapon's POW to its damage roll.

Power plus strength (P+S) — Melee weapons add both the weapon's POW and the model's STR to the damage roll. For quick reference, the P+S value provides the sum of these two stats.

Range (RNG) — The maximum distance in inches a model can make ranged attacks with this weapon. Measure range from the nearest edge of the attacking model's base to the nearest edge of the target model's base.

Rate of Fire (ROF) — The maximum number of times a model can make ranged attacks with this weapon during its activation. Reloading time limits most ranged weapons to only one attack per activation.

Area-of-Effect (AOE) — The diameter in inches of the template an *area-of-effect* (AOE) weapon uses for damage effects. When using an AOE weapon, center the template on the determined *point of impact*. All models covered by the template, even partially, potentially suffer the attack's effects. See Combat (pg. 38) for detailed rules on AOE weapons. Templates for AOE's can be found on pg. 208.

Location — A warbeast's weapon stat bars indicate where its weapons are located: left arm (LFT), right arm (RT), head (HD), or other location (—). These locations are used when resolving *head* and *weapon locks* (pg. 39).

Special Rules — In addition to their normal damage, many weapons have unique advantages or produce extraordinary effects explained by their special rules. A weapon with more than one such rule lists "Multi" along with a complete effects listing in the special rules section for the model.

SPECIAL RULES

Most HORDES combatants are highly specialized and trained to fill unique roles on the battlefield. To represent this, certain models have **special rules** that take precedence over the standard rules. Depending on their use, special rules are categorized as *abilities*, *feats*, *special actions*, *special attacks*, or *orders*.

A model's horde list entry and the back of its stat card summarize its special rules. In addition, Combat (pg. 38) and Warlocks, Warbeasts, and Fury (pg. 55) detail many special rules common to all warbeasts and warlocks that do not appear on the stat cards.

Abilities — An ability typically gives a benefit or capability that modifies how the standard rules apply to the model. Abilities are always in effect and apply every time a game situation warrants their use.

Feats — Each warlock has a unique feat he can use once per game. A warlock can use this feat freely at any time during his activation in addition to moving and performing an action.

Ancestral Guardian: Solo

Krueger the Stormwrath: Warlock

Carnivean: Heavy Warbeast

Farrow Brigands: Unit

Special Actions (★Action) — A special action lets a model perform an action normally unavailable to other models. A model can perform a special action instead of its combat action if it meets the specific requirements for its use.

Special Attacks (★Attack) — A special attack gives a model an attack option normally unavailable to other models. Warbeasts may also make a variety of punishing special attacks called *power attacks* described in Combat (pg. 38). A model may make one special attack instead of making any normal melee or ranged attacks during its combat action if it meets the specific requirements

Orders — An order lets a unit perform a specialized combat maneuver during its activation. A unit may receive an order from a model with the Commander ability prior to its activation or from its leader at the beginning of its activation.

DAMAGE CAPACITY AND LIFE SPIRALS

A model's **damage capacity** determines how many damage points it can suffer before being *destroyed*. Most troopers do not have a damage capacity; they are destroyed and removed from the table as soon as they suffer one damage point. The horde list entry for a more resilient model gives the total amount of damage it can suffer before being destroyed. Its stat card provides a row of **damage circles** for tracking the damage it receives. Unmarked damage circles are sometimes called **wounds**. A warbeast's damage circles are arranged in a **life spiral**.

Every time one of these models suffers damage, mark one damage circle for each damage point taken. A model with damage capacity is **destroyed** once all its damage circles are marked. However, a warbeast may lose *aspects* before its life spiral is completely filled. A

warbeast's life spiral is arranged into three **aspects**: Mind, Body, and Spirit. When all damage circles for a specific aspect have been marked, the warbeast loses the use of that aspect. See Combat (pg. 38) for detailed rules on recording damage and its effects.

BASE SIZE AND FACING

The physical model itself has a couple of properties important to game play: *base size* and *facing*.

Base Size

The physical size and mass of a model are reflected by its **base size**. There are three base sizes: **small base** (30mm), **medium base** (40mm), and **large base** (50mm). Generally speaking, lesser warbeasts and most human-sized warrior models have small bases, larger creatures and light warbeasts have medium bases, and very large creatures and heavy warbeasts have large bases. A model's horde list entry states its base size.

Facing

A model's **facing** is the direction indicated by its head's orientation. The 180° arc centered on the direction its head faces defines the model's **front arc**; the opposite 180° defines its **back arc**. You may want to make two small marks on either side of each of your models' bases to indicate where the front arc ends and the back arc begins.

A model's front arc determines its perspective of the battlefield. A model typically directs its *actions*, determines *line of sight*, and makes attacks through this arc. Likewise, a model is usually more vulnerable to attacks from its back arc due to a lack of awareness in that direction.

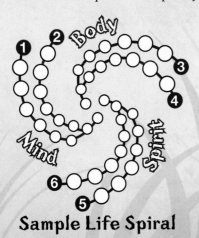

Sample Life Spiral

Model Facing

PREPARING FOR WAR

Building a Horde Suitable for Crushing Your Opponent

CREATING A HORDE

A warlock and his warbeasts form the central fighting group of every HORDES force. Units and solos with a variety of abilities further support the warlock and his warbeasts. In larger battles, you can even field multiple warlocks for greater might.

To create a horde, first decide on an *encounter level*, and then spend the allotted *horde points* to purchase models and units from your chosen faction's horde list and from minions that will work for that faction. Every horde list entry and stat card provides the model or unit's *point cost* and *field allowance* values to which you must adhere when designing your force. Specific *scenarios* may modify the standard horde creation rules.

ENCOUNTER LEVELS

HORDES battles are played at different encounter levels to allow for a diversity of horde sizes, strategies, and game experiences. Each encounter level gives the maximum number of horde points each player can spend when designing a horde. You need not spend every point available, but your horde cannot exceed the maximum number of points allowed by the selected level.

Each encounter level also limits the number of warlocks available to each player.

Duel

Max Warlocks: 1   Horde Points: 350
Est. Play Time: 30 Minutes

A duel occurs when two warlocks cross paths. Sometimes they are on special assignments, but other times they are out to settle vicious rivalries. Duels include only individual warlocks and their personal warbeasts. Duels are the perfect match for playing with the contents of a Warpack Box.

Rumble

Max Warlocks: 1   Horde Points: 500
Est. Play Time: 60 Minutes

A rumble is an encounter that includes a single warlock and his warbeasts supported by a small retinue of units and solos. Rumbles can occur over such things as routine border patrols or elite, surgical missions.

Grand Melee

Max Warlocks: 1   Horde Points: 750
Est. Play Time: 90 Minutes

As warfare ravages across the wilds, escalating hostilities rage unchecked and out of control. Each faction races to bring its most devastating beasts of war to the battlefield to ensure total victory. Everywhere hordes march to battle commanded by individual warlocks.

Battle Royale

Max Warlocks: 2   Horde Points: 1000
Est. Play Time: 2 hours

Battles decide the pivotal events in the course of a military campaign. With up to two warlocks in a horde, you can fully realize the opportunities for army customization and heavy firepower.

War

Max Warlocks: 3   Horde Points: 1500
Est. Play Time: 3 hours

When objectives can no longer be achieved by deploying small forces and when both sides refuse to yield, nothing less than war can resolve their differences. This huge game, in which each side fields up to three warlocks, allows your forces enough breadth and depth to inflict and recover from staggering blows as the fight seesaws back and forth.

Apocalypse

Max Warlocks: 4+   Horde Points: 2000+
Est. Play Time: 4+ hours

When a conflict rages so bitterly that war itself cannot resolve it, the final reckoning has arrived, for you have summoned the apocalypse. An apocalypse is a massive game employing four or more warlocks in each force. Although this vast endeavor should never be undertaken lightly, it yields game experiences that can be found in no other arena. One warlock may be added to a horde for each additional increment of 500 pts.

CHARACTERS

Some models represent unique individuals from the wilds of Immoren. These personalities receive proper names and are identified as **characters**. Characters follow the rules for their basic model type.

A horde may include only one model of each named character. For instance, you can never have two Madrak Ironhides in the same horde. However, two rival Trollblood players could each field Ironhide. How can this be?

In the chaos and tumult now cloaking war-torn Immoren, pretenders and imposters abound. Thus, you may find yourself fielding one or more warlocks who, impossibly, face their apparent counterparts across the field of battle. Who is the *real* Madrak Ironhide or Thagrosh, Prophet of Everblight? Victory alone can determine the answer.

POINT COSTS

A model's **point cost** indicates how many *horde points* you must spend to include one of these models (or in the case of units, one basic unit) in your horde. Some entries also include options to spend additional points for upgrades typically in the form of adding more troopers to a unit.

FIELD ALLOWANCE

Field allowance (FA) is the maximum number of models or units of a given type that may be included for each warlock in a horde. For example, Circle Tharn Ravagers have FA: 2, indicating that a horde may have up to two Tharn Ravager units for each warlock. A horde with two warlocks could have up to four Tharn Ravager units.

A field allowance of "U" means an unlimited number of these models or units may be fielded in a horde. A field allowance of "C" means the model is a character; only one of each named character is allowed per horde.

SETUP, DEPLOYMENT, AND VICTORY CONDITIONS

HORDES games can be played in a variety of ways. The primary influences on a game's setup are its encounter level, number of players, and victory conditions. Players may also agree to play a specific scenario or even design one of their own.

TWO-PLAYER GAMES

In a typical HORDES game, two players match forces across a 4' by 4' playing surface. After setting

Sample Horde

WE BUILT THE FOLLOWING HORDE TO ILLUSTRATE HORDES' FORCE CREATION CONCEPTS. THIS HORDE IS DESIGNED FOR THE BATTLE ROYALE ENCOUNTER LEVEL, MEANING A PLAYER CAN SPEND A MAXIMUM OF 1,000 HORDE POINTS AND FIELD UP TO TWO WARLOCKS.

WARLOCKS

KAYA THE WILDBORNE	59
KRUEGER THE STORMWRATH	61

WARBEASTS

2 WARPWOLF HEAVY WARBEASTS	216 (108 EA.)
1 WOLDWARDEN HEAVY WARBEAST	116
2 ARGUS LIGHT WARBEASTS	108 (54 EA.)
2 GORAX LIGHT WARBEASTS	114 (57 EA.)

SUPPORT

1 LORD OF THE FEAST (CHARACTER)	33
2 WOLVES OF ORBOROS UNITS (FA: 3) WITH 4 ADDITIONAL WOLVES EACH	166 (51+8+8+8+8 EACH)
2 THARN BLOODTRACKER UNITS (FA: 1)	120 (60 EACH)

TOTAL	993 POINTS

THE CHOSEN WARLOCKS ARE KAYA THE WILDBORNE AND KRUEGER THE STORMWRATH, AVOIDING DUPLICATION SINCE THEY ARE NAMED CHARACTERS. THE TWO UNITS OF WOLVES OF ORBOROS EACH HAVE FOUR ADDITIONAL WOLVES, THE MAXIMUM ALLOWED BY THE UNIT OPTIONS. WITH AN FA: 3 AND TWO WARLOCKS, THIS HORDE COULD INCLUDE UP TO SIX UNITS OF WOLVES OF ORBOROS. TWO UNITS OF THARN BLOODTRACKERS CAN BE INCLUDED DESPITE THEIR FA: 1 BECAUSE THERE ARE TWO WARLOCKS. YOU ARE ALLOWED ONE UNIT OF THARN BLOODTRACKERS PER WARLOCK. ON THE OTHER HAND, THERE CAN ONLY BE ONE LORD OF THE FEAST REGARDLESS OF THE NUMBER OF WARLOCKS BECAUSE HE IS A CHARACTER. THIS BRINGS THE TOTAL HORDE POINTS SPENT TO 993. SINCE NOTHING ELSE IS AVAILABLE FOR 7 POINTS OR LESS, THOSE POINTS REMAIN UNSPENT.

up the battlefield according to Terrain (pg. 63), players make a **starting roll**. To make a starting game roll, each player rolls a d6. The highest roller chooses any player, including himself, to be the **first player**. Once established, the turn order remains the same for the rest of the game.

Players then deploy their armies starting with the first player. The first player may choose any edge of the playing surface and deploy all his forces up to 10" in from that edge. Deploy units so that all of their troopers are *in formation*. The second player then deploys his

forces on the opposite side of the playing surface, following the same guidelines.

MULTIPLAYER GAMES

When playing multiplayer games of HORDES, players can choose to play either a team game or a free-for-all game. After agreeing on the type of game to be played, set up the battlefield and use the following guidelines to determine the game's turn order.

Team Games

Before beginning a team game, the players must split into two opposing sides. Decide the composition of the teams. Teams should be made up exclusively of models from the same faction and the minions that will work for that faction. Each team may only include one of any *character* model. To begin, have one player from each team roll a d6 to establish the turn order. The team that rolls highest gets to choose which team goes first; the first team gets to choose which of their players will be the first player. Once the first player is determined, the opposing team chooses which of their players will go next. The first team then nominates one of their players to be third, followed again by the opposing team. This continues until all players have a place in the turn order and ensures the turn order will alternate between players of opposing teams.

Force deployment should be done in turn order, following the above guidelines, with teammates sharing the same deployment zone opposite the battlefield from their opponents' deployment zone.

Free-for-all Games

You can also choose to play a multiplayer game in which each player fights independently in a free-for-all game. To establish turn order, each player rolls a d6. Starting with the highest roller and working to the lowest, each player gets to choose any available position in the turn order. Re-roll ties as they occur with the highest re-roller winning his choice of position, followed by the next highest re-roller, and so on. For example, Matt, Jason, Mike, and Steve roll 6, 5, 5, and 3 respectively for turn order. Matt chooses his position first. Then Jason and Mike re-roll their tie, getting a 4 and a 2. Jason chooses next, followed by Mike. As the lowest roller, Steve gets the remaining position in the turn order.

Use your best judgment to establish deployment zones based on the number of players and the size and shape of your playing surface. Deployment zones should be spaced such that no player gets a significant advantage or disadvantage—unless mutually agreed upon. As a starting point, for games with three or four players on a 4' by 4' playing surface, consider deploying forces within 10" of any corner of the playing area to ensure adequate separation.

SCENARIOS

If all players agree, you can set up the game according to a specific scenario. Scenarios add an extra layer of excitement by incorporating special circumstances and unique rules. A player wins a scenario by achieving its objectives, not necessarily by eliminating his opponent's forces. Certain scenarios have specific guidelines for playing-area size, terrain setup, deployment zones, and turn order. See Scenarios (pg. 67) for the scenario descriptions. If you feel particularly daring, you can randomly determine which scenario to play.

As long as all players agree, you can even design your own scenarios to create a unique battle experience. Just be sure to allow a minimum of 24" between rival deployment zones. Feel free to be creative when setting up your games. For instance, if you have three players, one player could set up in the middle of the table as a defender and the other two could attack from opposite edges. Furthermore, you could have a four-player team game with teammates deploying across from each other on opposite edges of the battlefield meaning everyone will have enemies on either side. Your imagination is the only limit.

VICTORY CONDITIONS

Establish victory conditions before deploying forces. Typically victory goes to the player or team who eliminates the opposition or accepts their surrender. A scenario defines specific objectives for each side. You can also use *victory points* to determine a game's winner.

Victory Points

Every model and unit is worth a set number of **victory points**. A player or team scores victory points for each of their opponents' models that have been *destroyed* or *removed from play*. Players and teams only score victory points for the casualties they inflict. Victory points for models destroyed or removed from play are awarded when the models leave the table. All other victory points for eliminating models are awarded at the end of the game. Additionally, award victory points at the end of the game to a player or team for each enemy warbeast that is *wild* as a result of the elimination of a warlock. Award these victory points only to the player or team that last caused the warbeast to become wild. Once a player has been awarded victory points for eliminating a model or unit, these points are never lost even if the model subsequently returns to play. If returned models are later eliminated, award victory points for them again. If a player accidentally or intentionally eliminates a friendly model, be it his own or a teammate's, award its full victory points to every opposing player or team.

Decide how victory points will be used, if at all, before starting the game. One option is to end the game after a chosen number of *game rounds*. Victory goes to the player or team with the most victory points at the end of the last game round. Another option is to end the game once any player or team accumulates a minimum number of victory points. Once a player or team reaches the victory point goal, the game will end at the conclusion of the current game round, and victory goes to the player or team with the most victory points at that time. If you run out of time while playing a game with other victory conditions, you may use victory points to determine the winner.

STARTING THE GAME

After establishing victory conditions and deploying forces, the first *game round* begins. Every warlock begins the game with a number *fury points* equal to his FURY stat. Starting with the first player, each player takes a turn in turn order. Game rounds continue until one side achieves its victory conditions and wins the game.

A HORDES battlefield before a battle commences

GAMEPLAY—THE RULES OF ENGAGEMENT

Turn Sequence, Movement, and Actions

THE GAME ROUND

HORDES battles are fought in a series of **game rounds**. Each game round, every player takes a turn in the order established during setup. Once the last player in the turn order completes his turn, the current game round ends. A new game round then begins starting again with the first player. Game rounds continue until one side wins the game.

For game effects, a **round** is measured from the current player's turn to the beginning of that player's next turn regardless of his location in the turn order. When put in play, a game effect with a duration of one round expires at the beginning of the current player's next turn. This means every player will take one turn while the effect is in play.

THE PLAYER TURN

A player's turn has three phases: *Maintenance*, *Control*, and *Activation*.

MAINTENANCE PHASE

During the Maintenance Phase, perform the following steps in order:

1) Remove any effects that expire at the beginning of your turn.

2) Remove fury points from your warlocks in excess of their FURY stats.

3) Resolve any compulsory effects on your models.

4) Check for expiration of *continuous effects* on any models you control and apply those that remain in play.

5) Activate *fleeing* models and fleeing units under your control. A fleeing model or unit may attempt to *rally* at the end of this activation. See Command (pg. 61) for detailed rules on fleeing and rallying. Make a *threshold check* for each of your *wild* warbeasts in the control area of any of your warlocks. Activate those that fail as well as any of your wild warbeasts that are outside all of your warlocks' control areas. See Warlock Death (pg. 53) for detailed rules on wild warbeasts.

CONTROL PHASE

During the Control Phase, perform the following steps in order:

1) Each of your warlocks may *leach* (pg. 57) any number of fury points up to his FURY stat from friendly warbeasts in his control area.

2) Each warlock may then spend the fury points required to keep his *upkeep spells* in play. If a warlock does not spend fury points on a spell requiring upkeep, it expires and its effects end immediately.

3) Make a *threshold check* (pg. 58) for each of your warbeasts with one or more fury points left on it. Any warbeasts that fail the check immediately *frenzy* (pg. 58).

4) Resolve any other effects that occur during the Control Phase.

ACTIVATION PHASE

The Activation Phase is the major portion of a player's turn. All models you control must be activated once per turn. This is usually done during the Activation Phase, but models may activate earlier in the turn due to fleeing, frenzy, or other effects. Independent models and units are activated one at a time in an order of your choosing. A model cannot forfeit its activation unless required to do so by a special rule.

An active model first moves (see Movement pg. 32) or forfeits its movement, and then it may perform one action (see Actions pg. 37) allowed by the movement option chosen.

ACTIVATING MODELS

Always completely resolve the active model or unit's movement before it performs any actions.

ACTIVATING INDEPENDENT MODELS

Independent models activate individually. Only one independent model can activate at a time. The active model must complete its movement and completely resolve its action before another model or unit can be activated.

ACTIVATING UNITS

Troopers do not activate individually. Instead, the entire unit activates at once. When a unit activates, every trooper in the unit must complete or forfeit its movement before any actions can be performed. After completing the entire unit's movement, each trooper may then perform an action, one trooper at a time.

Units require strong leadership and guidance to be effective on the battlefield. Since a unit operates as one body, it functions best when all members are in formation. A unit must receive an order from its leader or a nearby model with the Commander ability to run, charge, or perform a specialized combat maneuver. Additionally, a unit must end its movement with all members *in formation*.

LINE OF SIGHT

Many game situations such as charging, ranged attacks, and most magic attacks require a model to have **line of sight (LOS)** to its intended target. A model has line of sight to a target if you can draw a straight, unobstructed line from the center of its base at head height through its front arc to any part of the target model, including its base. Warrior models present a slight exception to this rule. Unlike warbeast models, items held in the hands of warrior models—such as their weapons or a banner pole—do not count as part of the model for determining line of sight. For example, a Pyg Bushwhacker does not have line of sight to a

Cataphract Cetratus if all he can see is the tip of a spear poking out from behind a wall.

Simply put, having line of sight means that the model can see its target. If a model's line of sight is questionable, it may be easiest for a player to position himself to see the table from his model's perspective. A laser pointer may also come in handy when determining line of sight.

INTERVENING MODELS

A model blocks line of sight to models that have equal or smaller-sized bases. If any line between the center of the attacking model's base at head height and the target passes over another model's base, that model is an **intervening model**. You cannot draw a line of sight across an intervening model's base to models that have equal or smaller-sized bases. However, you might still have a line of sight to the target if its base is not completely obscured by the intervening model's base.

An intervening model does not block line of sight to models that have larger bases. Ignore it when drawing line of sight.

> ## What does a model do when activated?
>
> AN ACTIVE MODEL FIRST MOVES OR FORFEITS ITS MOVEMENT. DEPENDING ON THE MOVEMENT OPTION CHOSEN, THE MODEL MAY BE ABLE TO PERFORM EITHER A COMBAT ACTION OR A SPECIAL ACTION. A COMBAT ACTION LETS A MODEL MAKE ATTACKS. A SPECIAL ACTION LETS A MODEL PERFORM A UNIQUE BATTLEFIELD FUNCTION SUCH AS DIGGING IN OR SPAWNING A LESSER WARBEAST.

SCREENING

A **screening model** is an intervening model that has an equal or larger-sized base than the target model and is within 1" of it. The target model is **screened** by a screening model and gains +2 DEF against ranged and magic attacks. The target does not gain this bonus if the intervening model has a smaller base, if the attacker's line of sight to the screening model is completely obstructed by terrain, or if the target's base is more than 1" away from the screening model's

Warrior held weapon: no line of sight

Warbeast weapon: clear line of sight

Clear line of sight

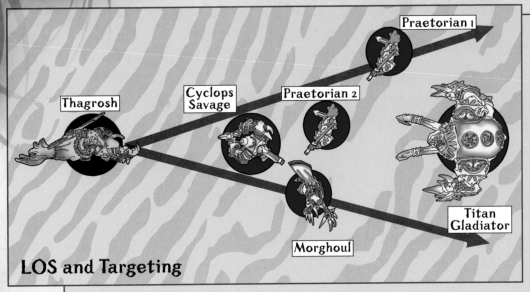

LOS and Targeting

This diagram highlights the LOS rules. Thagrosh has LOS to the Cyclops Savage. Since the Cyclops Savage has a medium base, it is an intervening model for other models with medium and small bases. Thagrosh has LOS to Praetorian 1 since he can draw a line of sight to it that does not cross the Cyclops Savage's base. On the other hand, Thagrosh does not have LOS to Praetorian 2 since he cannot draw a line to its base that does

not cross the Cyclops Savage's base. Praetorian 2 is within 1" of the intervening Cyclops Savage, so even if Thagrosh were on a higher elevation than those two models, he still would not have LOS to Praetorian 2 because it is screened by the Cyclops Savage.

Since they have smaller bases, the Cyclops Savage and the Praetorians are not intervening models for the Titan Gladiator. Thagrosh can draw a line of sight to the Titan Gladiator as if those models were not there.

The Cyclops Savage is an intervening model for Morghoul since it has a larger base, and Thagrosh has LOS to Morghoul since his base is not completely obscured, just like Praetorian 1. The difference is that Morghoul is within 1" of the intervening model, so he gains +2 DEF against Thagrosh's ranged and magic attacks because he is screened by the Cyclops Savage.

base regardless of base size. The screening bonus is only applied once regardless of the number of screening models.

ELEVATION AND LOS

When drawing line of sight from a model on a higher elevation than its target, ignore all intervening models on lower elevation than the attacking model except those that would normally screen the target. Additionally, you can draw a line of sight through screening models that have equal or smaller-sized bases than the attacking model, but the target still gets +2 DEF for being screened.

When drawing line of sight from a model on a lower elevation than its target, ignore all intervening models on a lower elevation than the target. A model on higher elevation than its attacker gains +2 DEF against ranged and magic attacks from that opponent. Models on lower elevations than the target do not provide *screening*.

MOVEMENT

The first part of a model's activation is movement. A model must use or forfeit its movement before performing any action. When moving a model, first declare the type of movement the model will perform, and then measure the distance. Make all movement measurements from

the front of a model's base. Determine the distance a model moves by measuring how far the front of its base travels. The distance moved is absolute; we suggest using a flexible measuring device to keep accurate track of a model's movement. Terrain, spells, and other effects can reduce a model's movement or prevent it completely. Movement penalties are cumulative, but a model allowed to move can always move at least 1". See Terrain (pg. 63) for full details on terrain features and how they affect movement.

A moving model's base may not pass over another model's base. It can move between models only if enough room exists for its base to pass between the other models' bases without touching them.

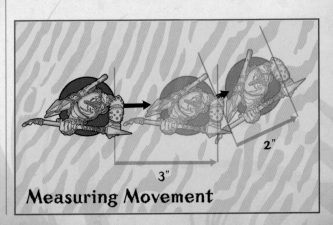

Measuring Movement

A model can voluntarily forfeit its movement by not changing its position or facing. If it does so, the model can perform one action and gains an aiming bonus for any ranged attacks made during this turn's combat action.

A model unable to move cannot change its position or facing. It may or may not be able to perform an action depending on the effect preventing its movement. A model that cannot move cannot forfeit its movement and therefore does not receive the aiming bonus for doing so.

There are three different types of movement: advancing, running, and charging.

The term *normal movement* refers to the movement a model makes during the movement portion of its activation, not to any movement due to other effects such as spells or being slammed. Some rules such as charging and slamming require a model to be able to move its full normal movement. Although a model's speed (SPD) may be modified during play, the model's unmodified SPD determines its normal movement. Whether due to a game effect, a spell, feat, or weapon effect, a terrain effect, or another modifier, a model suffering any penalty to its SPD or movement (regardless of offsetting bonuses) is unable to move its full normal movement.

ADVANCING

An advancing model may move up to its speed (SPD) in inches. An advancing model always faces its direction of movement, but it may change facing freely while moving and may face any direction after moving. After a model advances, it may perform one action.

RUNNING

A running model may move up to twice its current speed (SPD) in inches. Declare that a model or unit will run when you activate it. A running model always faces its direction of movement, but it may change facing freely while moving and may face any direction after moving. A model that runs cannot perform an action, cast spells, use animus, or use feats this turn. A running model's activation ends at the completion of its movement.

Some models must meet special requirements to run:

- A warlock or solo may always run instead of advancing.

- A warbeast must be *forced* to run.

- A trooper must receive a run order to run.

- An out-of-formation trooper may attempt to regain formation by running.

CHARGING

A charging model rushes into melee range with an opponent and takes advantage of its momentum to make a more powerful strike. A charge combines a model's movement and combat action. A model suffering a penalty to its SPD or movement for any reason, regardless of offsetting bonuses, or that is denied its movement or action cannot charge.

A model may attempt to charge any other model, friendly or enemy, in line of sight at the beginning of its normal movement. Declare a charge and its target before moving the model. After declaring a charge, the charging model turns to face any straight, unobstructed line that will let it move into melee range with its target. The charging model then moves its full SPD plus 3" along that line, stopping short at any point its target is in melee range. It must stop if it contacts another model, an obstacle, obstruction, or rough terrain. At the completion of its movement, the charging model turns to directly face the center of its target.

Some effects require a model to charge. A model required to charge cannot forfeit its activation, but it is not required to target another model. Instead, it may

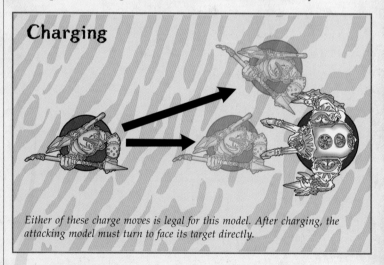

Charging

Either of these charge moves is legal for this model. After charging, the attacking model must turn to face its target directly.

make a charge move in any direction in its front arc and then immediately end its activation.

A charging model that ends its movement with its intended target in melee range performs a combat action. If the charging model moved at least 3", its first attack is a charge attack. This is not an extra attack in addition to a model's regular attack. Rather, it is simply the model's first attack after its charge movement. The attack roll is made normally and may be boosted. If the charge attack hits, add an additional die to the damage roll. This damage roll cannot be boosted. After the charge attack, the charging model makes the rest of its melee attacks normally and may spend fury points or be *forced* to make additional melee attacks. A model may not make *power attacks* or ranged attacks after charging.

If a charging model moved less than 3", it performs its combat action and attacks normally, but its first attack is not a charge attack because the model did not move far or fast enough to add sufficient momentum to its strike.

A charging model's activation ends if it contacts a terrain feature that obstructs or slows its movement or if its intended target is not in melee range after moving the full charge distance. Some models must meet special requirements to charge:

• A warlock or solo may always charge instead of advancing.

• A warbeast must be *forced* to charge. A warbeast cannot make a power attack after charging, but it may make other special attacks.

• A trooper must receive the charge order to charge. When a trooper receives a charge order, it must either run or charge. Troopers may charge the same target or multiple targets but must be in formation at the end of the unit's movement.

UNIT FORMATION

A horde's soldiers and support personnel are organized into units. Every member of a unit is similarly equipped and trained to fulfill a certain battlefield role. Some units specialize in melee combat, others excel with ranged weapons, and some provide critical or highly specialized capabilities. Regardless of their duties, one thing is certain. A unit is most effective when all of its members are in formation.

Wolves of Orboros in Skirmish Formation

Striders in Open Formation

A unit must operate as a single coherent force, but its formation may be of any size or shape. Troopers up to 3" apart are in **skirmish formation**.

Troopers up to 1" apart are in **open formation**. Troopers in open formation are close enough to coordinate attacks and provide each other mutual support.

Troopers that form up in ranks are in **tight formation**. A rank is a row of troopers in base-to-base contact, or as close as the actual models allow, all facing in the same direction perpendicular to the row of models. A tight formation may consist of any number of ranks, but each rank must be at least two troopers wide. Each rank after the front-most must be parallel to it and have at least one trooper in base-to-base contact with a trooper in the rank ahead of it, or as close as the actual models allow. Troopers in contact with the rank ahead must be lined up directly behind the trooper ahead of them.

Formations are not mutually exclusive. Troopers in tight formation are also in open and skirmish formation. Likewise, troopers in open formation are also in skirmish formation.

Some special rules require a group of troopers to be in a specific formation. This does not require every model in the unit to be in the specified formation, but only those models in that formation will gain the special rule's benefits. A group of troopers is in the specified formation when every model in the group can be connected by a chain of models also in the group and in the specified formation. For example, in the illustration on this page, troopers B and C form a group in open formation as do troopers D and E, but all four of them do not form a single open-formation group.

Out of Formation

A unit must begin the game in formation. A unit's leader is always **in formation**. The status of other troopers is based on their relationship to the unit's leader. The group of troopers in skirmish formation with the leader is in formation, while all others are **out**

Praetorians in Tight Formation

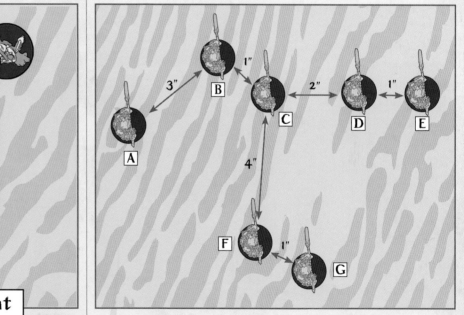

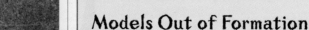

Models Out of Formation

Wolf of Orboros A is in skirmish formation with B. B and C are in open formation with each oehter. D is within 3" of C so is in skirmish formation with C. E is within 1" of D, so those two troopers are in open formation with each other. F and G are close enough to be in skirmish formation with each other. However, since neither of them are within 3" of a model in the largest coherent group of the unit, they are both out of formation.

of formation. If the unit has no leader or its leader is no longer in play, then the largest group of troopers in skirmish formation is in formation. If two or more groups have the largest number of troopers, their controller chooses which group is in formation. A lone surviving trooper of a unit is always in formation whether he is the leader or not.

At the beginning of a unit's activation, determine if any troopers are out of formation. Those who are will not receive any order given to their unit. An out-of-formation trooper must attempt to regain formation, but the desire to stay alive tempers this mandate. The trooper can advance or run in an effort to regain formation, but he must move by the most direct route that does not take him through a damaging effect or let enemies engage him. If enemy models obstruct a trooper's only path back to his unit, he must engage and attack them unless he has a ranged weapon. An out-of-formation trooper in this situation can stop moving once in range and make ranged attacks against those opponents. An out-of-formation trooper engaged by an opponent may either disengage or advance and attack.

At the end of a unit's activation, every out-of-formation trooper must make a command check or flee. Unlike most other command checks made by troopers, an out-of-formation trooper makes this command check and flees individually. An out-of-formation trooper in command range of a friendly model with the Commander ability may use that model's command (CMD) stat for the check instead of his own. See Command (pg. 61) for detailed rules on command checks and fleeing.

Moving Units

When you activate a unit, you are simulating that its members' movement and actions occur simultaneously even though each model moves and acts individually. A unit required to make a command check as a result of its movement does not do so until after every trooper has completed its movement. Troopers can move in any order, but they must be in formation after all troopers have completed their movement.

ACTIONS

An active model may be entitled to perform one action depending on the type of movement it made. There are two broad action types: combat and special. A combat action lets a model make one or more attacks. A special action lets a model perform a specialized function. A model forfeits its action if it does not use it during its activation. A model cannot move after performing any action unless a special rule specifically allows it to do so.

COMBAT ACTIONS

A model can perform a combat action after advancing, charging, or forfeiting its movement. A combat action lets a model make *attacks*. A model performing a combat action can choose one of the following options:

• A model can make one melee attack with each of its melee weapons in melee range.

• A model can make one special attack (★Attack) allowed by its special rules instead of making any other attacks. A model does not have to spend fury points or be *forced* to make a special attack.

• A warbeast that did not charge can be *forced* to make one power attack instead of making any other attack. A power attack is considered a melee attack.

• A model not *in melee* and that did not charge can make one *ranged attack* with each of its ranged weapons. Each ranged weapon only makes one attack at this point, regardless of its ROF.

A model making more than one attack may divide them among any eligible targets.

After resolving these attacks, a warlock may spend fury points to make additional attacks, one per fury point spent. Similarly, a warbeast may be *forced* to make additional attacks. Each additional attack may be made with any appropriate weapons the model possesses, including multiple attacks with the same weapon. However, a ranged weapon cannot exceed its rate of fire

(ROF) during a model's activation. Completely resolve each additional attack before spending another fury point or forcing a warbeast to make another additional attack.

Unless noted otherwise, a model cannot make both melee and ranged attacks in the same combat action. Additional attacks must be of the same type (melee or ranged) as the model's original attack. A model may make additional attacks after a special attack or power attack, but they, too, must correspond to the basic nature (either melee or ranged) of the original attack made. Some special attacks are neither melee attacks nor ranged attacks. The rules for these special attacks indicate the nature of any additional attacks that may be made afterwards. A model cannot make a special attack or a power attack as an additional attack.

See Combat (pg. 38) for detailed rules on making attacks and determining their results.

SPECIAL ACTIONS

Some models can perform a special action instead of a combat action. Unless otherwise noted, a model can perform a special action only after advancing or forfeiting its movement. A special action's description details its requirements and results.

COMBAT–THROWING DOWN

Melee attacks, Ranged Attacks, and Damage

COMBAT OVERVIEW

A model's combat action allows it to make attacks. An attack roll determines if an attack successfully hits its target. After a successful attack, a damage roll determines how much damage, if any, the target receives.

Unless stated otherwise, an attack can be made against any model, friendly or enemy, and against certain terrain features.

There are two broad categories of combat: melee combat and ranged combat. A model can only make attacks of the same type during its combat action. A model cannot make a ranged attack after making a melee attack, and it cannot make a melee attack after making a ranged attack.

MELEE COMBAT

A model using its combat action for melee attacks can make one attack with each of its melee weapons. Some models have special rules that allow additional melee attacks. Warlocks may use fury points and warbeasts may be forced to make additional melee attacks, for example. Each additional melee attack may be made with any melee weapon the model possesses with no limit to the number of attacks made per weapon.

A melee attack can be made against any target in melee range of the weapon being used. A model cannot make a melee attack through an intervening model (pg.

31). A model making more than one melee attack may divide its attacks among any eligible targets.

MELEE WEAPONS

Melee weapons include such implements as claws, fangs, spears, swords, hammers, flails, saws, and axes. A warbeast can also use its body as a melee weapon for attacks such as head-butts or slams.

A melee weapon's damage roll is 2d6+POW+STR.

MELEE RANGE

A model can make melee attacks against any target in melee range. A weapon's melee range extends 1/2" beyond the model's front arc for any type of melee attack. A reach weapon has a melee range of 2". Some effects and special rules may even increase a weapon's melee range beyond this. A model's melee range is the longest melee range of its usable melee weapons. A model possessing a reach weapon and another melee weapon can engage and attack an opponent up to 2" away with its reach weapon, but its other weapons can only be used to attack models within their normal 1/2" melee range. Models with no melee weapons have no melee range.

ENGAGED MODELS AND MODELS IN MELEE

When a model is within an enemy model's melee range, it is engaged in combat and primarily concerned with fighting its nearest threat. Both the engaged and engaging models are considered to be **in melee** and cannot make ranged attacks. An engaged model can move freely as long as it stays inside its opponent's melee range.

A model can **disengage** from melee by moving out of its enemy's melee range, but doing so is risky. A model disengaging from melee combat is subject to a *free strike* by the enemy model.

Free Strikes

When a model moves out of an enemy's melee range, the enemy model may immediately make a **free strike** against it just before it leaves melee range. The model makes one melee attack with any melee weapon that has sufficient melee range to reach the

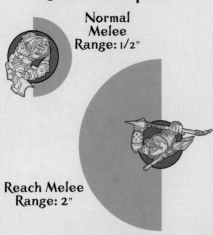

Melee Range, Engaged Models, and Reach Weapons

Normal Melee Range: 1/2"

Reach Melee Range: 2"

If a model is in melee range, it has engaged its opponent in melee combat. These appear to go hand-in-hand. When opposing models are in each other's melee range, they are both engaged. However, a model with a reach weapon can take advantage of its greater melee range to engage an opponent with only normal melee range weapons without becoming engaged intself. While both models are considered to be in melee, a model is engaged only if it is in its opoponent's melee range!

moving model and gains a +2 bonus to its melee attack roll. If the attack succeeds, add an additional die to the damage roll. A free strike's attack and damage rolls cannot be boosted.

A model may make a free strike against each enemy that moves out of its melee range.

MELEE ATTACK ROLLS

Determine a melee attack's success by making a melee attack roll. Roll 2d6 and add the attacking model's melee attack value (MAT). Boosted attack rolls add an additional die to this roll. Special rules and certain circumstances may modify the attack roll as well.

Melee Attack Roll = 2d6+MAT

An attack hits if the attack roll equals or exceeds the target's defense (DEF). If the attack roll is less than the target's DEF, the attack misses. A roll of all 1s on the dice causes an automatic miss. A roll of all 6s causes an automatic hit regardless of the attacker's MAT or his opponent's DEF, unless you are rolling only one die.

Completely resolve a melee attack's damage roll and special effects before applying any special rules from the target. The target model's special rules apply only if they are still usable.

Melee Attack Modifiers

The most common modifiers affecting a model's melee attack roll are summarized here for easy reference. Where necessary, additional detail can be found on the pages listed.

• Back strike (pg. 50): A melee attack against a target's back arc from a model that began its activation in the target's back arc gains a +2 bonus to the attack roll.

• Free strike (above): A melee attack against a disengaging model gains a +2 bonus to the attack roll and adds an additional die to the damage roll.

• Intervening Terrain: A model with any portion of its base obscured from its attacker by an obstacle or an obstruction gains +2 DEF against melee attacks from that opponent.

• Stationary Target (pg. 50): A melee attack against a stationary target hits automatically.

WARBEAST MELEE ATTACK OPTIONS

Warbeasts have melee attack options unavailable to all other model types. Unless otherwise noted, a warbeast can use any of the following attack options that its equipment and damage state allow.

POWER ATTACKS

Power attacks are special attacks that may be made by warbeasts. A warbeast must be *forced* to make a power attack. Unlike other special attacks, a warbeast cannot make a power attack after charging. A warbeast may make additional melee attacks after a power attack, but it must be *forced* to do so.

Headlock/Weapon Lock

As its combat action, a warbeast with at least one usable claw or jaw may be *forced* to seize another

warbeast's weapon or head and prevent its use. Declare what the warbeast is attempting to lock and which weapon it is using for the attempt before making a melee attack roll. A knocked down model cannot be targeted by a headlock or weapon lock. A hit keeps the target from using the named weapon along with all other weapons in the same location, but it does not cause any damage. Locking a weapon with a location of "—" has no effect on other weapons. Being held in a headlock prevents a warbeast from attacking with any weapons located in the head. A warbeast being held in a headlock or weapon lock may not perform special attacks

Once involved in a lock, the attacker cannot use the weapon with which it made the lock attempt, nor any other weapon in the same location. Maintaining a lock with a weapon with a location of "—" has not effect on the warbeast's other weapons. The attacker and the defender are free to attack with any of their other melee weapons.

For example, Rob's Titan Gladiator successfully locks the head of Erik's Argus with its right War Gauntlet. The Argus cannot make head-butt attacks or jaw attacks, and the Titan Gladiator cannot make attacks with its right War Gauntlet until the headlock is broken or released.

During its activation, a warbeast suffering a headlock or weapon lock must attempt to break the lock by performing a combat action. During this combat action, for each headlock and weapon lock that it is suffering, both models involved in the lock roll a d6 and add their STR. If the locked model's total exceeds that of the model holding it in the lock, the lock is broken. The warbeast may also make normal melee attacks with any usable melee weapons. After resolving these attacks and attempts to break free, a warbeast may be *forced* to make more attempts to break a lock or to make additional attacks with usable weapons. Once a lock is broken, the warbeast may use the weapons that were locked. It may not make normal attacks with those weapons during that combat action, but it may be *forced* to make additional melee attacks with them.

A warbeast may release a lock it is holding at any time during its own activation. Neither model may move while involved in a lock. Any effect that causes either model to move, knocks down the defender, or causes the attacker to become a stationary target automatically breaks the lock. A lock is also broken once either model is no longer on the playing area.

Head-butt

As its combat action, a warbeast may be *forced* to head-butt a model and drive it to the ground. The attacking model makes a melee attack roll which suffers a –2 penalty against a target with an equal or smaller-sized base and a –4 penalty against a target with a larger base. A hit causes a damage roll with a POW equal to the attacker's current STR and knocks the target model down.

A warbeast cannot make a head-butt if held in a headlock or is using its jaws to maintain a headlock or weapon lock.

Push

As its combat action, a warbeast may be *forced* to push another model. Both models roll a d6 and add their STR. If the defender's total is greater, it resists being pushed. If the attacker's total equals or exceeds the defender's, the defending model suffers no damage but is moved one full inch directly away from the attacker.

A pushed model moves at half rate through rough terrain, suffers the effects of any hazards, and stops if it comes in contact with an obstacle, obstruction, or a model with an equal or larger-sized base. Models with smaller bases do not stop the pushed model. The smaller model is pushed back as well. A pushed model cannot be targeted by free strikes during this movement.

A pushed model falls off elevated terrain if it ends its push movement with less than 1" of ground under its base. See Falling (pg. 50) for detailed rules on determining damage from a fall.

After a successful push, the attacker may immediately make a follow-up move toward the pushed model up to the distance the pushed model was moved.

Rend

As its combat action, a heavy warbeast may be *forced* to rip apart a smaller-based model. Instead of attacking normally, the warbeast makes one attack with a melee weapon against a living model with a small or medium base. If the target is destroyed by this attack, it is brutally torn apart. Enemy models/units within 5" of the attacking warbeast must pass a command check or flee.

Slam

A warbeast may be *forced* to slam a model by ramming it with the full force of its body to send it flying backward and knock it to the ground. A slam

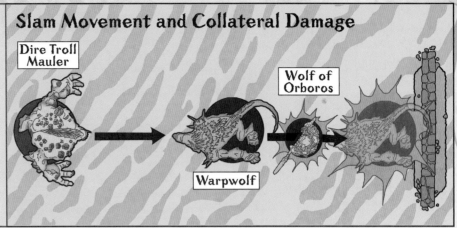

A Dire Troll Mauler declares a slam attack against a Warpwolf. Because it moved more than 3" to get into melee with the Warpwolf, the Dire Troll Mauler makes a slam attack. The attack succeeds, and the Warpwolf is knocked back d6". The roll comes up a 6, but the Warpwolf stops when it hits the wall 5" behind it. During the slam, the Warpwolf passes over a Wolf of Orboros, and the Wolf suffers collateral damage. In addition, because the Warpwolf was slammed into a wall, it suffers a damage roll of 3d6 plus the STR of the Mauler (2d6 plus an extra die for colliding with a solid terrain feature).

combines a warbeast's movement and combat action. A warbeast suffering a penalty to its SPD or movement for any reason, regardless of offsetting bonuses, or that is denied its movement or action cannot attempt a slam.

A warbeast may attempt to slam any other model, friendly or enemy, in line of sight at the beginning of its normal movement. Declare the slam attempt and its target before moving the warbeast. A slam cannot target a knocked down model. After declaring a slam, the warbeast turns to directly face the center of its target. The warbeast then moves its full SPD plus 3" directly toward the center of its target, stopping short at any point within 1/2" of its target. It must stop if it contacts another model, an obstacle, obstruction, or rough terrain. The slamming model cannot change its facing during or after this movement.

A warbeast that attempts a slam and ends its movement within 1/2" of its intended target and moved at least 3" performs a slam attack as its combat action. The attacking model makes a melee attack roll which suffers a –2 penalty against a target with an equal or smaller-sized base and a –4 penalty against a target with a larger base. If the slam attack hits, it causes the target to be slammed directly away from its attacker, knocked down, and then suffer damage as detailed under *Slam Damage*.

If a warbeast attempting a slam attack moved less than 3", it has not moved fast enough to get its full weight and power into the blow. The attack roll suffers a –2 penalty regardless of the target's base size. A hit does not move the target model, but it does cause the target to suffer damage as detailed under Slam Damage.

A slamming warbeast's activation ends if it contacts a terrain feature that obstructs or slows its movement or if it is not within ½" of its intended target after moving the full slam distance. It may not perform an action during this activation.

Being Slammed

A slammed model is moved d6 inches directly away from its attacker and is then knocked down. Halve the slam distance if the target has a larger base than the attacker. A slammed model moves at half rate through rough terrain, suffers any damaging effects it passes through, and stops if it contacts an obstacle, obstruction, or a model with an equal or larger-sized base. A slammed model cannot be targeted by free strikes during this movement.

A slammed model moves over a model with a smaller base. If its slam movement ends up on top of a smaller model, push the smaller model back to make room for the slammed model.

Super Slam!!!

A WARBEAST THAT SLAMS ITS TARGET INTO A SOLID TERRAIN FEATURE OR A MODEL WITH AN EQUAL OR LARGER-SIZED BASE ADDS AN ADDITIONAL DIE TO ITS DAMAGE ROLL FOR A TOTAL OF THREE DICE. THE WARBEAST MAY BE *FORCED* TO BOOST THIS DAMAGE ROLL AND ADD ANOTHER DIE, FOR A TOTAL OF FOUR DICE!

A slammed model falls off elevated terrain if it ends its slam movement with less than 1" of ground under its base. See Falling (pg. 50) for detailed rules on determining damage from a fall.

Slam Damage

Determine slam damage after moving the slammed model. A slammed model suffers a damage roll with a POW equal to the attacker's current STR. Add an additional die to the damage roll if the slammed model contacts an obstacle, obstruction, or a model with an equal or larger-sized base. Slam damage may be boosted.

Collateral Damage

If a slammed model contacts a model with an equal or smaller-sized base, that model is knocked down and

Example of a Throw

1 2 6 3 5 4

INTENDED POINT OF IMPACT

ACTUAL POINT OF IMPACT

A Warpwolf throws a Scattergunner. Since the Warpwolf has a STR of 10, measure 5" from the thrown model to determine the intended point of impact and determine deviation from that point. The Warpwolf rolls a 3 for deviation direction and a 6 for distance. On a d3, that comes to 3" of deviation. Measure 3" in the direction indicated by the deviation diagram to determine the actual point of impact. The Scattergunner moves from its current position directly toward the point of impact and ends its movement centered on that point.

suffers collateral damage. A model taking collateral damage suffers a damage roll with a POW equal to the attacker's current STR. Collateral damage cannot be boosted. A model with a larger-sized base than the thrown model does not suffer collateral damage.

Throw

As its combat action, a warbeast with a usable claw may be *forced* to pick up and throw a model with an equal or smaller-sized base. Knocked down models cannot be thrown. The attacking model makes a melee attack roll which suffers a –2 penalty. If the attack hits, both models roll a d6 and add their current STR. If the target's total is greater, it breaks free without taking any damage and avoids being thrown. If the attacker's total equals or exceeds the target's, the target model gets thrown, is knocked down, and then suffers damage as detailed in *Throw Damage*.

Being Thrown

After a successful throw attack, the attacker throws the target any direction within its front arc. Measure a distance from the target equal to half the attacker's current STR in the chosen direction. A large based model throwing a small based model adds 1" to this distance. From that point, determine where the thrown model actually lands by rolling for deviation. Referencing the deviation template (pg. 208), roll a d6 for direction and a d3 for distance in inches. The thrown model is moved

directly from its current location in a straight line to the determined point of impact, ending centered on that point. The thrown model is then knocked down.

Rough terrain and obstacles do not affect this movement, but the thrown model stops if it contacts an obstruction or a model with an equal or larger-sized base. A thrown model cannot be targeted by free strikes during this movement.

A thrown model moves over a model with a smaller base. If its impact point ends up on top of a smaller model, push the smaller model back to make room for the thrown model.

Throw Damage

Determine throw damage after moving the thrown model. A thrown model suffers a damage roll with a POW equal to the attacker's current STR . Add an additional die to the damage roll if the thrown model contacts an obstacle, obstruction or a model with an equal or larger-sized base. Throw damage may be boosted.

Collateral Damage

If a thrown model contacts a model with an equal or smaller-sized base, that model is knocked down and suffers collateral damage. A model taking collateral damage suffers a damage roll with a POW equal to the attacker's current STR. Collateral damage cannot be boosted. A model with a larger-sized base than the thrown model does not suffer collateral damage.

Double-Hand Throw

As its combat action, a warbeast with two usable claws may be *forced* to pick up and throw a model with an equal or smaller-sized base. The attacking model makes a melee attack roll. If the attack hits, the target rolls a d6 and adds its current STR. The attacker rolls 2d6 and adds its current STR. If the target's total is greater, it breaks free without taking any damage and avoids being thrown. If the attacker's total equals or exceeds the target's, the target model gets thrown, is knocked down, and then suffers damage as detailed in *Throw Damage*.

After a successful double-hand throw attack, the attacker may throw the target any direction within its front arc. Measure a distance from the target equal to half the attacker's current STR in inches. A large based model throwing a model with a small base adds 1" to this distance. From that point, determine where the thrown model actually lands by rolling for deviation. Referencing the deviation template (pg. 208), roll a d6 for direction and a d3 for distance in inches. The thrown model is moved directly from its current location in a straight line to the determined point of impact, ending centered on that point.

Instead of throwing its target at a spot on the ground after a successful attack, the attacker may throw it at another model within LOS. Ignore the model being thrown when selecting the target model. If this new target model is within the throw distance as described above, the attacker makes a ranged attack roll against it. On a hit, the thrown model is moved directly from its current location in a straight line to the center of the ranged attack roll's target. It ends this movement in base-to-base contact with the target and collides with it unless the movement is stopped by an obstruction or another model.

If the attack roll fails, determine the thrown model's point of impact by rolling deviation from the center of the target model. If the target model is beyond the throw distance, determine deviation from a point on the line to the target equal to the throw distance. Referencing the deviation template (pg. 208), roll a d6 for the direction and a d3 for distance in inches. The thrown model moves directly from its current location in a straight line to the determined point of impact, ending centered on that point.

Rough terrain and obstacles do not affect a thrown model's movement, but the model stops if it contacts an obstruction or a model with an equal or larger-sized base. A thrown model cannot be targeted by free strikes during this movement.

A thrown model moves over a model with a smaller base. If its impact point ends up on top of a smaller model, push the smaller model back to make room for the thrown model.

After moving the thrown model, it is knocked down and then suffers damage as detailed in Throw Damage, above. If a thrown model contacts another model with an equal or smaller-sized base, that model is knocked down and suffers damage as detailed in Collateral Damage, above

Trample

A heavy warbeast may be forced to trample over small-based models in its path. Trampling combines a warbeast's movement and combat action. A warbeast

that suffers a penalty to its SPD or movement for any reason, regardless of offsetting bonuses, or is denied its movement or action cannot make a trample power attack. Any effects that prevent charging also prevent a model from making a trample power attack.

Declare a trample attack at the beginning of the warbeast's activation. Choose a direction you wish to trample, and turn the model to face that direction. The warbeast then moves its SPD +3" in a straight line. It may move through any small-based model in its path if it has enough movement to move completely past the model's base. These models do not perform free strikes at this time. After the warbeast has finished its movement, it makes a melee attack against each small-based model through which it moved during this movement in the order it moved through them. Models hit cannot perform free strikes against the trampling model and suffer a damage roll with a POW equal to the current STR of the attacker. A model missed by the trample attack may make one free strike targeting the trampling warbeast immediately after the failed attack roll.

During a trample attack, the warbeast cannot move over terrain across which it could not also charge, and it cannot change its facing during or after its movement. After making all of its trample attacks, a warbeast may be forced to make additional melee attacks against any models in melee range.

RANGED COMBAT

Many would argue there is no honor in defeating an enemy without being close enough to look him in the eyes. However, when a rabid Warpwolf with a pair of enormous flesh-tearing claws bears down on you at blinding speeds, it is a good plan to keep your distance and consider your ranged attack options.

A model using its combat action for ranged attacks makes one attack with each of its ranged weapons. Some models have special rules that allow additional ranged attacks. Warlocks may spend fury points and warbeasts may be *forced* to make additional ranged attacks. Each additional attack may be made with any ranged weapon the model possesses, but a ranged weapon can never make more attacks in one activation than its rate of fire (ROF).

A ranged attack can be declared against any target in line of sight subject to the targeting rules. A model making more than one ranged attack may divide its attacks among any eligible targets. A model in melee cannot make ranged attacks.

Some spells and special rules let certain models make magic attacks. Magic attacks are similar to ranged attacks and follow most of the same rules. However, magic attacks are not affected by a rule that only effects ranged attacks. See Warlocks, Warbeasts & Fury (pg. 55) for full details on magic attacks.

RANGED WEAPONS

Ranged weapons include bows, rifles, and crossbows. A ranged weapon's damage roll is 2d6+POW.

DECLARING A TARGET

A ranged or magic attack can be declared against any target in the attacker's line of sight subject to the targeting rules. The attack must be declared before measuring the range to the intended target. Unless a model's special rules say otherwise, it can make ranged and magic attacks only through its front arc.

Targeting

A ranged or magic attack must be declared against a model or an object on the battlefield within LOS that can normally be damaged. For LOS rules, see page 31. Neither attack type can target open ground or a permanent terrain feature. A ranged attack need not target the nearest enemy model, but intervening models may prevent a model further away from being targeted.

Certain rules and effects create situations that specifically prevent a model from being targeted. A model that cannot be targeted by an attack still suffers its effects if inside the attack's area-of-effect. Other rules and effects, such as Stealth, only cause an attack to miss automatically. They do not prevent the model from being targeted by the attack.

Measuring Range

A ranged or magic attack must be declared against a legal target prior to measuring range. After declaring the attack, use a measuring device to see if the target is within Range (RNG) of the attack. Range is measured from the nearest edge of the attacking model's base to the nearest edge of the target model's base. If the target is in range, make a *ranged attack roll* or *magic attack roll*, as applicable. If the target is beyond maximum range, the attack automatically

Cover:
+4 DEF

Cover:
+4 DEF

Concealment:
+2 DEF

Concealment:
+2 DEF

Examples of Concealment and Cover

misses. If an area-of-effect (AOE) attack's target is out of range, it automatically misses, and its *point of impact* will deviate from the point on the line to its declared target at a distance equal to its RNG. See Area-of-Effect Attacks (pg. 48) for full details on these attacks and deviation.

RATE OF FIRE

A weapon's rate of fire (ROF) indicates the maximum number of ranged attacks it may make in an activation. Reloading time prevents most ranged weapons from being used more than once per activation. Some ranged weapons reload faster and may make multiple attacks if a model is able to make additional attacks. However, a ranged weapon may not make more attacks per activation than its rate of fire regardless of the number of additional attacks a model is entitled to make.

RANGED ATTACK ROLLS

Determine a ranged attack's success by making a ranged attack roll. Roll 2d6 and add the attacking model's Ranged Attack (RAT). A boosted attack roll adds an additional die to this roll. Special rules and certain circumstances may modify the attack roll as well.

Ranged Attack Roll = 2d6+RAT

An attack hits if the attack roll equals or exceeds the target's Defense (DEF). If the attack roll is less than the target's DEF, the attack misses. A roll of all 1s on the dice causes an automatic miss. A roll of all 6s causes an automatic hit regardless of the attacker's RAT or his opponent's DEF, unless you are rolling only one die.

Completely resolve a ranged attack's damage roll and special effects before applying any special rules from the target. The target model's special rules apply only if they are still usable.

Ranged Attack Modifiers

The most common modifiers affecting a model's ranged attack roll are summarized here for easy reference. Where necessary, additional detail can be found on the pages listed.

- *Aiming*: A model that voluntarily forfeits its movement by not changing its position or facing gains a +2 bonus to every ranged attack roll it makes as part of its combat action. A magic attack does not get the aiming bonus.

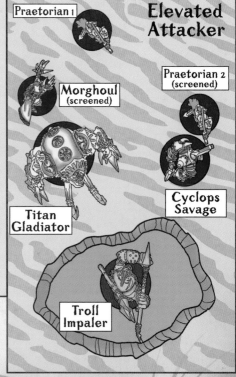

A Troll Impaler standing on top of a hill is choosing his target for a Thrown Spear ranged attack. Because the Titan Gladiator has a larger base than the Impaler and Morghoul is close enough to be screened by it, it blocks LOS to Morghoul. However, the Impaler can draw line of sight to all the other models because an elevated attacker ignores intervening models of equal or smaller base size on lower elevation. Even though the Impaler has LOS to him, Praetorian 2 still receives +2 DEF for being screened.

Elevated Attacker

Praetorian 1

Morghoul (screened)

Praetorian 2 (screened)

Titan Gladiator

Cyclops Savage

Troll Impaler

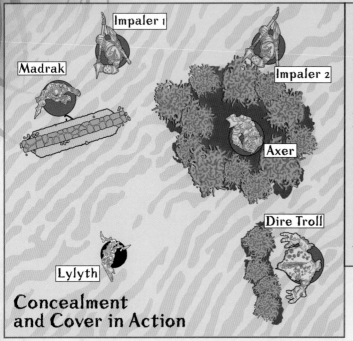

Concealment and Cover in Action

It may at first appear that Lylyth has several targets for Hellsinger, but many of them are actually quite well defended. Madrak is behind a stone wall and benefits from cover (+4 DEF). The forest and the hedge grant concealment (+2 DEF) to the Axer and Dire Troll. Because there is a forest between her an Impaler 2, Lylyth cannot draw LOS to Impaler 2 at all. Impaler 1 is behind a wall, but since he is more than 1" from the wall, he does not benefit from cover.

- *Back Strike* (pg. 50): A ranged or magic attack against target model's back arc from a model that began its activation in the target's back arc gains a +2 bonus to the attack roll.

- *Cloud Effect* (pg. 54): A model inside a cloud effect gains +2 DEF against all ranged and magic attacks.

- *Concealment* (pg. 46): A model with concealment in relation to its attacker gains +2 DEF against ranged and magic attacks from that opponent.

- *Cover* (pg. 46): A model with cover in relation to its attacker gains +4 DEF against ranged and magic attacks from that opponent.

- *Elevated Target*: When drawing line of sight from a model on a lower elevation than its target, ignore all intervening models on a lower elevation than the target. A model on higher elevation than its attacker gains +2 DEF against ranged and magic attacks from that opponent. Models on lower elevations than the target do not provide *screening*.

- *Elevated Attacker*: When drawing line of sight from a model on a higher elevation than its target, ignore all intervening models on lower elevation than the attacking model except those that would normally screen the target. Additionally, you can draw a line of sight through screening models that have equal or smaller-sized bases than the attacking model, but the target still gets +2 DEF for being screened.

- *Stationary Target* (pg. 50): A stationary target has a base DEF of 5 against ranged and magic attacks.

- *Screened Target* (pg. 31): A screened target gains +2 DEF against ranged and magic attacks.

- *Target in Melee* (pg. 46): A ranged or magic attack against a target in melee suffers a −4 penalty to the attack roll. If the attack misses its target, it may hit a nearby model instead.

CONCEALMENT AND COVER

Terrain features, spells, and other effects may make it more difficult to hit a model with a ranged or magic attack. A model within 1" of a terrain feature that obscures any portion of its base from an attacker gains either a concealment or cover bonus to its DEF against ranged or magic attacks from that opponent. Concealment and cover bonuses are not cumulative with themselves or each other, but they are cumulative with other effects that modify a model's DEF. See Terrain (pg. 63) for full details on terrain features and how they provide concealment or cover.

A model benefiting from concealment or cover may make ranged and magic attacks normally against targets in line of sight.

Some terrain features and special effects grant a model concealment by making it more difficult to be seen, but they are not actually dense enough to block an attack. Examples include low hedges or bushes. A model within 1" of a concealing terrain feature that obscures any portion of its base from an attacker gains +2 DEF against ranged and magic attacks from that opponent. Concealment provides no benefit against spray attacks.

Other terrain features and special effects grant a model cover by being physically solid enough to block an attack against it. Examples include stone walls, giant boulders, and buildings. A model within 1" of a covering terrain feature that obscures any portion of its base from an attacker gains +4 DEF against ranged and magic attacks from that opponent. Cover provides no benefit against spray attacks.

TARGETING A MODEL IN MELEE

A model making a ranged or magic attack against a target *in melee* risks hitting another model participating in the combat, including friendly models. The standard targeting rules, including line of sight and screening, must be observed when targeting a model that is in melee. *Combined ranged attacks* cannot target a model in melee; it is impossible to concentrate such firepower against a single target in a swirling fight.

In addition to any other attack modifiers, a ranged attack against a target in melee suffers a –4 penalty to the attack roll. All of the target's special rules and effects in play on it still apply. For instance, an attack targeting a model with the Stealth ability from greater than 5" away still automatically misses, and a magic attack by Lylyth targeting a model affected by her Witch Mark ability still automatically hits.

If the attack against the intended target misses, it may hit another combatant. The attacker must immediately re-roll his attack against another model in that combat. Randomly determine which other model in the combat (not including the intended target) becomes the new target. When determining the attack's new target, only the models that are in melee with the attack's original target and any other models in melee with those models are considered to be in the same combat. Every model meeting these criteria is eligible to become the new target, regardless of line of sight, with two exceptions: A model is ineligible to become the new target if it has a special rule preventing it from being targeted or if the attacker's line of sight to it is completely blocked by obstructing terrain. If multiple models in the combat are eligible targets, randomly determine which model becomes the new target.

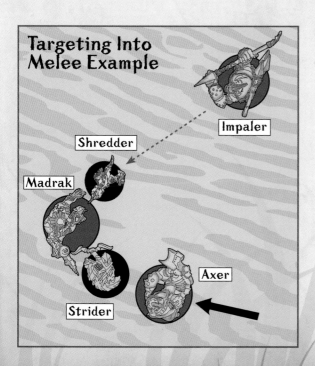

Targeting Into Melee Example

For example, using a d6, if there are three other models in the combat, the first model will become the new target on a 1 or 2, the second on a 3 or 4, and the third on a 5 or 6. However, if the attacker cannot draw a line of sight to one of those models due to an obstruction (e.g., it's around a corner), ignore that model and randomize the attack between the other two: It targets the first on a 1 through 3 or the second on a 4 through 6. If one of those two models cannot be targeted for some reason (such as being under the protection of a Warding Chant shamanic prayer), then only one model is an eligible target and a random roll is not necessary.

When re-rolling the attack against the new target, all modifiers affecting the attacker still apply such as a boost die, the aiming bonus, spell effects, and the –4 penalty for targeting a model in melee. All modifiers affecting the newly targeted model also apply, but ignore those that only applied to the intended target. If the attack against the new target misses, it misses completely without targeting any more models. For instance, Ironhide is in melee with a Woldwatcher affected by the Wind Storm spell. A Troll Impaler aims and targets the Woldwatcher with its thrown spear and is *forced* to boost its attack roll. The Impaler's attack roll gains a boost die and the aiming bonus and suffers the penalty for targeting a model in melee. In addition, the Woldwatcher's DEF against this attack is enhanced due to the spell affecting it. If the attack misses, the Impaler re-rolls the attack, this time targeting Ironhide. It still includes the boost die, aiming bonus, and the penalty for targeting a model in melee. If Ironhide is behind cover in relation to the Impaler, then he gains +4 DEF against this attack.

As a second example, Ironhide is in melee with a Strider and a Shredder. A Troll Axer enters the fight from the side to engage the Strider but not the Shredder. A Troll Impaler makes a ranged attack against the Shredder and misses. Since Ironhide is in melee with the Shredder and the Strider is in melee with Ironhide, they are both in the same combat as the intended target. The Troll Axer is not included because it is not in melee with the intended target (the Shredder) or with another model in melee with the intended target (Ironhide). It is far enough from the intended target not to be attacked accidentally. A random die roll determines that the Strider is the new target. Unfortunately, since the Impaler is more than 5" away from the Strider, his Stealth ability makes the attack automatically miss without even rolling. Even though Stealth prevents the Strider from being hit, he can still be targeted. Since the attack missed both its intended target and the new target, it misses completely with no further chance of hitting Ironhide or the Troll Axer.

An area-of-effect attack that misses a target in melee deviates normally instead of following these rules.

AREA-OF-EFFECT ATTACKS

An area-of-effect attack, such as from an explosive spell or a gas cloud, affects every model in an area centered on its point of impact. The attack covers an area with a diameter equal to its area-of-effect (AOE). Templates for AOEs can be found on page 208.

Target an AOE attack just like a normal ranged or magic attack. A successful attack roll indicates a direct hit on the intended target, which takes a direct hit damage roll of 2d6+POW. Center the AOE template over the point of impact—in the case of a direct hit, the center of the targeted model. Every other model with any part of its base covered by the AOE template is automatically hit by the attack and takes a blast damage roll of 2d6+1/2 POW. Make separate damage rolls against each model in the AOE; each roll must be boosted individually. Every model caught in an attack's area-of-effect is subject to its special effects.

An AOE attack that misses its target deviates a random direction and distance. An area-of-effect attack declared against a target out of range (RNG) automatically misses, and its point of impact deviates from the point on the line to its declared target at a distance equal to its RNG. An area-of-effect attack that misses a target in range deviates from the point directly over its intended target.

Deviation

When an AOE attack misses its target, determine its actual point of impact by rolling deviation. Referencing the deviation template (pg. 208), roll a d6 to determine the direction the attack deviates. For example, a roll of 1 means the attack goes long and a roll of 4 means the attack lands short. Roll another d6 to determine the deviation distance in inches. Determine the missed attack's point of impact by measuring the rolled distance from the center of the original target in the direction determined by the deviation roll. If the intended target is beyond the weapon's RNG, determine deviation from the point on the line to its declared target at a distance equal to its RNG.

An attack will not deviate further than half the distance from the attacker to its intended target. Use the exact value for this maximum—do not round it. For instance, an attack made at a target 5" away from

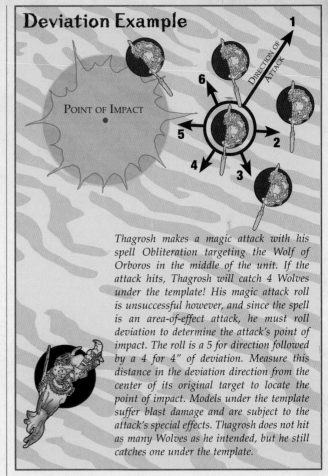

Deviation Example

POINT OF IMPACT

DIRECTION OF ATTACK

Thagrosh makes a magic attack with his spell Obliteration targeting the Wolf of Orboros in the middle of the unit. If the attack hits, Thagrosh will catch 4 Wolves under the template! His magic attack roll is unsuccessful however, and since the spell is an area-of-effect attack, he must roll deviation to determine the attack's point of impact. The roll is a 5 for direction followed by a 4 for 4" of deviation. Measure this distance in the deviation direction from the center of its original target to locate the point of impact. Models under the template suffer blast damage and are subject to the attack's special effects. Thagrosh does not hit as many Wolves as he intended, but he still catches one under the template.

the attacker will deviate a maximum of 2.5" even if the attacker rolls a 3, 4, 5, or 6 for deviation distance.

Terrain features, models, or other effects do not block deviating AOE attacks. They always take effect at the determined point of impact.

Center the AOE template over the point of impact. Every model with any part of its base covered by the AOE template is automatically hit by the attack and takes a blast damage roll of 2d6+1/2 POW. Make separate damage rolls against each model in the area-of-effect; each roll must be boosted individually. Every model caught in an attack's area-of-effect is subject to its special effects.

Deviating area-of-effect attacks never cause direct hits even if the point of impact is on top of a model.

An area-of-effect attack's point of impact determines the origin of the damage and effects for models not directly hit by the attack. For instance, suppose an AOE ranged attack targets a trooper benefiting from shield wall from the trooper's front arc, but the attack misses and deviates long. Since the point of impact is now behind the model and thus the blast damage originates in its rear arc, it does not benefit from the shield wall.

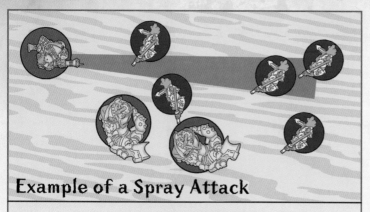

Example of a Spray Attack

A Scattergunner makes a spray attack against a group of Praetorians. The Trollblood player centers the spray template laterally over an eligible target. The player chooses the centermost Praetorian because that trooper's comrades are too far away to be intervening models. Targeting that trooper also lets the player cover the greatest number of Praetorians without covering his own nearby Axers. He rolls a ranged attack against each of the four Praetorians in the spray. Per the "Targeting a Model in Melee" rules, if the attack against the Praetorian in melee with the Axers misses, it will randomly hit one of the Axers instead, even though they are not actually under the spray template!

SPRAY ATTACKS

Some weapons and spells, such as scatterguns and a Fell Caller's Sonic Blast, make spray attacks. This devastating short-ranged attack can potentially hit several models. A spray attack has a RNG of "SP" and uses the spray template. The spray template can be found on page 208.

When making a spray attack, center the spray template laterally over an eligible target in the attacker's front arc with the narrow end of the template touching the nearest edge of the attacker's base. This target need not itself be under the template. The targeting rules apply when selecting the attack's primary target. Every model with any part of its base covered by the spray template may be hit by the attack.

Make separate ranged attack rolls against each target; each roll must be boosted individually. A model under the spray template does not receive any benefit from concealment, cover, or intervening models because the attack comes over, around, or—in some cases—through its protection.

A spray attack against a model in melee suffers a –4 penalty to its attack roll against those models. An attack that misses has the potential to hit another model in the combat, including those already affected by the spray and models that are not under the template at all. See Targeting a Model in Melee for full details on resolving this situation.

Terrain that obstructs LOS blocks spray attacks. A model under the spray template cannot be hit by the attack if the attacker's LOS is completely blocked by terrain.

Every model hit by a spray attack suffers the full effects of the attack. Make separate damage rolls against each model hit; each roll must be boosted individually. Every model hit by the spray is subject to its special effects.

SPECIAL COMBAT SITUATIONS

The chaos of a battlefield is constantly producing the unexpected. Although several situations can arise as a result of unique circumstances or a model's special rules, these rules should enable a smooth resolution. Savvy players will use these rules to their best advantage.

SPECIAL ATTACKS

Certain models have special rules allowing them to make special attacks. A model may make one special attack instead of making any normal melee or ranged attacks during its combat action if it meets the specific requirements for its use. Resolve the special attack following the rules for melee combat or ranged combat as applicable. Models may spend fury points or be *forced* to make additional attacks after a special attack, but they may only be normal melee or ranged attacks and must correspond to the nature of the special attack made.

Power attacks are a unique type of special attack.

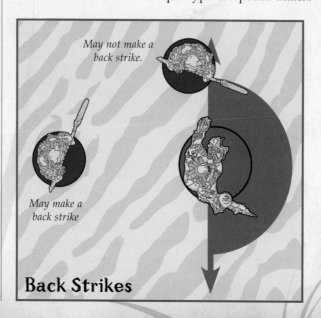

May not make a back strike.

May make a back strike

Back Strikes

Unlike other special attacks, power attacks cannot be made after charging.

BACK STRIKES

A back strike grants a +2 bonus to the attack roll of any melee, ranged, or magic attack made against a model from its back arc. To receive the back strike bonus, the attacking model must spend its entire activation up to the moment of its attack in the target's rear arc. If any portion of the attacking model's base enters the target's front arc, the attacker does not receive this bonus. A model only receives a back strike bonus during its activation.

EFFECTS WITH SIMULTANEOUS TIMING

If multiple special rules with contradictory effects are triggered at the same time, the attacker's special rule takes precedence.

ATTACKS THAT HIT OR MISS AUTOMATICALLY

Some special rules cause attacks to hit automatically or miss automatically. In cases of conflicting special rules, one causing an attack to hit automatically takes precedence over one causing an attack to miss automatically. For instance, Lylyth's Witch Mark ability allows her magic attacks to hit automatically, which overrides special rules that would otherwise cause an attack to miss automatically such as Stealth.

FALLING

A model slammed, pushed, or that otherwise moves off of an elevated surface greater than 1" high is knocked down and suffers a damage roll. A fall of up to 3" causes a POW 10 damage roll. Add an additional die to the damage roll for every additional increment of three inches the model falls, rounded up.

For example, a model falling 7" suffers a damage roll of 4d6+10!

STATIONARY TARGETS

A stationary target is an inanimate object or a model that has been knocked down or immobilized. A stationary target cannot move, perform actions, cast spells, use feats, give orders, use animus, or be *forced*. A stationary target does not have a melee range. A stationary target cannot engage other models or make attacks. A model can never be in melee with a stationary model. A stationary target does not engage other models nor does a model engage a stationary target.

A melee attack against a stationary target automatically hits. An attack roll may be made in an effort to score a critical hit, but the attacking model risks automatically missing if it rolls all 1s. A stationary target has a base DEF of 5 against ranged and magic attacks.

KNOCKDOWN

Some attacks and special rules cause a model to be **knocked down**. Mark a knocked-down model with a token. A knocked-down model is *stationary* and obeys those rules until it stands up. A knocked down model does not count as an intervening model and therefore it does not block LOS or provide screening. It may be ignored for targeting purposes. A knocked down model has no facing and no back arc; its front arc extends 360°. A knocked down model cannot be targeted by a throw, two handed throw, slam, headlock, or weapon lock.

A knocked-down model can stand up at the start of its next activation before doing anything else. However, if a model is knocked down during its controller's turn, it may not stand up until that player's next turn even if it has not been yet activated yet this turn.

To stand up, a model must forfeit either its movement or its action for that activation. A model may face any direction when it stands up. A model that forfeits its movement to stand can perform an action as if it had advanced, but it cannot make attacks involving movement such as a slam. A model that forfeits its action to stand can advance but cannot run or charge.

LEAVING THE PLAY AREA

A model that flees off the table or a *wild* warbeast that moves off the table is removed from play. A model that would leave the table for any other reason (such as being thrown or slammed) will stop at the table edge and remain in play. The table edge does not count as an obstacle; models do not take additional damage for stopping there.

COMBINED MELEE ATTACKS

Two or more troopers with this ability and in melee range of the same target may combine their attacks. In order to participate in a combined melee attack, a trooper must be able to declare a melee attack against the intended target. The trooper with the highest MAT in the attacking group makes one melee attack roll for the group, adding +1 to the attack and damage rolls for each model, including himself, participating in the attack. If multiple troopers participating in the attack have the same MAT, declare which model is the primary attacker.

A unit's melee attacks may be grouped in any manner, including multiple combined melee attacks. Troopers capable of multiple melee attacks can divide them among eligible targets and participate in multiple combined melee attacks.

Example: Four members of a Circle Wolves of Orboros unit, including their Huntsman, make a combined melee attack against a Legion Carnivean. Since the Huntsman has the highest MAT, he makes one melee attack for the group, adding +4 to his attack and damage rolls since there are four models participating in the attack. Two other troopers in the same Wolves of Orboros unit make a combined melee attack against a nearby Seraph. The trooper declared as the primary attacker makes one melee attack, gaining +2 to its attack and damage rolls.

If the target of a combined melee attack has a special rule or effect in play that affects its attackers, only the primary attacker—the model making the attack roll—suffers those effects.

COMBINED RANGED ATTACKS

Two or more troopers with this ability may combine their ranged attacks against the same target. In order to participate in a combined ranged attack, a trooper must be able to declare a ranged attack against the intended target and be in a single open formation group with the other participants. The trooper with the highest RAT in the attacking group makes one ranged attack roll for the group, gaining +1 to the attack and damage rolls for each model, including himself, participating in the attack. If multiple troopers participating in the attack have the same RAT, declare which model is the primary attacker.

Combined ranged attacks cannot target a model in melee.

If the target of a combined attack can claim concealment or cover in relation to any member of the attacking group, it gets the appropriate bonus against the attack. All other bonuses and penalties are based on the primary attacker.

After measuring range, any models found to be out of range of the target do not contribute to the attack and damage roll bonus, but are still considered to have made a ranged attack whether or not they contribute. If the primary attacker is out of range, the entire combined attack automatically misses regardless of bonuses. Similarly, models found to be more than 5" away from a target with the Stealth ability do not contribute, and the entire combined attack automatically misses if the primary attacker is more than 5" away from the target.

A unit's ranged attacks may be grouped in any manner, including multiple combined ranged attacks. Troopers capable of multiple ranged attacks can divide them among eligible targets and participate in multiple combined ranged attacks.

Example: Four members of a Legion Blighted Archers unit, including its Vassal, are in open formation and declare a combined ranged attack against a Dire Troll Mauler. When measuring range, the player discovers one archer is out of range and cannot participate in the attack. Since the Vassal has the highest RAT, he makes one ranged attack for the group, adding +3 to his attack and damage rolls since there are three models participating in the attack. Two other troopers in the same Blighted Archers unit could not participate in the combined attack because they are not in open formation. They declare individual ranged attacks against two Trollblood warriors nearby.

If the target of a combined ranged attack has a special rule or effect in play that affects its attackers, only the primary attacker—the model making the attack roll—suffers those effects.

SOUL TOKENS

Certain models can claim a model's soul, represented by a soul token, when it is destroyed. Only living models generate soul tokens. A model only has one soul. If more than one model is eligible to claim its soul, the model nearest the destroyed model receives the token. Refer to a model's special rules for how it utilizes soul tokens. Models removed from play for any reason do not generate soul tokens.

WEAPON CREWS

Weapon crews are small units that operate large or cumbersome weapons. Weapon crews are made up of a gunner and one or more crewmen. Unlike other units, weapon crews do not have leaders. A weapon crew cannot run or charge. The gunner gains +2" of movement for each crewman from his own unit in base-to-base contact with him when he begins his activation. If the gunner takes sufficient damage to be destroyed, a crewman within 1" can take the destroyed gunner's place immediately and become the new gunner. Remove the crewman from the table instead of the gunner. Any effects, animi, or spells on the damaged gunner expire. Any effects, animi, or spells on the removed crewman are applied to the new gunner.

Even though the gunner is on a larger-sized base, he is treated as a small-based model. A gunner only blocks line of sight to models with small bases. He does not block line of sight to a model with a medium-sized or larger base, nor does he screen such a model from a ranged or magic attack. Intervening models of any base size block line of sight to a gunner and screen him.

DAMAGE

Warlocks, warbeasts, and some other models can take a tremendous amount of damage before they fall in combat. What may be an incapacitating or mortal wound to a regular trooper will just bruise a warbeast or be deflected by a warlock's arcane protections.

DAMAGE ROLLS

Determine how much damage a successful attack causes by making a **damage roll**. Roll 2d6 and add the attack's Power (POW). Melee attacks also add the attacker's STR. A boosted damage roll adds an additional die to this roll. Special rules for certain circumstances may modify the damage roll as well.

Damage roll = 2d6 + POW (+STR if applicable)

Compare this total against the target's Armor (ARM) stat. The target takes one **damage point** for every point that the damage roll exceeds its ARM.

Completely resolve an attack's damage roll and special rules before applying any special rules from the target. The target's special rules apply only if they are still usable.

An attack is one use of a weapon or offensive spell even if it generates multiple attack rolls and/or damage rolls. For these attacks, completely resolve all of the attack and damage rolls just like an attack with only one attack and damage roll before applying the target's special rules. For example, suppose a Scattergunner makes a spray attack against some Venators under the effect of Hexeris' Death March spell. Venators destroyed by the attack do not make the movement and attack that Death March grants them until after all of the attack and damage rolls generated by the spray attack have been resolved.

RECORDING DAMAGE

A model's horde list entry gives the total amount of damage it can take before being *destroyed*. Most models are destroyed after suffering one damage point. A model resilient enough to take more than one point of damage will have a row of **damage circles** on its stat card for tracking damage it receives. Record its damage left to right, marking one damage circle for each damage point taken. A model is destroyed once all of its damage circles have been marked. Every fifth damage circle is colored for ease of counting. Unmarked damage circles are often called **wounds**.

A warbeast has a **life spiral** consisting of six **branches** of damage circles labeled 1 through 6. Life spirals vary in the number of damage boxes from warbeast to warbeast, but they serve the same function. When a warbeast suffers damage, roll a d6 to determine the branch on which to record the damage. Starting with the outermost empty circle in that branch working inwards, mark one damage circle per damage point suffered. Once a branch is full, continue recording damage in the next branch clockwise that contains unmarked damage boxes. Continue shifting branches as required until every damage point has been recorded.

DAMAGING ASPECTS

The branches of a warbeast's life spiral are grouped into three **aspects** that may be lost as they suffer damage. As a warbeast loses aspects, its performance on the battlefield suffers. An aspect is lost when all the damage circles corresponding to that aspect have been marked. The effects of lost aspects are as follows:

Lost Body: The warbeast rolls one fewer die on damage rolls.

Lost Mind: The warbeast rolls one fewer die on attack rolls. If the warbeast only rolls one die and the result is a six (6), it does not automatically hit its target.

Lost Spirit: The warbeast cannot be *forced*.

A warbeast is *destroyed* once all of its damage circles have been marked.

DESTROYED VS. REMOVED FROM PLAY

When a model suffers sufficient damage to be eliminated from play, it is **destroyed**. A model without damage capacity is destroyed as soon as it takes one *damage point*. Models with damage circles are **destroyed** when all their damage circles have been filled. Destroyed models are cleared from the play area and set aside. It is possible for destroyed models to return to play.

Occasionally models will be outright **removed from play**, sometimes instead of being destroyed, at other times in addition to being destroyed. A model removed from play cannot return to the table for any reason.

WARLOCK DEATH

Should a warlock be unfortunate enough to be destroyed or removed from play, his entire horde will suffer from the harsh blow. Upkeep spells cast by the warlock immediately expire.

Due to the loss of the warlock's guiding influence over his beasts, friendly faction warbeasts in the control area of the warlock that was destroyed or removed from play will go *wild* unless they are also in the control area of another friendly faction warlock. Additionally, friendly faction warbeasts not in the control area of a friendly faction warlock will also go wild if the closest friendly faction warlock to them was the warlock that was destroyed or removed from play. A **wild** warbeast cannot perform actions, cannot be forced, and cannot have damage transferred to it. Wild warbeasts never frenzy, and a warlock cannot tap a wild warbeast's animus.

During your Maintenance Phase, make a threshold check for each of your wild warbeasts in the control area of any friendly faction warlock. Note that this is a separate check from the one made during the Control Phase to see if a warbeast will frenzy. On a successful check, the warbeast is no longer wild. If the check fails, or if a wild warbeast is not in any friendly faction warlock's control area, it activates immediately and runs without being forced toward the nearest table edge using the most direct route that does not take it through a damaging effect or allow enemies to engage it.

A wild warbeast that leaves the table is removed from play. A wild warbeast with no escape route will cower in place, forfeiting its activation.

SPECIAL EFFECTS

Many attacks cause special effects in addition to causing damage. Each special effect is unique in its

A Lesson in Abstraction

Obviously a warbeast's spirit could never be literally damaged. These rules are an abstraction of the effects of damage suffered by a warbeast. For instance, as a warbeast suffers damage on the battlefield, its physical wellbeing may be compromised (*body aspect*) or it may lose the will to fight (*spirit aspect*).

application. There are four categories of special effects: automatic effects, critical effects, continuous effects, and cloud effects. A special effect may belong to more than one category, and its category may change depending on the weapon. For instance, one weapon may cause fire automatically on a successful hit, but another may require a critical hit to cause fire.

Pay close attention to the exact wording for each model's special effects. Even though the effect may be the same for different models with the same weapon or ability, it may require different conditions to function. Some model's special effects function if the target is hit, others require the target to take damage, and critical effects require a critical hit on the attack roll.

Automatic Effects

Apply an automatic effect every time it meets the conditions required to function.

Critical Effects

Apply a critical effect if any two dice in the attack roll show the same number and the attack hits—this is a **critical hit**. The target model suffers the special effect even if it takes no damage from the damage roll unless the specific effect requires that it do so. An *area-of-effect attack's* critical effect only functions with a *direct hit,* and every model under the template will suffer the critical effect.

A weapon with a critical effect has the label "Critical" to distinguish it from an automatic damage effect.

Continuous Effects

Continuous effects remain on a model and have the potential to damage or affect it some other way on subsequent turns. A model can have multiple continuous effects on it at once, but it can have only one of each continuous effect type on it at a time.

Resolve continuous effects on models you control during the maintenance phase of your turn. Roll a d6—if the result is a 1 or 2, the continuous effect immediately expires without further effect. On a 3 through 6, it remains in play and the model immediately suffers its effects.

Continuous effects do not require fury for *upkeep* and cannot be removed voluntarily. Remove a continuous effect only when it expires, a special situation causes it to end, or the affected model is removed from the table.

For example, a Pyre Troll attacks a Gorax with its Spew Fire attack and gets a critical hit. The Gorax is now on fire. It takes no damage from the fire at this point. During its controller's next Maintenance Phase, he rolls

a d6. The result is a 5, so the Gorax suffers a POW 12 damage from the fire. The Pyre Troll attacks it again on its turn, scoring another critical hit, but since the Gorax is already on fire, there is no further effect from the critical hit. When the Gorax's controller's Maintenance Phase comes around again, he rolls another d6 for the fire. This time, the result is a 1, so the fire goes out without doing any more damage to the Gorax.

Cloud Effects

A cloud effect produces an area of dense smoke or gas that remains in play at its *point of impact*. Use an area-of-effect template of the appropriate diameter to represent the cloud. Consider every model with any part of its base covered by the cloud's template to be inside the cloud and susceptible to its effects.

In addition to being affected by a cloud's special rules, a model inside a cloud effect gains +2 DEF against ranged and magic attacks, which is cumulative with *concealment* or *cover*. A model in a cloud effect may target models outside of it normally. For a model outside of it, the cloud effect completely obstructs line of sight to anything beyond it. Thus, a model can see into or out of a cloud effect but not through one. A cloud effect provides no protection from melee attacks.

A model that enters an existing cloud effect suffers its effects immediately. A model that begins its activation inside an existing cloud effect and does not move out of it suffers its effects at the end of its activation.

Remove a cloud effect when it expires or if a special situation causes it to end.

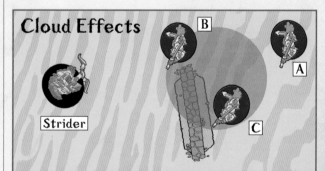

Cloud Effects

The Strider has LOS to models B and C, but they both gain +2 DEF against any ranged or magic attacks from the Strider for being in the cloud effect. The Strider's LOS to model C crosses a solid terrain feature, so model C also gains +4 DEF from cover for a total of +6 DEF against the Strider's attacks. The Strider and model A do not have LOS to each other since LOS cannot be drawn through a cloud effect.

Models B and C can make ranged or magic attacks agaisnt the Strider at no penalty. However, models B and C do gain +2 DEF against attacks from each other.

WARLOCKS, WARBEASTS, AND FURY
Special Rules, Managing Fury Points, and Casting Spells

The warlock is the single most important model in a player's horde. In large games, you can employ multiple warlocks, but each should be considered significant and essential to the success of any battle.

Warlocks are the most powerful models represented in HORDES. They are powerful shamans and deadly warriors as effective in martial combat as when wielding arcane forces. However, a warlock's greatest talent lies in harnessing the raw primal power contained within his warbeasts. If a warlock is the most potent model in a horde, warbeasts are his greatest assets. Without warbeasts, a warlock's power is greatly diminished.

Battles are won or lost purely by how well a warlock manages his abilities, *forces* warbeasts when appropriate, and draws upon the *fury* generated. HORDES is a game of risk management pure and simple. A warlock is not only required to know where he needs to boost an attack or cast a spell but also how far he is willing to push his warbeasts to keep them under control. Choosing poorly can result in frenzied warbeasts rushing far ahead of the warlock, or worse they could turn around and assault the warlock in their blind rage.

WARLOCK SPECIAL RULES

All warlocks have the following special rules in common:

DAMAGE TRANSFERENCE

Whenever a warlock suffers damage, he may immediately spend a fury point to **transfer** the damage to a friendly faction warbeast in his control area. The warbeast suffers all damage from that attack instead of the warlock. Determine where to mark the damage normally. Transferred damage exceeding the warbeast's unmarked damage circles is applied to the warlock and cannot be transferred to another warbeast. A warlock cannot transfer damage to a *frenzied* warbeast, a *wild* warbeast, or a warbeast that already has a number of fury points equal to its FURY stat. The warlock is still considered to have suffered damage even if the damage is transferred.

FEARLESS

A warlock never flees.

FEATS

Each warlock has a unique feat that can turn the tide of battle if used at the right time. A feat can freely be used any time during a warlock's activation in addition to his movement and action. A warlock cannot use his feat if he runs. A warlock can only use his feat once per game.

FORCING

Warlocks are adept at manipulating the primal nature of the warbeasts in their hordes. Warlocks are able to *force* their warbeasts to run, charge, perform power attacks, use special abilities, boost combat abilities, or make extra attacks. Each time a warbeast is *forced*, it gains one or more *fury points*.

HEALING

A warlock can spend fury points during his activation to heal damage done to himself or his warbeasts.

COMMANDER

A friendly model or unit in the warlock's *command range* may use the warlock's Command (CMD) stat for any *command checks*. A warlock can attempt to *rally* any *fleeing* friendly units in his command range. A warlock can *give orders* to one friendly unit in his command range during his activation. See Command (pg. 61) for full details on command checks, fleeing, and giving orders.

FURY MANIPULATION

A warlock is able to *leach* and manipulate fury points drawn from friendly faction warbeasts of his horde. Every turn a warlock is able to leach a number of fury points up to his FURY stat. Fury points can be used to cast spells, heal himself or his warbeasts, make extra attacks, transfer damage to a warbeast, or boost the combat abilities of the warlock.

In addition, a warlock can **discard fury**. During his activation, a warlock may remove any number of fury points from himself.

SPELL CASTER

A warlock can use fury points to cast spells any time during his activation in addition to his movement and action. A warlock cannot cast spells if he runs.

WARBEAST SPECIAL RULES

Warbeasts have a number of special rules in common:

CONTROLLED

Warbeasts are constantly under the control of their warlocks. Both a strength and weakness, a warbeast serves its master more efficiently than the best-trained animal imaginable, but it lacks freedom enjoyed by lesser creatures with freer wills. A warbeast cannot run, charge, or perform power attacks unless *forced* to do so by a friendly faction warlock.

FEARLESS

A warbeast never flees.

ANIMUS

Warbeasts have dormant arcane abilities called animi that can be tapped by friendly faction warlocks.

A warbeast may be *forced* to use its animus, or a friendly faction warlock may treat the animus as if it were one his own spells while the warbeast is in the warlock's control area.

Some warbeasts have a FURY stat too low for them to use their animus. These animi exist simply to be tapped by friendly warlocks as spells.

THRESHOLD AND FRENZY

Tapping into the primal energies of vicious warbeasts is not without its inherent risks. During their controller's Maintenance Phase, warbeasts with one or more fury points must pass a threshold check or frenzy (see Threshold Checks, pg. 58). The more fury points a warbeast has, the more likely it is to frenzy. A frenzied warbeast acts on its own according to the rules on pg. 58.

FURY & FORCING

A warlock's greatest resource is the primal energy known as *fury*. He draws fury points from the warbeasts in his horde during the control phase and uses them to cast spells, boost rolls, and heal or transfer damage. Warbeasts generate fury when they are *forced* during their activations. A warlock can only *force, reave,* or *leach* from friendly faction warbeasts in his *control area*. Unspent fury points remain on a model from turn to turn, although a warlock will lose fury points in excess of his FURY stat during his controller's Maintenance Phase.

CONTROL AREA

A warlock's **control area** extends out from the warlock in all directions for a distance equal to twice his FURY stat in inches. Measure this distance from the edge of the warlock's base. A warlock is always considered to be in his own control area. When a spell or special rule changes a warlock's FURY stat, his control area changes accordingly. Some spells and feats use the warlock's control area as their *area of effect*.

A warbeast must be within a friendly warlock's control area to be *healed, forced, leached, reaved* or for the warlock to *tap* the warbeast's animus, but it does not have to be within line of sight.

Measuring Control Areas

A player may measure his warlock's control area at any time for any reason. While measuring a warlock's control area, the controller may determine the proximity of other models to his warlock. Specifically, a player may measure the distance from his warlock to any other model within the warlock's control area at any time.

For control area effects against opposing models, a player does not have to measure his warlock's control area until after the enemy model commits to its movement or action.

FORCING

A warbeast within a friendly faction warlock's control area may be *forced* during its activation, but it need not be in line of sight. To *force* a warbeast, declare the desired effect and place one fury point on it. This fury point does not come from the warlock. A warbeast may be *forced* several times during its activation, but it can never have a total number of fury points higher than its FURY stat. If a warbeast's FURY stat is reduced for any reason, immediately remove excess fury points. It cannot be *forced* if the fury point gain would cause it to exceed this limit. *Wild* warbeasts cannot be *forced*. Fury points remain on warbeasts until removed by leaching, reaving, or a special rule.

A warbeast may be *forced* during its activation for any of the following effects:

Additional Attack

A warbeast may be *forced* to make an additional melee or ranged attack as part of its combat action. The warbeast may make one additional attack each time it is *forced*. A warbeast *forced* to make additional ranged attacks cannot exceed a weapon's *rate of fire* (ROF). A warbeast cannot be *forced* to make additional special attacks.

Boosting Attack & Damage Rolls

A warbeast may be *forced* to add one die to any attack roll or damage roll. Boosting must be declared before rolling any dice. Each attack or damage roll can only be boosted once, but a model can boost multiple rolls during its activation. When an attack affects several models, the attack and damage rolls against each individual model must be boosted separately.

Use Animus

In addition to its movement and action, a warbeast may be *forced* to use its animus any time during its activation. A warbeast may only use its animus once per activation and may not use its animus at all if it runs. Instead of gaining one fury point, it gains a number of fury points equal to the animus' cost. Resolve the effects of the animus immediately. Though using an animus

often creates a spell effect, it is not casting a spell. See Casting Spells & Using Animi on pg. 59.

Run, Charge, and Power Attacks

A warbeast must be *forced* in order to run, charge, or make a power attack. A warbeast does not need to be *forced* to use a special attack granted by the warbeast's special rules.

Rile

A warbeast may be *forced* for the sole purpose of gaining fury points. When a warbeast is riled, it may gain any number of fury points, but the resulting total may not exceed its FURY stat. A warbeast may be riled even if it runs.

Think Before Measuring
KEEP IN MIND THAT IF YOU MEASURE YOUR WARLOCK'S CONTROL AREA, THE INFORMATION MUST BE SHARED WITH YOUR OPPONENT AS WELL, SO HE WILL ALSO KNOW EXACTLY HOW CLOSE YOU ARE TO HIS MODEL. FREQUENTLY MEASURING CONTROL AREAS CAN ALSO TELEGRAPH YOUR INTENTIONS TO YOUR OPPONENT.

LEACHING

Warlocks can use the fury generated by their warbeasts for a variety of actions, but they do not receive it automatically. A warlock must **leach** fury points from friendly faction warbeasts in his control area during the warlock's controller's Control Phase. Fury points leached from a warbeast are removed from it and placed on the warlock.

A warlock may also leach fury points from his own life force during his controller's Control Phase. For each fury pointed he leaches from himself, a warlock takes one damage point. This damage cannot be transferred to a warbeast.

A warlock may leach any number of fury points, but his fury point total cannot exceed his FURY stat when leaching. Leaching is performed at the start of the Control Phase before *threshold checks* are made or fury is spent to upkeep spells. Some circumstances may allow a warlock to have more fury points than his FURY stat normally allows. During his controller's Maintenance Phase, a warlock loses all fury points in excess of his FURY stat.

Fury Points Stick Around!
THAT'S RIGHT JACKHEAD! FURY POINTS ARE NOT REMOVED ARBITRARILY DURING THE CONTROL PHASE LIKE FOCUS POINTS WOULD BE IN WARMACHINE. ONLY FURY POINTS ON THE WARLOCK EXCEEDING HIS FURY (FURY) STAT ARE REMOVED DURING THE MAINTENANCE PHASE. AIN'T IT NICE WE CALLED THAT TO YOUR ATTENTION?

For example, Hoarluk Doomshaper has a FURY stat of seven (7). If he begins his controller's turn with two fury points, he may leach up to five (5) additional fury points from friendly Trollblood warbeasts in his control area, but he cannot leach more than five because the additional points would exceed his FURY.

A warlock begins the game with a number of fury points equal to his FURY stat.

Reaving

Warlocks are able to capture the life essence of their warbeasts as they die. When a friendly faction warbeast is destroyed within a warlock's control area, he may **reave** the warbeast's fury points. Immediately transfer the destroyed warbeast's fury points to the warlock. A warlock cannot have a higher fury point total that his FURY stat as a result of reaving. Excess fury points gained from reaving are lost. A destroyed warbeast's fury can only be reaved by one warlock.

Discarding Fury

During his activation, a warlock may remove any number of fury points from himself. A warlock may discard fury even if he runs.

Using Fury Points

A warlock has many powerful uses for fury points at his disposal. The real trick is knowing which use is best depending on what dire circumstances his horde faces. A fury point may be spent any time during a warlock's activation for any of the following effects:

Additional Attack

A warlock may spend a fury point to make an additional melee or ranged attack as part of his combat action. The warlock may make one additional attack for each fury point he spends. A warlock using fury to make additional ranged attacks cannot exceed a weapon's *rate of fire* (ROF). A warlock cannot spend fury points to make additional special attacks.

Boosting Attack & Damage Rolls

A warlock may spend a fury point to add one die to any attack roll or damage roll. Boosting must be declared before rolling any dice. Each attack or damage roll can only be boosted once, but a model can boost multiple rolls during its activation. When an attack affects several models, the attack and damage rolls against each individual model must be boosted separately.

Cast Spell

In addition to its movement and action, a warlock may cast a spell any time during its activation by simply spending the appropriate number of fury points and immediately resolving its effects. A warlock may cast any number of spells during his activation provided he has enough fury points to do so. See Casting Spells & Using Animi on page 59.

Healing

A warlock may spend fury points during his activation to remove damage points from himself or from a friendly faction warbeast in his control area during his activation. For each fury point spent, the warlock may remove one damage point. Damage may be removed from anywhere on the warbeast's life spiral.

Threshold Checks & Frenzy

Forcing warbeasts does not come without inherent risks. The fury generated by pushing warbeasts can potentially send them into blind rages causing the warbeasts to frenzy.

During each Control Phase, after warlocks have leached fury from their warbeasts and spent fury to upkeep their spells, each warbeast with one or more fury points must make a successful threshold check or frenzy. To make a threshold check, roll 2d6 and add one to the roll for each fury point on the warbeast. If the roll exceeds the warbeast's current Threshold (THR) stat, it fails.

For example, during his Control Phase Rob makes a threshold check for his Dire Troll that has three (3) fury points left. Rob rolls 2d6 and adds three to the roll for the Dire Troll's fury points. He then compares the result to the Dire Troll's THR of 11. If Rob rolls 8 or less, nothing happens since 8 plus 3 for the fury points is 11, which is equal to the Dire Troll's THR. If Rob rolls 9 or more, the Dire Troll frenzies because the result exceeds the Dire Troll's THR.

A frenzied warbeast immediately activates and attempts to attack another model. If there are models in melee range, it will attack one of them, enemy models first. If there are no models in the warbeast's melee range but there are models engaging it, the warbeast will advance toward and attack the closest, enemy models first. Otherwise, the frenzied warbeast will charge and attack the nearest model in line of sight, friendly or enemy. If the frenzied warbeast cannot charge, it will advance toward the selected model instead. If there are no models in the frenzied warbeast's line of sight, it will advance toward and attack the nearest model, friendly or enemy. When there is a choice of models, select one of them at random. A frenzied warbeast that is knocked down will forfeit its movement to stand up and attack if possible. Otherwise it will forfeit its action and advance toward the nearest model.

A frenzied warbeast never makes special attacks. It makes one attack with each of its melee weapons, and its melee attack and melee damage rolls are automatically boosted. If it destroys its target before it has made all of its attacks, it will attack another model in melee range, enemy models first.

A frenzied warbeast cannot be forced nor can it have damage transferred to it. Because a frenzied warbeast activates in the Control Phase, it cannot be activated in the following Activation Phase. Frenzy lasts for one round.

Casting Spells & Using Animi

Warlocks have the ability to cast spells and tap the dormant primal power of a warbeast known as an animus. A warlock may tap the animus of a friendly faction warbeast in his control area and cast it as if it were a spell of his own. A warbeast can be *forced* to use its animus. When a warbeast uses its animus, it is not considered to be casting a spell, but when a warlock taps a warbeast's animus, he is considered to be casting a spell.

Unless noted otherwise, spells and animi that target a model other than the warlock casting the spell or the warbeast using the animus require line of sight to their targets.

Warlock Spell Casting

A warlock may cast a spell any time during his activation by spending a number of fury points equal to the spell's fury cost. Any spell, including offensive spells, may be cast while the warlock is in melee. Resolve the spell's effects immediately. A warlock may cast as many spells during his activation for which he can pay the fury cost. The same spell may be cast multiple times during the warlock's activation. A warlock may cast spells before movement or after movement but not during movement, nor may he interrupt an attack or special action to cast a spell. A warlock cannot cast a spell if he runs during his activation.

For example, a warlock could cast a spell, move, use his combat action to make a melee attack, cast two more spells and then spend another fury point to make another melee attack.

Animus

Warbeasts have dormant arcane abilities that may be tapped by friendly faction warlocks. In addition to its movement and actions, a warbeast may be *forced* to use its animus any time during its activation. A warbeast may only be *forced* to use an animus once per activation.

A warbeast may be *forced* to use its animus while in melee. Resolve the effects immediately. A warbeast may be *forced* to use its animus before movement or after movement but not during movement, nor may it interrupt an attack or special action to use its animus. A warbeast cannot be *forced* to use its animus if it runs during its activation.

When a warbeast uses its animus, it gains a number of fury points equal to the casting cost. Immediately resolve the effects of the animus. A warbeast cannot exceed its Fury (FURY) stat when using its animus. If the fury points gained by using its animus would cause a warbeast's fury point total to exceed its FURY stat, it cannot use the animus.

A warbeast may not have a FURY stat high enough for it to use its animus at all. However, a friendly faction warlock may still tap it if the warbeast is in his control area.

A model/unit may only have one friendly animus in play on it at a time regardless of whether it was cast by a warlock or used by a warbeast. A friendly animus already in play on a model/unit immediately expires and is replaced by the newer one.

Offensive Spells & Magic Attacks

An *offensive spell* or animus requires that the model casting the spell or using the animus succeed in a magic attack roll to put its effects in play. Magic attacks are similar to *ranged attacks* and follow most of the same rules. Determine a magic attack's success by making a **magic attack roll**. Roll 2d6 and add the attacking model's FURY. A *boosted* attack roll adds an additional die to this roll. Special rules and certain circumstances may modify the attack roll as well.

Magic Attack Roll = 2d6 + FURY

An attack hits its target if the attack roll equals or exceeds the target's DEF. If the attack roll is less than the target's DEF, the attack misses. A roll of all 1s on the dice causes an automatic miss. A roll of all 6s causes an automatic hit regardless of the attacker's FURY or his opponent's DEF, unless you are rolling only one die.

Unless stated otherwise, a model making a magic attack must obey the *targeting* rules when declaring a target. A model may not target itself with an offensive spell or animus. A magic attack's target may benefit from such modifiers as *concealment* and *cover*, however, magic attacks are not affected by rules that only apply to ranged attacks. A model does not benefit from *aiming* when making a magic attack.

A magic attack does not suffer the *target in melee* attack roll penalty when the attacker is in melee with the target. However, if such an attack misses and there are multiple models in the combat, the attack may still hit another random model in the combat, excluding the attacker and the original target. Resolve these situations per the *Targeting a Model in Melee* rules on page 46. An AOE spell that misses in this situation will deviate normally.

UPKEEP SPELLS

Upkeep spells can be maintained for more than one round. During the Control Phase, after leaching but before making threshold checks, warlocks may spend fury points to keep any of their upkeep spells in play. Each upkeep spell requires the expenditure of one fury point. A warlock can upkeep his spells even if the spell's effects are outside his control area. If a fury point is not spent to upkeep the spell at this time, it immediately expires and its effects end.

A warlock may only have one of each specific upkeep spell in play at a time, but he can maintain any number of different upkeep spells simultaneously if he has enough fury points to spend. A model or unit may only have one friendly and one enemy upkeep spell in play on it at one time. If another upkeep spell is cast on a model that already has one from the same side— friendly or enemy—the old upkeep spell expires and is replaced by the newly cast one.

A warlock may recast any of his upkeep spells already in play. When a warlock does so, the spell's previous casting immediately expires and its effects end.

For example, a unit of Cataphract Arcuarii currently has Defender's Ward in play on it. The Skorne player decides that it would be more beneficial to have the Savagery spell cast on the unit instead, which immediately removes the Defender's Ward spell once cast. During the Trollblood player's turn, Doomshaper casts the Vexation spell on the unit, which does not remove the Savagery spell because an enemy upkeep spell does not replace a friendly one.

SPELL & ANIMUS STATISTICS

A spell or animus is defined by the following six statistics:

- **Cost:** The number of fury points that must be spent to cast the spell or the number of fury points a warbeast gains when it is *forced* to use the animus. A warbeast cannot use its animus if doing so would cause its fury point total to exceed its FURY stat.

- **Range (RNG):** The maximum distance in inches that a spell/animus can be used against a target. Range is measured from the nearest edge of the attacking model's base to the nearest edge of the target model's base. A RNG of "Self" indicates that the spell/animus can only be cast on the model casting or using it.

- **Power (POW):** The base amount of damage a spell/animus inflicts. Add a spell's/animus' POW to its damage roll.

- **Area-of-Effect (AOE):** The diameter in inches of the template an area-of-effect spell/animus uses for damage effects. When using an AOE spell, center the template on the determined point of impact. Models covered by the template potentially suffer the spell's effects. See Combat (pg. 48) for detailed rules on AOE attacks. Templates for AOEs can be found on page 208. A spell with an AOE of "CTRL" is centered on the warlock and affects every model in his control area.

- **Upkeep (UP):** An upkeep spell remains in play if the warlock who cast it allocates a fury point to it during his controller's Control Phase.

- **Offensive (OFF):** An offensive spell/animus requires a successful magic attack roll to take effect. If the attack roll fails, the attack misses and the spell/animus has no effect. A failed attack roll for a spell/animus with an area of effect deviates according to those rules instead.

COMMAND–OF MICE AND MEN

Command Checks, Fleeing, and Orders

Regardless of a soldier's skill at arms, his real worth is measured by his will to fight. Warriors may break and flee after suffering massive casualties or when confronted by terrifying entities while manipulative spells can warp the minds of the weak-willed and cause them to attack their allies. The inspiring presence of a nearby warlock or a unit's leader can steel the nerves of warriors faced with these mental assaults and even rally them before their panic becomes a full-blown rout. Command checks determine the outcome of these game situations that test a combatant's discipline or mental resolve.

COMMAND CHECKS

There are several different circumstances that require a model or unit to make a command check: *massive casualties*, *terrifying entities*, and a spell or other attack's special rules.

Massive Casualties

A unit suffers massive casualties when it loses 50% or more of the models in it at the beginning of the current turn. The unit must immediately pass a command check or *flee*.

Terrifying Entity

A terrifying entity is one with either the *terror* or *abomination* special ability. A model/unit in *melee range* of an enemy model with terror, a model/unit with an enemy model with terror in its melee range, or a model/unit within 3" of an abomination—friendly or enemy—must pass a command check or flee. Make this command check after the active model or unit completes it movement but before it performs any actions.

For instance, if Thagrosh moves into melee with a Skorne Praetor, the Praetor's unit makes a command check as soon as Thagrosh ends his movement. However, if a Praetor moves into melee with Thagrosh, make a command check for his unit after every trooper in the unit finishes moving. In either case, make the command check before any model performs an action.

A model or unit that passes a command check caused by its proximity to a terrifying entity does not make further command checks as a result of proximity to that entity as long as it remains inside the range that triggered the effect. If these models become separated and encounter each other again later, another command

check will be required. A unit that consists of terrifying entities counts as a single terrifying entity for the purpose of these rules. A model/unit need only make a single command check for encountering the unit regardless of how many of its troopers it actually encounters.

Special Rules

Some spells and other attacks cause an individual model or an entire unit to make a command check. Reference the specific description to determine the attack's eligible targets and effects. Though fleeing is the most common outcome of a failed command check, some spells and effects have more sinister effects.

When one of these situations requires a model or unit to make a command check, roll 2d6. If the result is equal to or less than its Command (CMD) stat, it passes the check. In most cases, this means the model or unit continues to function normally or rallies if it was fleeing. If the roll is greater than its CMD, the check fails and the model or unit suffers the consequences. When a unit fails a command check, every trooper in that unit suffers the effects, including out-of-formation troopers.

For example, a Scattergunner has a CMD of 6. The Scattergunner passes a command check on a 2d6 roll of 6 or less.

A model or unit that fails a command check against massive casualties or terrifying entities immediately flees; one that fails a command check against a spell suffers the associated effect.

An independent model makes a command check on an individual basis using its own CMD. It may use the CMD of a friendly model with the Commander ability instead of its own if it is in that model's command range.

In most cases, troopers make command checks at the unit level. Some exceptions include troopers that end their activations out of formation and spells that specifically target single models. Make one command check for the entire unit using the unit leader's CMD if he is still in play, and apply its results to every trooper in that unit, unless stated otherwise. A unit making a command check within command range of a friendly model with the Commander ability may use that model's CMD stat instead. A trooper making an individual command check may use his leader's CMD if he is in formation or the CMD or a friendly model with the Commander ability if he is within that model's command range.

COMMAND RANGE

A model with the Commander ability, such as a warlock has a command range equal to his CMD in inches. A friendly model or unit in such a model's command range may use that model's CMD when making a command check, but it is not required to do so. Only one model in a unit must be in a warlock's command range for the entire unit to be considered in command range.

A unit leader can *rally* and *give orders* only to his troopers in formation, but a model with the Commander ability can rally any friendly model or unit and give orders to any friendly unit in his command range. A trooper out of formation cannot be rallied by his unit leader or receive any orders. A trooper making an individual command check may use his leader's CMD if he is in formation or the CMD of a friendly model with the Commander ability if he is within its command range.

FLEEING

A model or unit that fails a command check against fleeing immediately turns to face directly away from the threat that caused the command check. If this occurs during the model or unit's activation, its activation immediately ends. Other than changing facing, the fleeing model does not move until its next activation.

A fleeing model activates during its controller's Maintenance Phase. A fleeing model automatically runs away from its nearest threat toward its horde's deployment edge using the most direct route that does not take it through a damaging effect or allows enemies to engage it. When playing games without defined deployment edges, fleeing models run toward the nearest table edge. Fleeing troopers are not required to remain in formation. A fleeing model cannot perform any actions.

A fleeing model that leaves the battlefield is *removed from play*. A fleeing model with no escape route will cower in its current position and forfeit its activation.

After its mandatory movement, a fleeing model can attempt to *rally* if it is in formation with its unit leader or if it is within the command range of a friendly model with the Commander special ability, such as a warlock.

RALLYING

A fleeing model or unit can make a command check after its mandatory movement in the Maintenance Phase if in formation with its leader or if in command range of a friendly model with the Commander ability. If it passes the command check, the model or unit rallies and turns to face its nearest opponents. This ends its activation and the unit or model cannot activate again this turn, but it may function normally next turn. If the fleeing model fails the command check, it continues to flee during its controller's next Maintenance Phase.

FEARLESS MODELS

A model with the *fearless* special ability never flees. However, the model is still subject to command checks that have penalties other than fleeing.

ISSUING ORDERS

An order lets a model make a specialized combat maneuver during its activation. Unlike other warrior models, troopers cannot automatically choose to run or charge—they must receive an order to do so. A unit may receive an order from a friendly model with the Commander ability prior to its activation or from its leader at the beginning of its activation. Alternatively, the unit's leader may issue an order granted by his special rules such as a Tharn Bloodtracker Huntress giving an ambuscade order. A unit whose leader is no longer in play cannot use its leader's unique orders.

A unit can receive only one order per activation. Every trooper in formation receives the order and must obey it. An out-of-formation trooper cannot receive an order and does not perform the task or gain its benefits. A unit not given a specific order can advance and perform its actions normally. A unit must be given new orders for each activation. Orders do not carry over from one activation to another.

At any time during its activation, a model with the Commander ability can give a run or charge order to one friendly unit in his command range, but if the unit has already activated, the order expires at the end of the turn.

TERRAIN—YOUR BEST FRIEND

The Battlefield, Hazards, and Structures

The lay of the land has a tremendous impact on a horde's ability to maneuver. The most cunning commanders use the terrain conditions to their best advantage. These terrain rules provide guidelines for establishing the effects and restrictions a battlefield's objects and environment can have on a game. Players should discuss the terrain prior to a game and agree on the characteristics for different terrain features. Covering the rules for every possible terrain type would be an endless task, so players themselves must determine the exact nature of each terrain feature on the battlefield before the game begins.

BATTLEFIELD SETUP

Use the amount of terrain that suits the type of game you wish to play. A table with few terrain features favors ranged attacks and swift movement while having more terrain features shifts the emphasis toward melee combat.

Give consideration to model base sizes when placing terrain features close together since a model can move between terrain features only if its base will fit between them. With careful placement, you can create narrow passages that can be accessed only by models with smaller bases.

All players should agree upon terrain setup. When placing terrain, strive for a visually appealing and tactically challenging battlefield. These qualities provide the most exciting and memorable games. Battlefield setup and terrain placement is not a competitive portion of the game—players should not strategically place terrain features in a manner that unfairly aids or penalizes a specific horde. However, a published or homemade scenario might dictate doing so to represent, for example, an overmatched horde defending a village or mountain pass. In such a scenario, giving the defending horde a strong defensive position would be one way to make up for being outclassed by its opponent.

If all players are involved with the battlefield setup, or if an impartial third party sets up the terrain, establish turn order and deploy forces normally. If only one player or team sets up the battlefield, then the opposing player or team chooses on which table edge to deploy his forces before determining turn order.

Before the game begins, all players should agree on each terrain feature's game effects.

TERRAIN

A model's movement can be penalized depending on the type of ground over which it moves. In HORDES, traversable terrain falls into one of three categories: *open, rough,* and *impassable.*

Open terrain is mostly smooth, even ground. Examples include grassy plains, barren fields, dirt roads, and paved surfaces. A model moves across open terrain without penalty.

Rough terrain can be traversed but at a significantly slower pace than open terrain. Examples include thick brush, rocky areas, murky bogs, shallow water, and deep snow. As long as any part of its base is in rough terrain, a model moves at 1/2 normal movement rate. Therefore, a model in rough terrain actually moves only 1/2" for every 1" of its movement used.

Impassable terrain is natural terrain that completely prohibits movement. This includes cliff faces, lava, and deep water. A model cannot move across impassable terrain.

TERRAIN FEATURES

Natural and man-made objects on the battlefield are terrain features. Each terrain feature is unique, so you must decide its exact qualities before staring the game. Terrain features are virtually limitless in their variety, but you can quantify each by how it affects movement, the type of protection it affords, and any adverse effects it causes.

In addition to hindering movement, terrain features can also provide protection against ranged and magic attacks. A terrain feature such as a hedge or a mesh fence grants a model *concealment* by making it more difficult to be seen even though it is not dense enough actually to block an attack. A terrain feature such as a stone wall, a giant boulder, or a building grants a model *cover* by being physically solid enough to block an attack.

Obstacles & Obstructions

Obstacles and obstructions are terrain features that affect a model's movement, provide protection from ranged attacks, and serve as *intervening terrain* during melee combat.

An obstacle is any terrain feature up to 1" tall. Obstacles are low enough that they can be climbed upon or, in some cases, easily crossed. A model can climb atop and stand on an obstacle at least 1" thick such as a raised platform or the sides of a ziggurat.

An advancing or running model can climb atop an obstacle by using 2" of its movement. A model cannot climb an obstacle if it does not have at least 2" of movement remaining. Place a model that climbs an obstacle atop it with the front of the model's base making only 1" of forward progress. Once atop an obstacle, the model may continue with the remainder of its movement.

Realize that a model on a medium or large base may have trouble balancing atop an obstacle if it does not continue moving after initially climbing it. With only 1" of forward progress, the back of the model's base will hang off the back end of the obstacle. This is fine—just prop up the model with some extra dice until it can move again.

An advancing or running model can descend an obstacle without any penalty to its forward progress.

A **linear obstacle** is an obstacle up to 1" tall but less than 1" thick such as a wall or hedge. An advancing or running model can cross a linear obstacle at no penalty as long as the model has enough movement remaining to end its move with its base completely clear of the obstacle. If it does not, the model must stop short of the linear obstacle. A model cannot partially cross or stand atop a linear obstacle. A charging model cannot cross a linear obstacle.

In some rare cases, a model may be posed with its head so low that it has no line of sight over an obstacle. If this model's base touches an obstacle or if it is as close as its pose allows, assume the model is standing in a manner allowing it to see and attack over the obstacle. When this occurs, determine the model's *line of sight* from a point directly over the center of its base at the height of the wall. However, enemy models that have line of sight to that point may attack this model as well.

An obstruction is a terrain feature greater than 1" tall such as a high wall, a building, or a gigantic boulder. Treat obstructions as *impassable terrain*.

Forest

A typical forest has many trees and dense underbrush, but any terrain feature that hinders movement and makes a model inside it difficult to see can also follow these guidelines. A forest is considered *rough terrain* but also provides *concealment* to a model with any part of its base inside its perimeter.

A model can draw *line of sight* through up to 3" of forest, but anything more obstructs line of sight. For a model outside of it, the forest completely obstructs line of sight to anything beyond it. Thus, a model can see into or out of a forest but not completely through one no matter how thick it is. A forest provides no protection from melee attacks.

Hills

A hill is a terrain feature representing a gentle rise or drop in elevation. Since many terrain pieces use stepped sides instead of gradual slopes to represent a hill's elevations, be sure to declare whether the terrain feature is a hill or an obstacle for movement purposes.

A hill may be open or rough terrain depending on the ground's nature. Unlike obstacles, hills do not impose any additional movement penalties. A model can charge up or down a hill in open terrain at no penalty.

Elevation

Models can take advantage of hills, platforms, and some obstacles that provide elevations above table level. When drawing line of sight from a model on a higher elevation than its target, ignore intervening models on lower elevation than the attacking model except those that would normally screen the target. Additionally, you can draw a line of sight through screening models that have equal or smaller-sized bases than the attacking model, but the target still gets +2 DEF for being screened. A model on higher elevation than its attacker gains +2 DEF against ranged and magic attacks from that opponent.

Hazards

Many things on a battlefield can kill just as quickly as an opponent can. These hazards could include water or flowing magma. Immediately apply a hazard's effects to a model as soon as any portion of its base enters the hazard's perimeter.

Water

Depending on its nature, water can be hazardous to both warriors and warbeasts. When placing a water terrain feature, declare whether it is deep or shallow.

Deep water cannot be entered voluntarily. However, a model may be slammed, thrown, or otherwise forced to move into deep water.

A model in deep water can advance at half its normal movement rate but cannot run or charge. It cannot perform actions, cast spells, use feats, or give orders until it is completely out of the deep water. A model in deep water cannot engage other models or make attacks. A warlock in deep water can leach fury points and use them to maintain upkeep spells.

A model in deep water has a base DEF of 7 against all attacks. A warrior or warbeast ending its activation in deep water automatically takes one damage point.

Shallow water is rough terrain that can be crossed by any model. Other than hindering movement, shallow water poses no threat.

STRUCTURES

Structures present unique opportunities for terrain arrangement and tactical play. A structure is any large terrain feature that can be damaged and destroyed. The most common structures are buildings, but you can use these guidelines for fortress walls, bridges, and similar constructions as well. A single house in a field or a bridge over a chasm can be a scenario's major objective, and a series of buildings can be arranged to create a completely urban environment.

All structures are *solid obstructions*. A warrior can enter a structure through any entryway such as a door or window regardless of the model's base size. A warbeast can enter a building only through an opening big enough for its base to pass through unobstructed.

Playing In Enclosed Structures

Models function normally inside a structure, but how you represent this may change depending upon the nature of the terrain. If the terrain piece is open-topped or has a removable roof, move models about the interior of the structure to their actual positions. Normal rules apply. A model partially obscured by a door or window benefits from cover.

If the terrain piece representing the structure has a closed top or is otherwise unsuitable for moving models inside it, a more abstract method must be used. If a model enters such a structure, remove the model from the table and place a marker outside the building where the model entered.

When using these abstract rules, declare a model's position inside the structure at the end of its movement. When a model first enters a building, declare whether it is staying clear of all openings or using its entryway as cover. On subsequent activations, the model can move up or down one level and can either stay clear of entryways or choose to occupy a specific one. Instead of changing levels, a model can exit a structure through any entryway on the same level.

A model staying clear of openings does not have line of sight to anything outside the structure, but models outside cannot target it either. A model standing at a specific opening can draw line of sight out of it to make attacks, but it may be attacked in turn by any model with line of sight to its location. The model benefits from cover against attacks from outside the building.

When using this abstract method of interior movement, a model can engage an opponent in a structure simply by entering that building on the same level. Area-of-effect attacks and spray attacks against any model in a closed structure affect every model on that level of the building.

Bringing Down the House

DIFFERENT MATERIALS HAVE DIFFERENT ARM STATS:

WOOD—ARM 12

REINFORCED WOOD—ARM 14

BRICK—ARM 16

STONE— ARM 18

IRON—ARM 20

STEEL—ARM 22

Realize that these abstract rules take a very liberal approach. If you have very large structures, you may wish to divide them into several sectors to maintain some balance. If this does not provide an acceptable level of precision, we suggest placing a properly scaled floor plan for each structure near the playing area and placing the models on them in their actual locations once they enter a building. If you choose this latter method, play according to the normal rules.

Damaging and Destroying Structures

A model that would rather blast its way through the side of a structure than use an entryway will need to inflict substantial damage to it. An attack against a structure in range automatically hits. Not all weapons are effective against structures, so a model must have a weapon that will do the job if it intends to punch through. Ranged weapons such as handguns, rifles, and crossbows are all but useless. A ranged weapon must have a POW of at least 14 to damage a structure. However, melee and magic attacks, area-of-effect attacks, and attacks that cause fire or corrosion do full damage against structures. A magic attack only does its normal damage to a structure. Ignore a spell's special rules when it targets a structure.

Every structure has an Armor (ARM) stat corresponding to its composition. See the "Bringing Down the House" callout on the previous page for the ARM assigned to the most common forms of construction.

A structure can only suffer so much damage before being destroyed. Determine a structure's damage capacity based on its composition and thickness. For instance, a wooden gate is destroyed when it suffers 5 damage points and a small stone obelisk is destroyed when it suffers 10 damage points. Damage suffered by a structure is cumulative.

Large structures such as buildings, walls, and bridges can be destroyed in segments. A typical building wall can suffer 5 damage points per inch of width. Fortified or very thick walls could suffer 20 or more damage points or more per inch of width depending on its composition. When a specific segment of a structure suffers its total damage capacity, that portion of it is destroyed. If a single attack causes massive damage, it destroys an appropriate amount of the structure. We suggest having some graph paper handy to diagram a structure and record the damage it suffers. For example, a wooden wall with ARM 14 suffers 18 damage points from a damage roll of 32, so the attack destroys 3" of the wall.

A model with a small base can move through a 1" wide hole, and a model with a medium or large base can move through a hole at least 2" wide.

Undamaged portions of a wall or other freestanding structure remain intact as the structure suffers damage. However, complex structures such as buildings and bridges rely on the support of all segments to remain standing. A building collapses when half of its total wall length is destroyed, regardless of the proximity of the destroyed segments. For instance, a 3" x 6" building collapses as soon as 9" of its walls are destroyed. Remove the building from play and replace it with an equal-sized ruin. A model inside a building when it collapses suffers a damage roll with Power (POW) equal to the building's ARM and is knocked down. A ruined building is rough terrain and provides cover to a model with any portion of its base inside the ruin's perimeter.

These guidelines should be tailored to each individual structure. For instance, a rope bridge could be destroyed by any successful melee attack. A small wooden bridge should suffer damage and have segments destroyed as if it were a wall. Each support of a large stone bridge could suffer 20 damage points before being destroyed, and the entire bridge could collapse once two supports are gone.

SCENARIOS–
WHY WE CAN'T ALL BE FRIENDS

Six Variations of Gameplay

There are as many reasons for war as there are wars themselves. Sides seldom clash with only the intent to eliminate one another. It could be a skirmish over boundaries, a fight over resources, or an attempt to hold important strategic ground. Conceiving a reason for your conflicts can greatly enhance your HORDES gaming experiences.

Here you will find six scenarios ready to play. Each occurs on a balanced playing field conveying no specific advantage to any one player. You can agree with your opponent on which scenario to play, or prior to building your horde, roll a d6 and play the scenario indicated below:

1–Pendulum	4–Domination
2–Wild Fires	5–King of the Hill
3–Crossed Lines	6–Claw & Fang

Each scenario provides special rules that describe how to handle the unique circumstances of the scenario. Certain scenarios will also have restrictions on horde composition as well as how the game table should be set up. Most scenarios can be played on any scale you choose. Experiment with different combinations, and feel free to create variations or unique scenarios of your own!

PENDULUM

War always comes down to the line. You need to hold yours and break the enemy's. This has nothing to do with the ground where you're fighting. It's about what happens when the foe breaks a bloody hole through your warriors and floods through the breach like a river rupturing the dam, sweeping you from the field.

—GRISSEL BLOODSONG, TROLLBLOOD WARLOCK AND FELL CALLER

DESCRIPTION

The back and forth rhythm of warfare often leads to decisive moments as enemy lines are crossed. In a Pendulum battle both forces fight for control over the battlefield by holding their own half of the table and invading the enemy's region of control.

SPECIAL RULES

Divide the table in half with a line running east to west through the center. Using a piece of string is a good method for marking the centerline. The objective of Pendulum is for a player to get one or more of his models across the centerline onto his opponent's side of the table while keeping his opponent's models from crossing the centerline onto his side of the table. The first player to have models on his opponent's side of the table while there are none of his opponent's models on his own side for three (3) consecutive rounds wins the game.

For example, Matt and Rob play the Pendulum scenario. Matt wins if he has models on Rob's side of the table while Rob has no models on Matt's side of the table for three consecutive rounds.

HORDE SELECTION

Players agree on the size of the battle as normal.

SET UP

The table should be thick with terrain. Players take turns placing terrain features until one player wishes to stop placing terrain. The other player is then allowed to place one additional terrain feature. Each player must place a minimum of four (4) terrain features.

BEGINNING

At the start of the game, each player rolls a d6 and the high roller chooses who goes first. The first player gets his choice of deployment zones and takes the first turn. Players deploy their forces up to 10" from the table's edge.

VICTORY CONDITIONS

To win the game, a player needs to have models on his opponent's side of the table while none of his opponent's models are on his own side for three consecutive rounds.

MULTIPLAYER GAME

Pendulum is not suitable for multiplayer play.

WILD FIRE

There's no man or beast that wants to fight in fire—use that against the enemy. Do not fear the chaos of a forest ablaze. Use its wild power to advantage, and let it eat the enemy's flank and be a wall to shield you. Just don't expect it to behave; flame is a fickle friend at best.

—KRUEGER THE STORMWRATH, POTENT OF THE CIRCLE ORBOROS

DESCRIPTION

Fires rage out of control across the battlefield. It is best to destroy your enemy before your horde is consumed in the flames.

SPECIAL RULES AND SET UP

Players take turns placing terrain features until one player wishes to stop placing terrain. The other player may then place one additional terrain feature. Each player must place a minimum of three (3) terrain features.

Players then take turns, each placing two (2) fire markers within 14" of a table edge but not within 2" of a deployment zone. A fire marker may not be placed within 11" of another fire marker.

Fire markers represent fast growing fires that expand throughout the game. At the start of the game, each marker represents a fire with a 3" radius. Beginning with the second round, the radius of each fire increases by d3" each round before the start of the placing player's turn. Any model moving into an AOE or ending its movement in the AOE immediately suffers a POW 12 damage roll.

For example, Rob and Eric are playing Wild Fire. Before the start of each of Rob's turns beginning with the second turn, the radius of fires he placed each increase by d3". Likewise, the radius of the fires Eric placed increase before the start of each of his turns after the first.

Measuring Fires

FIRES CAN BE MARKED ON THE TABLE WITH A LOOP OF STRING. SIMPLY EXPAND THE LOOP AS THE FIRES GROW OUT OF CONTROL.

Models completely within shallow or deep water take no damage from the fires.

HORDE SELECTION

Players agree on the size of the battle as normal.

BEGINNING

At the start of the game, each player rolls a d6 and the high roller chooses who goes first. The first player gets his choice of deployment zones and takes the first turn. Players deploy their forces up to 10" from the table's edge.

VICTORY CONDITIONS

A player wins the game when he has the only remaining warlock(s) in play.

MULTIPLAYER GAME

In multiplayer Wildfire, all players should be equidistant from each other and have comparable deployment zones. Each player places one (1) fire marker.

CROSSED LINES

It happened as we left the Gnarls to head east to join with Ironhide's forces. Blackclads had expected us but did not know our exact path, spreading themselves thin in the brush and fog. We'd also become spread out, and by the time we knew we were under attack, things had become a jumble. Neither of us had lines anymore and it was utter chaos.

—CHAMPION JUSSIKA OF THE GURLOS KRIEL IN THE GNARLS

DESCRIPTION

Sometimes rival forces inadvertently stumble across one another. These clashes quickly become disorganized brawls rather than the orchestrated battles preferred by most commanders, and they typically involve close-quarter fighting in urban settings where battles might be taken structure-to-structure or in dense forests where one never knows what lies beyond the next copse of trees.

SPECIAL RULES

No models from either side are allowed to use the Advance Deployment special ability.

HORDE SELECTION

Players agree on the size of the battle normally.

SET UP

The table should be thick with terrain. Players take turns placing terrain until one player wishes to stop placing terrain. The other player is then allowed to place one additional piece. Each player must place a minimum of four (4) terrain features.

BEGINNING

Players roll to determine who chooses the first deployment point and then alternate choosing deployment points anywhere on the table. Each player chooses three deployment points, and players may not choose a point within 12" of a point selected by their opponent.

Players then alternate arranging one model or unit at a time anywhere completely within 6" of one of their deployment points. A player may choose to deploy all of his solos instead of setting up a model or unit. Players arrange their models and units in the same order they chose deployment points. After all forces are deployed, the players roll again, and the high roller chooses who goes first.

VICTORY CONDITIONS

A player wins the game when he has the only remaining warlock(s) is play.

MULTIPLAYER GAME

Crossed Lines is a truly chaotic multiplayer game. It is also very easy to adapt to multiplayer play because there are no deployment zones to worry about. Players should simply follow the rules detailed above.

DOMINATION

We cannot attack in one place by overwhelming force. Victory will come only if we are able to capture key points on the battlefield. If we leave any of them open, the enemy can flank us and attack our vulnerable lines.

—Archdomina Makeda of the Western Reaches to her tyrants

DESCRIPTION

Often in battle the goal is to gain control over the majority of the land, and it results in much back and forth conflict. Domination pits rival forces against each other in a struggle to capture and hold as much of the battlefield as possible.

SPECIAL RULES

Domination lasts for eight (8) game rounds as players rush to capture specific coordinates on the table. A player captures a coordinate when a model stands directly on top of it. If a model leaves the coordinate, it remains under its horde's control until an enemy model moves on top of it. Only one model may be on top of a coordinate at any time.

HORDE SELECTION

Players agree on a size of the battle as normal.

SET UP

Domination is best played on a 4'x4' table. Players decide how much terrain to use and then take turns placing terrain.

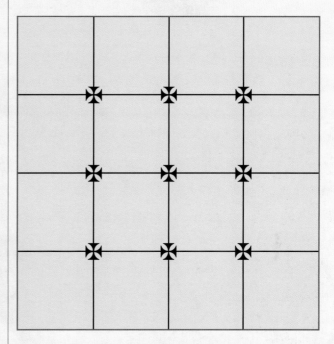

Divide the table into 1-foot squares and place coordinates at the vertices of each intersection according to the diagram.

BEGINNING

At the start of the game, each player rolls 1d6 and the high roller chooses who goes first. The first player gets his choice of deployment zone and takes the first turn. Players are allowed to place their forces up to 10" from the table's edge.

VICTORY CONDITIONS

The game ends at the completion of the eighth game round. The player controlling the most coordinates wins the game. In case of a tie, the player who accumulated the most victory points wins.

MULTIPLAYER GAME

Domination requires some care in set up for multiplayer scenarios. All players must be equidistant from each other, and each must have the same size deployment zone.

KING OF THE HILL

As we made our approach on the Fane, our most trying battle was against the bulk of the Aeryn tribe when we simultaneously arrived at Jilsyr hill. It was a race to take the high ground while each side rained arrows on the other. It was the Teraphs that gained our victory, taking the summit and holding it despite all their efforts to dislodge them.

—VAYL, DISCIPLE OF EVERBLIGHT

DESCRIPTION

Many battles are fought over strategic locations of uncertain value, but military strategists know the benefit in taking a monumental hill before securing ancillary vantage points. King of the Hill is one such battle. In this scenario, both forces scrabble over land and rush up the hillside to claim the spot for their faction.

SPECIAL RULES

The obvious objective of King of the Hill is to take the hill. At the end of each player's turn, the player with more models on the hill than his opponent scores a victory point. A unit counts as one model for the purposes of calculating who has more models on the hill. The first player to reach five points wins the game.

HORDE SELECTION

Players agree on a size of the battle normally.

SET UP

Place a hill in the center of the table. Players take turns placing terrain until one player wishes to stop. The other player is then allowed to place one additional piece. Each player must place a minimum of two terrain features.

BEGINNING

At the start of the game, each player rolls 1d6 and the high roller chooses who goes first. The first player gets his choice of deployment zone and takes the first turn. Players are allowed to place their forces up to 10" from the table's edge.

VICTORY CONDITIONS

The game ends when one player accumulates five points.

MULTIPLAYER GAME

In multiplayer King of the Hill, all players should be equidistant from each other and have the same-sized deployment zone.

CLAW & FANG

I only require beasts at my side for battle brought together as a single pack to stalk and slay by my will. Men get in the way, never do what they are told, and then lose their nerve when needed most.

—KAYA THE WILDBORNE, OVERSEER OF THE CIRCLE ORBOROS

DESCRIPTION

Claw & Fang is a brutal gladiatorial contest between rival warlocks and their 'beasts. This scenario is an all-out unrestrained bloodbath where the only goal is to survive.

SPECIAL RULES

None.

HORDE SELECTION

Players agree on a point limit and then purchase their forces as normal, except each player is only allowed a single warlock regardless of the size of the game. Points may only be spent on the warlock and his warbeasts; units and solos have no place in Claw & Fang.

SET UP

Claw & Fang may be played on any size table, but a smaller table works better. Each player is allowed to place two terrain features on the table.

BEGINNING

At the start of the game, each player rolls 1d6 and the high roller chooses who goes first. The first player gets his choice of deployment zones and takes the first turn. Players are allowed to place their force up to 10" from the table's edge.

VICTORY CONDITIONS

The game ends with either the death of a warlock or when all warbeasts on either side have been destroyed or removed from play.

MULTIPLAYER GAME

In multiplayer Claw & Fang, all players should be equidistant from each other and have comparable deployment zones.

MANDRYK
2005

The Trollbloods

Grissel Bloodsong peered down from the hill where her kin gathered crouched behind a barricade of irregular boulders. She eyed the mass of red and gold armored figures scattered across the field at the hill's base just out of range of even their best pyg sharpshooters. They were regrouping for another charge. Her kin had formed a long line across the top of the hill ridge overlooking the Claysoil Wash—a trickling stream north of the Castle of the Keys— to establish a commanding position. The sun baked the rocks, but the trollkin were becoming used to the heat.

Looking over her shoulder Grissel saw wounded trollkin huddled in whatever shade they could find and sucking on beer casks or wine skins amid blood-soaked garments and armor. They had endured several charges up the hill by the tenacious skorne, and red armored forms littered the steep slope. It was difficult to discern where the blood ended and the red tattered banners began.

The familiar bulk of a leading scattergunner hunkered next to her. "Lo, Grissel." She could recognize the distinct smell of his cigars and the sound of his creaking boots.

The sight of his weathered face prompted a small smile. "Lo, Murok. Is the line ready?"

He snorted. "They're too tired to move."

She pulled herself up on one elbow and turned to face him with fierce eyes. "Just one more." Her eyes flicked to the skorne clustered below. "They're nearly spent."

"Grissel, *we* are spent. Nothing but dust in these veins. No food, little water, and few have powder for their weapons."

Grissel's eyes narrowed, and her face set in a way he did not like but knew well. "Any word from Hasset?" Hasset was one of the elders in charge of moving their people out of the village along the lake's shore, packing them up to head for Chief Ironhide's fastnesses to the west.

Murok stuck another cigar in his lips and spent time lighting it so he did not have to look her in the eye. "She said one more day."

"We can't leave. There is no place to retreat; we'll not find a better spot to fight than this. If we last one more charge, they'll back off."

He puffed the rancid smoke and refused to answer, looking down.

She stood, turned to face the wounded kin, and let loose a great bellow which startled them all. Pygmies and kin scrambled for rifles and looked up in alarm. Pyre trolls who had taken a moment to recline on the baking rocks scrambled to their feet with narrowed eyes. The sound rolled forth across the rocks and echoed down below. As the echoes began to fade, she spoke.

"Murok says you are spent. I don't believe it! Do you think Grissel Bloodsong is tired? Of course she is! That's not going to stop her from adding notches to this hammer! Our enemy thinks they can take this hill. We have high ground and good guns. Our kinfolk need us to hold here to the last. They move west, to safety, to Chief Ironhide. They need time. The skorne will enslave your mothers, your sons, and your daughters. If you lack powder to fire your guns, charge to impale. If you're too tired to lift a weapon, raise fists instead. The enemy is tired. They don't have the spirit. They aren't breaking through. This is *our* hill! By kriel and kith, by quill and quitari, we will hold!"

She saw their spirits flickering to life, and they clutched their weapons with a renewed light in their eyes. They raised axes and guns into the air and gave a great cry in the name of the kriel. Grissel's shout exceeded them all. It rang across the hilltops and down onto the plain just as the skorne answered with their horns and began the steady march up the steep hill.

Legacy of Kriels, Legacy of Stone

Transcribed from the words of elder fell caller Genlas Gnarlheart at a gathering of the scattered kriels, Winter 606 AR.

We face a grim truth, for bloody days are ahead of us. We must answer the call of war or we will fade as a people and leave behind only our legacy of stone. We do not meddle in the decisions of distant elders, but today we put aside territorial claims to pool our wisdom and our strength. I will not tell you how to raise your young, but I will ask you to lift your blades with mine against our common enemies.

Even as I speak, warring armies tear apart the Thornwood Forest. We have heard the tales of Chieftain

Madrak Ironhide and his brave people. Our own forest has seen the passage of dark terrors erupting from the southern islands as flies stirred from a corpse. Villages have been annihilated, kriels decimated, and thousands uprooted. In the northern mountains a new and unholy disease brings death and corruption to the Scarsfell. Strange invaders attack from the east to enslave our kin near the Scarleforth Lake and Hawksmire River.

Why do we care what happens to kith in the Thornwood or the Scarsfell? Why do they care about our troubles? Some say we should face these threats as they arise, each kriel alone. I say that is cowardice, for we are all of one blood!

We have not been a single people since the ancient Molgur terrorized all of western Immoren thousands of years ago. Molgur was a name shared by many untamed tribes with nothing in common but their religion, and it was a vast and barbaric empire. There has never been anything like the Molgur, and there never will be again—humans, ogrun, goblins, and trollkin called by a single name descending on villages with bloodthirsty abandon. Our races shared an appetite for cruelty and malice, feasting in the darkness under the stars while sacrificing captured enemies to the Devourer Wurm—He who sired our races in the dawn of time by ravaging Dhunia. Our birth as a species arose from violence, and we were drawn to mimic our untamed father.

Some elders speak of the Molgur as a golden era, but it was a time of savagery. We must accept the darkness of our past. In the Molgur age we fought as one blood but forsook our goddess Dhunia. The Devourer Wurm is a cruel father not satisfied no matter how much blood spilled in His name. The Beast of All Shapes leaves behind nothing but ruin. We did not learn the lessons of civilization until the destruction of the Molgur and the scattering of the tribes.

Now some of our kin have become *too* civilized. Let us embrace the rage our ancestors knew and turn it against our foes. As we gather, let none turn their backs on our kin, even those who wander as orphans in human cities. Let us rise up united like the Molgur but cry the name of Dhunia and leave a stronger legacy for our young.

The Molgur left us our shared tongue: Molgur-Trul, but humanity stole the Molgur rune alphabet from our people. This tongue is rich and varied although we record only the core meaning in runes. Its runes are not for record keeping but for immortalizing heroes. Learning the languages of mankind is inevitable for trade, but this is our true tongue. *Kith* describes both close and distant blood-kin and also means home. *Kriel* describes an entire tribe of the gathered people. *Shen* means both brotherhood and the lustful dangers of youth unbound and untied to community. *Quitari* describes the patterns in woven cloth linked to a community and once stood for tribal tattoos. The *Tohmaak Mahkeiri* or "Glimpse of the Mind" is a unique gift allowing us to peer deeply into the thoughts of another kin. Only our language holds the rich meaning of these words; it is far superior to the clumsy bastard tongues of man.

Other than giving us our language and a legacy of fierce warriors, the Molgur proved that mindless brutality is no way to govern and no way to create a lasting people. Humans learned this through the cruel example of their unforgiving god Menoth. The Menite priest-kings brought humanity in line with a stern hand and the barbed lash, and they built walls, organized armies, and annihilated entire tribes. This is not our way, but we must recognize why mankind has come to dominate.

We face a grim truth, for bloody days are ahead of us. We must answer the call of war or we will fade as a people and leave behind only our legacy of stone.

Never forget the lessons of sword and flame brought by Priest-King Golivant of Calacia. The humans and their worshipful histories never describe how brutally Golivant slaughtered our kind. Humans could convert to his religion, but he put Dhunia's children to the sword without question. The greatest Molgur chieftain was Horfar Grimmr, and he led a massive doomed attack against the long wall called the Shield of Thrace near the Murkham River in 2200 BR. In this epic battle tens of thousands of Molgur crashed against the wall like waves breaking on a shore. The Murkham River bled for weeks after this battle, but the Molgur were broken, and Grimmr was captured. The Menites wracked Horfar for a month before his life ended, hoping to break him and weaken the memory of his deeds among our people. They could not force a single word from his lips and he died defiant, but the time of the Molgur had ended. To Golivant, mass graves were too much honor for the carcasses of our people. He burned them instead in great bonfires or dumped them into the sea. In the far north, the priest-king Khardovic arose after Golivant and proved equally cruel. He enslaved entire tribes and worked them to death before sacrificing the survivors in Menoth's name at the conclusion of their labor.

Cygnar retired their colossals because of us and our ability to defeat them.

By the end, the Molgur were shattered and divided. Each race once called Molgur turned to their elders. Most of our people settled in the dense forests, but some spread to the mountains, islands, and marshes—any land the humans found difficult to tame. After Golivant, many kin fled west to the Scharde Islands, others headed deep into the Wyrmwall Mountains, but many more undertook the trek north among the Gnarls and the Thornwood. These two forests have become the greatest homes of our people. Other brave kriels continued further north and east to settle in the northern Scarsfell and Rimeshaws Forests or the fringes of the Bloodstone Marches.

Separated by distance and the barriers of man, our people returned to the lessons of Dhunia. Upon enduring krielstones we scribed the rites of our people and described the deeds of warriors and the decisions of the elders of each kriel. We continue this tradition of marking new stones to immortalize heroic acts while preserving those passed down to us by the ancients. Our history will never be a dusty list of endless names and dates.

Fighting among neighboring kriels has always been common, and it is not something we condemn. Each kith and kriel rightfully looks to its interests; in cases of disputes, bloodshed is honorable. This strife has strengthened our people, for we have never lost the love of battle or the willingness to stand up for our beliefs. Despite small disagreements we must stand together now against the greater threats.

I have heard this is the way of things among the dwarves of Rhul, and their example is one I am not shamed to borrow. It is no wonder so many ogrun—also children of Dhunia—have bound their fate to that race. The ogrun too were once Molgur, but we have little contact with their conclaves today, so do not expect assistance from them. Nor should you expect help from the unreliable goblins. Too many of them eagerly accept their lot as servants to humanity. We share little in common with these races today other than our respect for the Ravaged Mother.

We battled the Orgoth when they invaded, but to us they were humans of another tribe. Our withdrawal from human lands gave us some protection, and the invaders felt little need to intrude on our wilds. We fought them when they paved roads through our lands to connect their empire or when they befouled our sacred sites with their death magic. We made them pay dearly for every inch they gained.

We did not escape the Orgoth lash, however, for they recognized our stamina and our mastery over stone. Our kin erected many of the greatest Orgoth fortresses and stone temples. They were foul places, but we can take pride in how long our skill endured. Some of these places still stand, and even the colossals of the Rebellion army and the Orgoth Scourge could not break all our stonework to dust.

Certain heroes of our blood have risen to such greatness that even humanity remembers their deeds. Consider Grindar of the Tolok Kriel who became a general among the Rebellion army in the last battles against the Orgoth. He led mixed armies against the western strongholds of those dark invaders. Through his cunning ambushes the Rebellion was victorious, and Grindar earned a seat on the Council of Ten at the Corvis Treaties. His name is there on the document which birthed the human kingdoms. You will see his image in all paintings of that gathering, and his face frowns on Cygnar's kings from their throne room.

Grindar's time with humans clouded his judgment, but he worked to help his people. He used his influence to force all these new kingdoms to agree that trollkin could own their lands and tax certain roads and waterways. Few of those promises withstood the test of time though. Whenever they choose, human kings will deny the oaths of their forefathers. They honored Grindar with one breath and tore apart his life's work with another.

Four decades after the Corvis Treaties, trollkin had already lost these rights. Human towns near Point Bourne and Corvis sent loggers deep into the southern

Thornwood Forest ignoring all marks of territory. Here in this forest, Ceryl's caravans refused tolls on the Gnarlwood Trail. Along the Dragon's Tongue River merchant ship captains laughed at our demands. When we fought to enforce our lawful demands, Cygnar marched soldiers on our villages.

Sending elders to speak to their leaders did not help. They told us we lived at *their* whim and our forests belonged to them. They told our elders we should thank them since they did not demand taxes or other tribute from us—all this while Grindar watched from their walls. This is what we learned of human promises. It is futile to try to earn respect by words alone. War is the only language humanity understands, and we answered them in kind.

Cygnar thought our people primitive; they felt we could not challenge them. They did not understand the deep ties we have with our cousins, the full-blood trolls who are more like us than we admit. When starved, full-blood trolls seem mindless and untamable. Our Dhunian shamans have known how to speak their simple tongues and long ago forged lasting pacts with their tribes.

When Cygnar's nobles sent soldiers to cow us, we remembered our blood. Old pacts were renewed and trolls returned to the kriels. Trolls and trollkin came together as armies, equipped and trained for war. Freed from the need to hunt for prey, the trolls were not so different from us, and we learned to use their hunger as a weapon.

In 242 AR the kriels of both the Thornwood and the Gnarls gathered great forces and set upon the garrisons of the Cygnaran King Benewic II and the Ordic forces sent to their aid. Battles raged across Cygnar and Ord that engulfed Armandor, Tarna, Fellig, and Point Bourne and isolated Ceryl and Corvis. The uprising had no single leader but many strong chieftains who dealt blows to Cygnar. Cygnar won victories but only by overwhelming numbers. Fought one to one, or even two to one, we never saw defeat.

Finally they unleashed their colossals. Tales of those towering giants of iron survive the generations. Today we see the smaller descendants of those colossals, but our ancestors had seen nothing to match them. A coal-fed inferno roared inside the belly of each metal giant as it belched steam and smoke into the sky and crushed anything in its path. Colossals were slow and clumsy but utterly unstoppable. Axes and blades bounced off their armored shells, and even the strength of trolls was not enough to stand against them. Only those who have seen slaughters of our people can imagine the terror. I am proud of my ancestors for pushing Cygnar so hard they chose to unleash their mightiest weapons, but in those years we suffered a bitter defeat. Our elders withdrew from the fight and sued for peace in 247 AR.

Mankind has always been its own worst enemy. The nations of Cygnar and Khador have never needed excuses to spill blood. King Benewic II built Deepwood Tower in the Thornwood to house several of his gigantic guardians hoping to protect Cygnar from us, but Khador could not bear to have colossals so close to its border and attacked. Three years later the region was embroiled in the Colossal War which raged for seven years. In that time many trollkin suffered when their villages were turned into convenient ground for the clash of metal giants.

We did not give Cygnar time to enjoy their peace, and our war to regain our rights continued in 262 AR. They called this the Second Trollkin War, but it was the same fight as before—nothing had changed. Chief Modr rose to lead our kin and proved the power and the strength of trolls. He did not let the colossals pick the battlefields. Instead he lead them into traps and ambushes and showed our people that these giants can be enraged to charge into pits or ravines to be crushed to death by their own weight. We led them into bad ground and tore the colossals apart piece by piece. Trollkin and trolls alike swarmed them and hammered them with a hundred blows. After the first colossal fell, our people forgot their fear and tackled the second, and then the third.

Never forget this lesson of Modr. Cygnar retired their colossals because of *us* and our ability to defeat them. They created the smaller warjacks to fight us better, and *still* they are not equal to the task. A full-blood troll is more cunning, ruthless, and just as fearless. Warjacks are heavy, slow, and rely on coal and water. Can the warjack swim across a river and attack in silence by the dead of night? Can a warjack return from the brink of death by feasting on the bodies of the slain? Do not fear human technology. We borrow from them that which is useful, such as rifles, but we can defeat all of their tricks by strength and cunning.

By the end of Modr's war, Cygnar accepted all our demands, and the promises sworn at the Corvis Treaties were renewed. In 267 AR, we thought death and toil had won a lasting respect, but time has proven that human memories are short and subject to convenient change.

Peace sometimes brings old foes together and mingles tribes. After Modr's war, many *shen* journeyed to human cities. Cygnar's southern city of Mercir suffered a great fire in 415 AR, and thousands of trollkin moved there to rebuild it. Over the centuries there have been more city dwelling kin forgetting how to speak our language or participate in our rites. We need to bring them back to their kriels and to their families. The lore they have learned can serve us now, and we need every weapon in the hard times to come.

Every human war has brought hardship and casualties to our kin. Consider the Thornwood War in 511 AR between Khador and Cygnar. Lacking a force strong enough in their forest to confront the Khadorans, Cygnar tricked the massive Khadoran army to march into our largest and most ancient community, Tolok Kriel. They cared nothing for the innocents they destroyed, and hundreds of trollkin were slaughtered in the heart of our lands in spite of every oath between the Cygnaran throne and our elders.

Tolok Kriel no longer exists—the Khadorans ravaged its villages to feed their soldiers and burned everything behind them as they marched on. Our surviving warriors harried their advance by striking from the trees. As much human blood as trollkin soaked the ground to mark their passage. Later we learned it was Cygnarans who led them to us. Nothing so clearly shows what the humans think of our kind. To them we are nothing more than animals to be used or killed at whim when it serves them.

We of the Gnarls have kept this lesson to heart while those in the Thornwood are different, but let us not dismiss their trials. It is easy for us to preserve the ancient ways, for few are willing to violate our great forest, yet the Thornwood has been in the path of constant human warfare. Locked between Khador and Cygnar, their kin have a legacy as noble as ours but more tragic. Benefits have occasionally come from deals with humans, but the gains are short and betrayal is never far away. I speak now of the ties between Cygnar's King Leto and the Thornwood Chieftain Madrak Ironhide. Rumors of their agreements have spread to our forest, and in upcoming fights we cannot allow enemies to turn our kriels against each other.

Our two forests have been bastions of our kind since the fall of the Molgur. Consider now the scope of tragedy that forced the Thornwood kriels to abandon everything. Nothing in earlier wars can compare to the destruction seen in the last year in the Thornwood from not only Khador fighting Cygnar but also horrors from Cryx and fanatic Menites converging there. This is what Madrak Ironhide faced. We must understand that Chief Ironhide went to King Leto for aid. It is easy for us to point to the inevitable outcome. I know Chief Ironhide. He is as great a war-chief as has ever walked Caen. Like Grindar, from whom his blood flows, he counted on friendship with a human king to buy help for our kind.

To his merit, Ironhide's talks did bear fruit. Aid came to the Thornwood kriels when servants of Cygnar's king eased their exodus from the Thornwood to the Glimmerwood and Widower's Wood, a region unclaimed by nations. Chief Ironhide shrewdly gained considerable supplies, which is remarkable in a time of war. King Leto's orders brought blasting powder, firearms, raw metal, lumber, and other supplies. Ironhide organized his kin and the pygmies who allied with them into trained soldiers, the equal of any Cygnar has sent to war.

These acts by Cygnar were not a kindness; they put Ironhide's people in harm's way. The king told Ironhide to protect Cygnar's border from southern fanatics who might cross that region, but all the while King Leto knew that another threat approached from the east—the invaders that had attacked Corvis just three years ago. The king lied to Ironhide and promised him better lands *within* Cygnar at the price of vigilance along the border.

Despite the lives lost in the protection of that border, King Leto has given nothing to Ironhide's kriels. When Ironhide returned to claim the reward for his tireless battles, King Leto was swayed by the greed and prejudice of his nobles and refused. Again humans decided to make promises and later ignore them. Let this be the *last* time we are so easily fooled! No small gains are worth the cost in lives. No number of firearms, no barrels of blasting powder, and no tons of iron are worth so many deaths, but while we learn this hard lesson, do not hold Ironhide to blame.

The only humans upon whom we have relied have been the mystics who share our fondness for the wild places. I speak of the wilderness prophets, the blackclad messengers who call themselves druids. We have fought them over specific holy sites but maintained a general accord. In the past they earned trust by offering good advice to our elders. I was one who listened to their words and welcomed them to our most sacred places. Even my honored peer, Shaman Hoarluk Doomshaper—so vocal in his scorn of humanity—has listened to these messengers in the past.

We know the great betrayal two months ago in the Glimmerwood, for it is on the tongues of all the kriels. By this treacherous attack the friendly face of the druids proved false, and their advice has been poison. They wanted us to fight their battles for them, but this is no different from Cygnar leading enemies into our kriels. Druids would do this smiling and pretending to give us honor.

In recent months one of the great leaders of the druids came among our people and gathered *shen* to his side. He plotted to set the Gnarls at war with our Thornwood kin. They would slay the greatest war-chief of the Thornwood—that same Ironhide, descendant of Grindar, of the blood of the vanished Tolok kriel, and wielder of the axe of Grimmr! This chief was too mighty for them to stomach and was unwilling to heed their poison advice. The druid Ergonus took our kin to strike Ironhide down. This is how druids repay our honor. You roar in anger, but consider how close we came to this—how easy it was for them to recruit our *shen*.

By the example of Doomshaper and Ironhide, let us show them why any who come against our kin should fear us.

Hoarluk Doomshaper went east to unravel this plot and to save our youth from themselves. There by the Glimmerwood the druids bent their might to slay these two great war-chiefs, but they failed. The axe of Grimmr clove Ergonus, and he did not rise again. It was the druids and their allies fleeing into the trees while our people stood triumphant. We must not stop with this victory, for they have declared themselves our enemies. We cannot rest until we reclaim those places they have stolen from us over the centuries.

The druids alone recognized our potential, and they worked to prevent our coming together. By the example of Doomshaper and Ironhide, let us show them why any who come against our kin should fear us. No more will we hide in the forests and withdraw from battles allowing our enemies to steal our lands piece by piece. We in the Gnarls have the greatest power to bring strength to the battles of our scattered kin. The Gnarls is the last great gathering of our kin and the heart of our power. Like a beating heart, we must send blood to the furthest reaches to sustain our kin. It is time to reclaim our birthright. By Dhunia's gifts, the blood of trolls, we go to war!

Madrak Ironhide, Thornwood Chieftain
Trollblood Trollkin Warlock Character

Ironhide is the strongest trollkin leader to arise in four centuries. We cannot suffer him to live.

— Omnipotent Ergonus of the Circle, now deceased

Even as Madrak reached a pinnacle as the greatest leader in the history of the eastern trollkin, his life was recently darkened by ill omens and setbacks that would crush the spirit of a lesser chief. He has endured assassination attempts, his people have been forced from their ancestral home, and his blood brother has betrayed his trust. Somehow Madrak finds the strength to fight on and hopes to lead his people to a safer path.

As a youth Madrak earned renown for his ability to outfight his peers atop the *kuor* dueling platform in contests of arms or brawn, for such skill with weapons was unprecedented in an albino trollkin sorcerer. He pushed his limits exploring the ominous Thornwood Forest until one day a band of Tharn ambushed the young trollkin. Hopelessly outnumbered, he drew his axes and screamed the battle cry of his kriel. In this moment of doom, a crackle of thunder split the air, and lightning consumed the leading Tharn. Madrak's unlikely saviors were Cygnarans led by a young human bearing the Cygnus. Back at his kriel, Madrak honored the youth at a feast and evoked a ceremony called *kulgat* that made them blood brothers for life. In later decades this prince became King Leto, the ruler of Cygnar.

Madrak demonstrat-ed an ability to unite his fellow kin by fostering fellow chiefs and warriors, but full war between Khador and Cygnar fell on the Thornwood like darkness and interrupted his efforts. Bloodshed tore kriels apart as hundreds of innocents died in the crossfire. The situation reached a crisis when horrors from Cryx invaded the forest and slaughtered entire villages in the path of their advance. The displaced tribes turned to Chief Ironhide begging for help.

In late 605 AR Madrak reluctantly undertook a pilgrimage to a special *kuor* serving as the resting place for an ancient weapon, the axe Rathrok originally wielded by Horfar Grimmr of the Molgur. Its name means "World Ender." Legends proclaimed that this weapon was so mighty that if it were wielded, a dire curse would fall upon the world to herald the end of days and unleash the Devourer Wurm. Knowing his people faced annihilation, Ironhide grasped its hilt and brought the weapon forth against the darkness invading the forest.

Even with Rathrok's power, Madrak slowly lost ground against the inexhaustible reserves of the enemy. Desperate, he sought audience with King Leto, his blood brother, and negotiated what he thought would be the salvation of his people. King Leto encouraged Madrak to move into the unused lands east of the Black River and swore to grant substantial fertile lands if Madrak protected the border. Torn between abandoning his ancestral homeland and offering his people a new chance at survival, the chief ultimately concluded that accepting the king's offer was his people's best hope. With a heavy heart, he convinced his people to abandon their homes and move east.

Leaving the forest unwittingly put Madrak's people directly in the path of the invading skorne. After a bloody season of countless battles dutifully fulfilling his obligation to protect Cygnar's eastern border, Madrak returned to King Leto to demand the lands promised to his kriels. Swayed by the aristocracy claiming that land, Leto made excuses. Returning to his people with only failure to show, Ironhide was greeted by a vicious assassination attempt at the hands of not only his long time allies, the Druids of Orboros, but trusted kriel kin as well. Betrayed on all sides, the strongest trollkin chief of his age turned his anger to the battlefield, desperately hoping that with the last drops of blood, his people might once again find solace. In a final act of resolve that cost the chief more pain as any mortal wound, Madrak swore binding pacts with Hoarluk Doomshaper to carve a safe place for the kriels even if it unleashes a river of bloodshed and invokes the doom of World Ender.

SPECIAL RULES

Feat: Crusher - The greatest chieftain ever to rise to dominance from the Thornwood Forest, Madrak Ironhide eagerly fights alongside his kin in battle. His mere presence inspires allies to tremendous feats of courage and ferocity as they crush one enemy after another in a frenzied succession of blows.

While within Ironhide's control area this round, friendly Trollblood models that destroy an enemy model with a melee attack may immediately move up to 1" and make an additional melee attack without spending a fury point or being forced. While making a special attack a model only benefits from Crusher once regardless of the number of attacks generated or models destroyed by the special attack. Completely resolve all attacks generated by the special attack before making the Crusher move and attack.

IRONHIDE

Scroll of Grindar's Perseverance - Once per game, Ironhide may avoid suffering any damage and effects from a melee or ranged attack. Declare use of the scroll after damage has been determined.

Talisman of Subdual - Ironhide cannot be charged or slammed by a warbeast that began its activation in his front arc. If a warbeast frenzies and would normally charge Ironhide, it advances its current SPD in inches toward him instead.

Tough - When Ironhide suffers sufficient damage to be destroyed, his controller rolls a d6. On a 5 or 6, Ironhide is knocked down instead of being destroyed. If Ironhide is not destroyed, he is reduced to one wound.

IRONHIDE				CMD 9	
SPD	STR	MAT	RAT	DEF	ARM
6	8	7	5	14	16

THROWN AXE

RNG	ROF	AOE	POW
8	1	—	7

RATHROK

SPECIAL	POW	P+S
Multi	7	15

FURY	5
DAMAGE	18
FIELD ALLOWANCE	C
VICTORY POINTS	5
POINT COST	64
BASE SIZE	MEDIUM

THROWN AXE

Critical Fatality - On a critical hit, target warlock cannot transfer damage suffered from the attack.

Ricochet - After resolving a successful attack with the Thrown Axe, Ironhide may immediately make one additional Thrown Axe attack targeting another model in Ironhide's LOS and within 4" of the original target.

Thrown - Add Ironhide's current STR to the POW of his Thrown Axe ranged attacks.

Wraith Bane - Thrown Axe attacks may damage models only affected by magic attacks.

RATHROK

Critical Fatality - On a critical hit, target warlock cannot transfer damage suffered from the attack.

Wraith Bane - Rathrok attacks may damage models only affected by magic attacks.

SPELL	COST	RNG	AOE	POW	UP	OFF
GUIDED HAND	2	6	-	-		

Target friendly model/unit rolls an additional die on each model's first melee attack roll this turn.

SPELL	COST	RNG	AOE	POW	UP	OFF
STONE FALL	3	8	4	13		X

On a critical hit, models in the AOE suffer Concussion. A model suffering Concussion forfeits its next activation and cannot allocate focus for one round.

SPELL	COST	RNG	AOE	POW	UP	OFF
SURE FOOT	3	6	-	-		

Target friendly Trollblood model gains +2 DEF and cannot be knocked down. While within 3" of the affected model, friendly Trollblood models also gain +2 DEF and cannot be knocked down. Sure Foot lasts for one round.

Hoarluk Doomshaper, Shaman of the Gnarls

Trollblood Trollkin Warlock Character

There is no warlock more tied to the blood of trolls. The strength he brings in our blackest hour may carry us through. If we endure, it will be a testament to the Doomshaper's works.

—Chieftain Madrak Ironhide discussing his rival after the attempt on his life

The Dhunian shaman Hoarluk Doomshaper is a walking legend who has explored the face of Caen for over a hundred years. Though some elders are older than Doomshaper, few are so vigorous and irrepressible. Hoarluk wades into battle with mad fortitude and refuses to die regardless of the punishment inflicted by the weapons of his enemies. Many of the younger kin who have watched him in battle are convinced he is completely impervious to pain and has learned to regenerate like a full-blood troll.

Hoarluk has an obsessive fascination with the mystical power of the blood tie shared by troll breeds, and he believes in the superiority of troll blood over the diluted substance in the veins of other races. Resentment and awareness of the waning of his species fuels his scorn of humanity. Even in the Gnarls outsiders have encroached on trollkin lands to steal what is theirs by ancient right, and Doomshaper intends to strike back with a vengeance. The time for war is overdue.

Few are willing to speak against Doomshaper, and those who disagree do so quietly. The mighty shaman is prone to outbursts of temper and scathing indictments of those he considers foolish. Hoarluk has challenged countless elders to duels and has never yet been defeated, cruelly humiliating those who fall beneath his staff. Many consider him insane, yet even his detractors agree Dhunia chose the old shaman and try to avoid his wrath. He has spent his life working to embolden the trollkin of the Gnarls against human interlopers.

Even before recent troubles, Doomshaper traveled from kriel to kriel gathering recruits and leading strikes against any humans or other species foolish enough to plunder the Gnarls. He has obliterated at least two

logging companies that began to poach beyond the marked trees and slaughtered no less than three tribes of bogrin who attempted to settle near his home. His acts have put him at odds with more temperate trollkin, like Chief Ironhide of the Thornwood, until the druids' recently foiled plot forced an uneasy alliance. Though Hoarluk is not a chief, he carries tremendous influence over all the tribes inhabiting the length and breadth of the Gnarls, the mightiest surviving bastion of trollkin tradition. No chief of the Gnarls dares ignore his words.

This wizened elder has spent decades recovering lost krielstones and deciphering ancient runes. He feels the weight of his ancestors on his shoulders where he keeps a collection of transcribed lore. This interest is not academic but the key to great untapped powers the shaman intends to recover and use as weapons in the battles ahead.

By his lifelong effort and force of will, Doomshaper has gained unequalled power over full-blood trolls. He has spoken to all troll breeds, and they listen to him as if he were kin. Bearing bloodstones those brutes recognize as sacred, he has reinforced ancient pacts between species. Hoarluk earned immortality when he strode unarmed into the forest and returned with several dire trolls in tow. The beasts had never heeded the requests of their lesser cousins, and word of this deed has spread to every tribe, for these creatures have become the greatest weapons of the desperate trollkin.

Trolls are the chosen wrath of Dhunia, and this is the age where they will make their stand. Doomshaper enters every battle as if it were armageddon and as if the salvation of all troll-kind hinges on its outcome. Some elders whisper that the roots of the fire burning in his eyes trace back to the death of his daughters killed decades ago, but Hoarluk will not speak of these things. Whatever drives him, the emergence of Doomshaper from the forests of the Gnarls is a dire omen for those who have earned the wrath of the trollkin.

SPECIAL RULES

Feat: Dhunia's Wrath - One of Dhunia's eldest war shamans, Doomshaper can invoke the raw rage of the Ravaged Mother to bring a dread reckoning on the enemies of the Trollbloods. At his call, enemy beasts and warlocks are stricken with excruciating pain fueled by lingering primal energies that tears them apart from within.

While in Doomshaper's control area this round, enemy models take d3 damage points for each fury or focus point they spend. While in Doomshaper's control area this round, enemy warbeasts take d3 damage points each time they are forced.

DOOMSHAPER				CMD 7	
SPD	STR	MAT	RAT	DEF	ARM
5	6	5	4	13	14

GNARLROOT		
SPECIAL	POW	P+S
Multi	5	11

FURY	7
DAMAGE	16
FIELD ALLOWANCE	C
VICTORY POINTS	5
POINT COST	54
BASE SIZE	MEDIUM

DOOMSHAPER

Calming Effect - When a friendly Dire Troll in Doomshaper's control area frenzies, it never selects a friendly model to attack.

Scroll of the Will of Balasar - Once per game, Doomshaper may use the Scroll of the Will of Balasar to cause a warbeast that frenzies within his control area to charge a legal target chosen by Doomshaper's controller instead of frenzying normally.

Tough - When Doomshaper suffers sufficient damage to be destroyed, his controller rolls a d6. On a 5 or 6, Doomshaper is knocked down instead of being destroyed. If Doomshaper is not destroyed, he is reduced to one wound.

GNARLROOT

Furious Might - Add +1 to the damage roll for each unspent fury point on Doomshaper.

Reach - 2" melee range.

Withered Staff - Doomshaper may upkeep one spell in play without paying a fury point.

SPELL	COST	RNG	AOE	POW	UP	OFF
ACCURSED	3	10	-	12		X

Target model damaged by Accursed must forfeit either its movement or action during its next activation.

DISSOLUTION	3	SELF	CTRL	-		

When the spell is cast, enemy warbeasts and warjacks in Doomshaper's control area that have an enemy upkeep spell on them take d3 damage points. Each enemy warrior model/unit currently in Doomshaper's control area that has an enemy upkeep spell on it must pass a command check or forfeit its next activation. Enemy upkeep spells in Doomshaper's control area then expire.

FORTUNE	2	6	-		X	

Target friendly Trollblood model/unit may re-roll failed attack rolls. Each attack roll may be re-rolled once.

RAMPAGER	2	10	-	-		X

Target enemy warbeast must make an additional threshold check during its controller's next Maintenance Phase. If the check fails, the warbeast immediately frenzies and does not make a threshold check during the Control Phase. If the check succeeds, the warbeast may still have to make a threshold check during its controller's Control Phase as normal. This spell may be cast once per activation.

VEXATION	2	8	-	-	X	X

At the start of opponent's Activation Phase, Doomshaper's controller decides whether target enemy model/unit will activate first or last. Vexation cannot be cast on warcasters or warlocks.

GRISSEL BLOODSONG, FELL CALLER

TROLLBLOOD TROLLKIN WARLOCK CHARACTER

'Tis beauty and terror alike in that haunting voice o' hers, but glad I am to fight by'er side. Grissel's song makes this ol' mud slogger feel like a dire troll among whelps.

—Champion Horthol of the northern Thornwood

Fell callers are powerful trollkin warriors boasting voices capable of shattering stone and making the sky itself tremble. Female fell callers are rare, but Grissel Bloodsong is a perfect representation of one who has gained singular power through the mastery of this ability. Her mate's recent death left a hole in her heart that she now fills with a passion for fighting to save her people.

Bloodsong was born in the far north near Ohk but was overcome with wanderlust. She sailed the length of the western coast and spent several years of her youth in human port cities working as a mercenary. Tasked aboard Cygnaran merchant ships to battle pirates at sea, she crushed more than one Cryxian raider with her hammer Resounder in brave boarding maneuvers. She enjoyed life at sea, but her returns to the city felt stifling. Eventually she lost her patience entirely for human cities in sprawling Caspia where the teeming masses pressed around her and the stench of humans made it hard for her to breathe. She fled north on the Black River and found happiness for a time battling river bandits and the occasional savage tribe along its length.

After visiting Ternon Crag, Grissel found an unexpected challenge: the relentless advances of a fierce and proud trollkin named Turgol Redeye. She refused him, but he continued to pursue her hoping to tame her fiery heart. At one point after she had enough of his foolishness, they got into a drunken tavern brawl that tore the place to its foundations. Still, he doggedly refused to be intimidated and came to her the next day with a smile and a quip. He gained

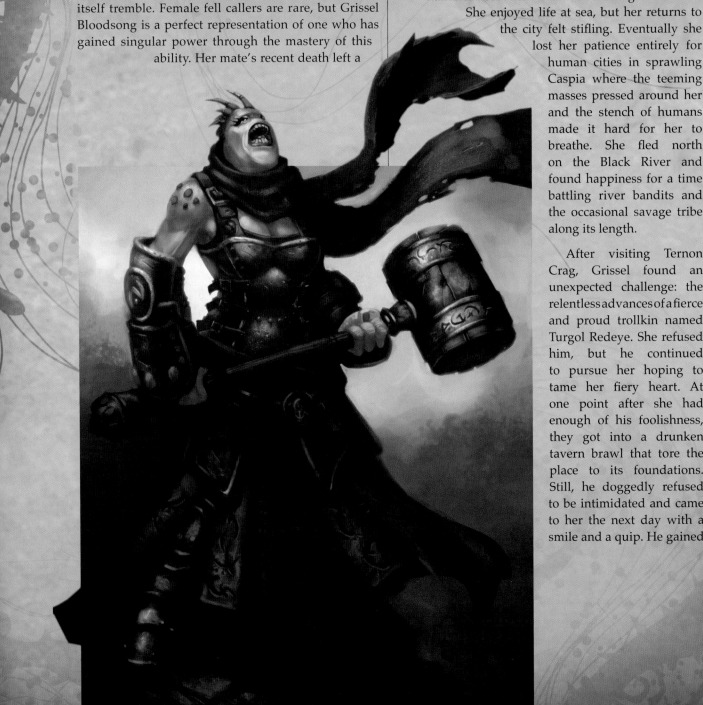

ground through quiet humor, his skill with the blade, and irrepressible optimism. For the first time in her life she considered settling down, and the two of them journeyed up to the bank of Scarleforth Lake where several trollkin kriels had villages near the Claysoil Wash River.

Without warning, the skorne arrived from the east bringing enslavement and death. In the course of the chaotic brawl, Turgol tore away from Grissel's side to thrust himself heroically between a trio of cyclops savages and a trollkin mother with two tiny infants. Turgol traded blows with each of them in turn, dispatching one and then another, but his hide was not as thick as his resolve. Before Grissel could disengage to aid him, Turgol fell to a mighty sword stroke that cleaved the brave trollkin in twain before his mate's very eyes. Grissel flew into a blood rage and belted forth her calls to blast the skorne out of her way. This trauma unlocked her warlock potential, and nearby pyre trolls heard her mental cry. With them she beat back the skorne, but it was too late for Turgol.

Something changed in Grissel Bloodsong with his death. She began to wage a personal war against the skorne and became an icon among the war-ravaged trollkin of the Scarleforth region. She has remained on the battlefront, and the sight of her is a comfort to rank and file trollkin who eagerly volunteer to follow her lead.

Contact with Chief Madrak Ironhide has renewed Grissel's hopes for a trollkin victory. Grissel has persuaded her people to join Ironhide's displaced Thornwood kriels knowing their only chance of survival will come from working together against this shared threat. She feels a part of a larger community as she walks among the rugged and courageous soldiers in Madrak's new army. She fights now not for empty coin, as when she was a mercenary, but for trollkin preservation. This purpose has given her strength to endure the fresh grief of the loss of her mate, which she feels keenly in the calm nights in the aftermath of battle.

SPECIAL RULES

Feat: Fell Chorus - Boasting an utter mastery of fell calling, Grissel is able to layer her calls one atop another, bellowing a sustained chant resounding like three voices engaged in song. The powerful sonic onslaught leaves foes faltering, almost deafened, and unable to heed their leaders while the weariest allies surge forward with renewed hope and tireless energy.

Bloodsong simultaneously uses all of her Fell Calls this activation. Enemy models/units within her control area suffer the effects of Cacophony. Friendly Trollblood models/units in her control area that have not been targeted by a friendly Fell Call this turn gain the benefits of both Heroic Ballad and Hoof It. Affected friendly Trollblood models cannot be targeted by additional Fell Calls this turn. Bloodsong cannot make a Fell Call in the same turn she uses Fell Chorus.

BLOODSONG

Tough - When Bloodsong suffers sufficient damage to be destroyed, her controller rolls a d6. On a 5 or 6, Bloodsong is knocked down instead of being destroyed. If Bloodsong is not destroyed, she is reduced to one wound.

RESOUNDER

Deafen - Target model hit by Resounder becomes Deaf for one round. A Deaf model moves at half rate, suffers –2 to attack rolls, cannot make free strikes, and cannot target models that were not in its front arc at the start of its activation with attacks.

BLOODSONG				CMD 9	
SPD	STR	MAT	RAT	DEF	ARM
6	7	6	5	15	16

HAND CANNON			
RNG	ROF	AOE	POW
12	1	—	12

RESOUNDER		
SPECIAL	POW	P+S
Deafen	7	14

FURY	6
DAMAGE	17
FIELD ALLOWANCE	C
VICTORY POINTS	5
POINT COST	70
BASE SIZE	MEDIUM

FELL CALLS

Bloodsong may make one of the following calls any time during her activation. A friendly Trollblood model/unit can only be affected by one Fell Call each turn.

- **Cacophony** - Enemy models/units currently in Bloodsong's command range suffer –2 CMD, cannot give or receive orders, and cannot cast spells. Cacophony lasts for one round.

- **Heroic Ballad** - Target friendly Trollblood warrior model/unit currently in Bloodsong's command range becomes Fearless and may make one additional melee attack without spending fury during its activation this round. Fearless models never flee. Heroic Ballad lasts for one round.

- **Hoof It** - Target friendly Trollblood warrior model/unit currently in Bloodsong's command range may move up to its SPD in inches at the end of this turn after all friendly models have completed their normal activations. During this movement, affected models cannot be targeted by free strikes.

SPELL	COST	RNG	AOE	POW	UP	OFF
CALAMITY	3	8	-	-	X	X

A model making an attack against target model/unit gains +2 to its attack and damage rolls.

UPROAR	3	8	3	14		X

Bloodsong blows enemies apart with the force of her will.

TROLL AXER

TROLLBLOOD LIGHT WARBEAST

TROLL AXER				CMD 6	
SPD	STR	MAT	RAT	DEF	ARM
5	9	6	4	12	18

—	GREAT AXE		
	SPECIAL	POW	P+S
	Thresher	6	15

FURY	3
THRESHOLD	9
FIELD ALLOWANCE	U
VICTORY POINTS	2
POINT COST	72
BASE SIZE	MEDIUM

Troll Axer

Regeneration [d3] - The Troll Axer may be forced to remove d3 damage points from anywhere on its life spiral once per activation. The Troll Axer cannot regenerate during an activation it runs.

Great Axe

Thresher (★Attack) - The Troll Axer may make one melee attack with its Great Axe against every model within melee range in its front arc. Completely resolve each attack individually and apply the targets' special rules immediately as each attack is resolved. Determine damage normally.

Lock your shields and stand ready. One of these beasts can carve through three of us with a single blow. Ready halberds to keep them at bay!

—Primus Kunguul, Cataphract Cetratus of the First Cohort

With its weapon gripped in both hands, a troll axer eagerly charges into battle while its corded muscles leverage the chopping edge with brutal power. An axer is capable of cleaving through a wall of men in a single swipe, and hacked off pieces of foes make for easy portions. It is not unknown for a troll to savor an arm or leg while its victim watches in horror and bleeds out on the ground.

Trolls are carnivorous humanoids that tower over the mightiest trollkin. Their tissues are so regenerative that if not immediately reattached, a severed limb may grow into a short-lived degenerate miniature troll called a "whelp," which may be consumed on the battlefield as a quick meal. Trolls are smarter than most realize and have a simple language allowing them to work effectively in groups. Trollkin leaders like Madrak Ironhide have made extensive use of the axers to bolster the lines of his trollkin warriors.

The trollkin train their larger cousins to be disciplined comrades in war outfitted with powerful oversized iron axes. Though trolls in the wild are capable of making crude axes from improvised materials, those used in modern battles are crafted

ANIMUS	COST	RNG	AOE	POW	UP	OFF
RUSH	2	6	-	-		

Target friendly model's next activation is a charge at SPD +5" that crosses rough terrain and obstacles without penalty.

by the trollkin specifically to cleave through bone and sinew. Trolls chosen and trained as axers are those with an inner primal strength which warlocks can tap to invigorate the limbs of their allies with a quick burst of speed, allowing troll or trollkin to charge through forests or up the steepest incline without tiring.

Full-blood trolls fighting alongside trollkin is a tradition dating back to the uprisings of 247 and 262 AR when the trollkin made an organized effort to create pacts with the trolls and enlist them as barely controlled forces of rampaging destruction. In the remote wilderness kriels of the Scarsfell, the Gnarls, and pockets of the Thornwood, chiefs and shamans have maintained these old pacts and can call the trolls to war.

ANIMUS	COST	RNG	AOE	POW	UP	OFF
FAR STRIKE	2	6	-	-		

INCREASE TARGET MODEL'S RANGED WEAPONS' RNG BY 4".

Pitching enormous spears with bone crushing force, impalers are the living ballistae of the trolls. Each carries a quiver of massive wood and iron projectiles bearing only functional similarity to the puny twigs men call spears. The impact from these weighty implements can send impaled victims flying back into walls, trees, or other combatants. These great piercing weapons are just as effective in close quarters and allow the impaler to inflict horrendous wounds on any who try to close within their reach.

Impalers are the same species as their axe-wielding kin. They are distinguished primarily by different training and equipment, and they have the same great powers of regeneration and a similarly ravenous appetite. Trollkin have learned to keep their troll allies well stocked and often load them down with meat and drink to discourage them from turning on their own warriors in the chaos of battle.

Do not underestimate the heft and weight of those spears. I've seen one lift a warpwolf and pin it to a tree.

—Baldur the Stonecleaver

Attempts have been made to teach the trolls to feast only on the bodies of enemies since most pious trollkin expect proper funereal rites for slain kin. However, these efforts are not always effective, particularly on trolls battered within an inch of death at a warlock's goading. A few missing bodies at the end of battle is an inevitable price of calling on trolls to fight.

Those trained as impalers have a keen eye and better-than-average coordination. Chief Ironhide insists the impalers are the smartest of the trolls although it has never been proven conclusively. Between battles the impalers enjoy testing their prowess against one another by competing in throwing contests and trying to impale difficult moving targets such as deer or even rabbits with a single throw. It can be dangerous to walk in the vicinity of these brutal contests, for the trolls have little awareness of pain or injury due to their regenerative capability.

TROLL IMPALER				CMD	6
SPD	STR	MAT	RAT	DEF	ARM
5	9	5	5	13	16

THROWN SPEAR			
RNG	ROF	AOE	POW
8	1	—	4

BATTLE SPEAR		
SPECIAL	POW	P+S
Reach	4	13

FURY	3
THRESHOLD	9
FIELD ALLOWANCE	U
VICTORY POINTS	2
POINT COST	75
BASE SIZE	MEDIUM

Troll Impaler

Regeneration [d3] - The Troll Impaler may be forced to remove d3 damage points from anywhere on its life spiral once per activation. The Troll Impaler cannot regenerate during an activation it runs.

Thrown Spear

Critical Slam - On a critical hit, instead of making a normal damage roll, the Troll Impaler may slam the target model d6" directly away from him. The model suffers a damage roll equal to the Troll Impaler's current STR plus the POW of the Thrown Spear. If the slammed model contacts a model with an equal or smaller-sized base, that model suffers a collateral damage roll equal to the Troll Impaler's current STR.

Thrown - Add the Troll Impaler's current STR to the POW of its Thrown Spear ranged attacks.

Battle Spear

Reach - 2" melee range.

Pyre Troll

Trollblood Light Warbeast

PYRE TROLL				CMD	6
SPD	STR	MAT	RAT	DEF	ARM
5	9	5	4	13	15

HD	SPEW FIRE			
	RNG	ROF	AOE	POW
	8	1	3	12

LFT	CLAW		
	SPECIAL	POW	P+S
	—	2	11

RT	CLAW		
	SPECIAL	POW	P+S
	—	2	11

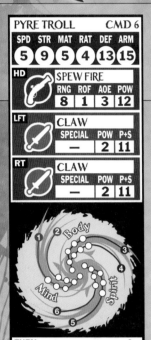

FURY	3
THRESHOLD	9
FIELD ALLOWANCE	U
VICTORY POINTS	2
POINT COST	68
BASE SIZE	MEDIUM

Pyre Troll

Regeneration [d3] - The Pyre Troll may be forced to remove d3 damage points from anywhere on its life spiral once per activation. The Pyre Troll cannot regenerate during an activation it runs.

Spew Fire

Critical Fire - On a critical hit, each model hit suffers Fire. Fire is a continuous effect that sets the target ablaze. A model on fire suffers a POW 12 damage roll each turn during its controller's Maintenance Phase until the Fire expires on a d6 roll of 1 or 2. Fire effects are alchemical substances or magical in nature and are not affected by water.

Nothing wakes up the enemy like a splash of fire hitting their tents before dawn!

—Grissel Bloodsong

These dangerous beasts can belch forth a gout of combustible liquid which ignites in air, sticks to flesh, and burns at terribly high temperatures. A pyre troll's skin continually smolders with heat, and the air ripples around them in a continual haze that warns of the inferno to come. After softening a foe with a great burst of blazing spittle, the pyre troll wades into battle with brutal enthusiasm and uses its thick-nailed claws to tear man or beast apart.

Trolls are a highly adaptable species able to find a niche in almost any environment. Pyre trolls are a bizarre and dangerous evolution of the "pitch trolls" more common along the fringes of the Marches, particularly east of Ternon Crag and near Scarleforth Lake. To blend in with the red sands and better stalk their prey, these trolls have a dark burgundy to ochre color. They prefer climates of extreme heat and are found in the most sweltering desert sunning themselves on hot rocks. They are noticeably less intelligent than most trolls and demonstrate no aptitude for wielding weapons. Perhaps their unnatural temperatures and strange eating habits have addled their brains.

No one has taken the time to study pyre trolls properly to determine how their flaming expectoration evolved. It seems likely it is the byproduct of a horrible internal digestive distress caused by the poisonous and toxic

ANIMUS	COST	RNG	AOE	POW	UP	OFF
FLAMING FISTS	2	6	-	-	-	'

TARGET MODEL GAINS CRITICAL FIRE ON MELEE ATTACKS AND +2 TO ITS MELEE DAMAGE ROLLS DURING ITS NEXT ACTIVATION THIS TURN. WHEN A MODEL WITH CRITICAL FIRE ROLLS A CRITICAL HIT, ITS TARGET SUFFERS FIRE. FIRE IS A CONTINUOUS EFFECT THAT SETS THE TARGET ABLAZE. A MODEL ON FIRE SUFFERS A POW 12 DAMAGE ROLL EACH TURN DURING ITS CONTROLLER'S MAINTENANCE PHASE UNTIL THE FIRE EXPIRES ON A D6 ROLL OF 1 OR 2. FIRE EFFECTS ARE ALCHEMICAL SUBSTANCES OR MAGICAL IN NATURE AND ARE NOT AFFECTED BY WATER.

substances these trolls eat indiscriminately. They have been witnessed swallowing rocks, metal, oil, and plants considered deadly to most species. They seem to enjoy drinking a thick brackish fluid that bubbles up from the soil in the northern Marches which could be similar to what is used to create "Menoth's Fury" further south in the Protectorate of Menoth. Grissel Bloodsong is an advocate of these beasts and has accumulated a supply of the foul-smelling tar they like to drink. Whatever the source of their blazing regurgitation is, it causes horrendous wounds on the battlefield and sends foes running and screaming while desperately trying to extinguish the persistent flames.

DIRE TROLL MAULER

TROLLBLOOD HEAVY WARBEAST

ANIMUS	COST	RNG	AOE	POW	UP	OFF
RAGE	2	6	-	-		

Target friendly Trollblood model gains +3 STR for one round.

Standing up to eighteen feet tall with bodies of thickened muscle and clawed hands nearly the size of a man, the awesome dire troll has few peers. In ancient days when these monsters came from the forest to stuff their fanged maws with screaming victims, it was proof to the primitive tribes of man that terror had flesh and walked among them. Even today there is no fighting these beasts and no defense against them except to run gibbering and hope it gluts itself on friends or family before retreating, sated, back to the trees. Their big meaty fists can rend metal or effortlessly rip a body to shreds.

Even at the height of the uprisings when the trollkin were beset by human colossals, no chiefs or shamans were foolhardy enough to seek the dire trolls. They have always been considered nothing less than a menace to all life. Every unpleasant attribute of a regular troll is

They are almost unstoppable and pose a grave threat to our order. Slay them immediately wherever you find them no matter what it takes or who must be sacrificed.

—Omnipotent Ergonus of the Circle, now deceased

magnified ten-fold in these bipedal terrors. In epics they are termed deathless and tireless.

Only the shaman Hoarluk Doomshaper had the power, will, and courage to bring the dire trolls to the Trollbloods. The maulers are among the largest and most brutal of the species— those so fierce and savage they cannot be trusted with weapons other than their teeth and hands. Whether the dire trolls speak a language is debatable, but they use a small range of verbal utterances and can learn to obey Molgur-Trul. They speak a word reserved only for Hoarluk Doomshaper: "Krol," which may represent worship or deification. Many chiefs are uneasy about his reckless decision to utilize the creatures and are still terrified of them, but maulers bring tremendous raw power to the allied kriels. As long as the old shaman can keep them controlled, they may offer the Trollbloods their greatest chance of victory.

DIRE TROLL MAULER CMD 5					
SPD	STR	MAT	RAT	DEF	ARM
5	12	5	3	12	18

LFT	BIG MEATY FIST		
	SPECIAL	POW	P+S
	Claw	4	16

RT	BIG MEATY FIST		
	SPECIAL	POW	P+S
	Claw	4	16

FURY	5
THRESHOLD	11
FIELD ALLOWANCE	U
VICTORY POINTS	3
POINT COST	111
BASE SIZE	LARGE

Dire Troll Mauler

Chain Attack–Chomp - If the Dire Troll Mauler hits with both of its initial Big Meaty Fist attacks against the same target in the same activation, after resolving the attacks it may immediately make an additional melee attack against the target. If the attack succeeds, it immediately suffers a damage roll equal to the Dire Troll's current STR. When damaging a warjack, the Dire Troll Mauler's controller chooses which column takes this damage. When damaging a warbeast, the Dire Troll Mauler's controller chooses which branch takes the damage.

Regeneration [d3] - The Dire Troll Mauler may be forced to remove d3 damage points from anywhere on its life spiral once per activation. The Dire Troll Mauler cannot regenerate during an activation it runs.

Snacking - When the Dire Troll Mauler destroys a living model with a melee attack, it may remove d3 damage points from anywhere on its life spiral.

Big Meaty Fists

Claw - The Dire Troll Mauler's Big Meaty Fists have the abilities of Claws.

DIRE TROLL BLITZER

TROLLBLOOD HEAVY WARBEAST

DIRE TROLL BLITZER	CMD 5				
SPD	STR	MAT	RAT	DEF	ARM
5	12	5	5	12	18

—	SLUGGER			
	RNG	ROF	AOE	POW
	12	*	—	13

LFT	CLAW		
	SPECIAL	POW	P+S
	—	3	15

RT	CLAW		
	SPECIAL	POW	P+S
	—	3	15

FURY	4
THRESHOLD	10
FIELD ALLOWANCE	U
VICTORY POINTS	3
POINT COST	118
BASE SIZE	LARGE

I see this wall of troll-flesh out of the corner of my eye, so I turn to look at it. Way up on top there's this chortling pyg with a cannon gunning down anything it sees! It was beautiful.

—Grissel Bloodsong on her first fight alongside a Blitzer

There has never been anything like the dire troll blitzer—an incarnation of mad trollkin inspiration plumbed from the depths of their desperate struggles. When Chief Ironhide acquired surplus Cygnaran weapons from King Leto, the king could never have anticipated their ultimate application. By mounting rapid-fire "slugger" cannons atop mammoth dire trolls, the trollkin effectively created a walking siege engine. As the dire troll bounds across the field toward the enemy, the pyg ace atop his back unleashes a devastating hail of fire.

There has always been a strange affinity between pygmies, commonly called pygs, and dire trolls inasmuch as any creature can endure the towering behemoths. Dire trolls seem genuinely to enjoy the company of the diminutive pygs and will not generally eat them unless they run out of other food. It is believed these

ANIMUS	COST	RNG	AOE	POW	UP	OFF
REPULSION	2	SELF	-	-		

MODELS WITHIN 2" OF THE MODEL USING THIS ANIMUS ARE PUSHED 1" DIRECTLY AWAY FROM IT IN AN ORDER DETERMINED BY ITS CONTROLLER. MODELS CANNOT BE TARGETED BY FREE STRIKES DURING THIS MOVEMENT.

tiny cousins exert a calming influence. After the dire trolls proved so effective, many chiefs schemed to find a way to utilize this bond in battle.

When the pygs proved their skill with rifles, it was only natural that they operate the sluggers (the trollkin name for the Cygnaran weapons). In what was undoubtedly an episode of drunken bravado, a slugger was strapped to the back of a slumbering dire troll. Surprisingly this outlandish scheme actually worked, but it did result in the maiming of a few pygs with more courage than sense. The combination of firearms and dire trolls held obvious merit, and the problem was solved by having the dire troll endure having its arms chained so it could not reach over its head to grab its pyg ace and gobble him up. The pygs have embraced this concept with surprising enthusiasm, and riding atop a dire troll is now an instant means to gain prestige among their tribes. The pygs treat blitzer aces as heroic champions.

Dire Troll Blitzer

Pyg Ace - The Dire Troll Blitzer may make Slugger attacks and melee attacks in the same activation. The Dire Troll Blitzer may make Slugger attacks while in melee or if it runs, charges, or slams, but it cannot target a model in its melee range. Intervening models in the Dire Troll Blitzer's melee range do not block LOS when it makes Slugger attacks, but they may still provide screening to models targeted. The Dire Troll Blitzer cannot be forced to make additional Slugger ranged attacks or boost Slugger ranged attack or ranged damage rolls. Slugger attacks are unaffected by the Dire Troll Blitzer's lost aspects.

Regeneration [d3] - The Dire Troll Blitzer may be forced to remove d3 damage points from anywhere on its life spiral once per activation. The Dire Troll Blitzer cannot regenerate during an activation it runs.

Snacking - When the Dire Troll Blitzer destroys a living model with a melee attack, it may remove d3 damage points from anywhere on its life spiral.

Slugger

Rapid Fire [d3] - The Dire Troll Blitzer may make d3 ranged attacks with the Slugger without being forced.

TROLLKIN CHAMPIONS

TROLLBLOOD TROLLKIN UNIT

The champions are hardened and experienced veterans who rise as the great heroes of their kriels. A tight bond and an awareness that theirs is a greater destiny link them, and they formalize these ties with the *kulgat* blood oath. They learn to draw strength from their brothers and fight with seamless precision side by side. As the fight for survival continues, even more of these brave champions' stories will end in tragic deaths, but before they fall, they distinguish themselves on the front line by hacking into enemies with a weapon in each hand. Their powerful blows hit their mark and send their foes back with grievous wounds.

With brawn rivaling the ogrun, only the largest and strongest trollkin warriors can become champions. As masters of all weapons, they are equally at ease with axes, blades, clubs, or other implements of war. The bond between these champions goes beyond a normal *kulgat*, and in battle they fight almost with one mind, perfectly anticipating the moves of their brothers to exploit opportunities in their enemies' defenses.

Leaders of the champions take the name "kithkar" which means "firstborn" among trollkin siblings. They are the eldest and most skilled of their group. Many kithkar were chieftains of lesser kriels but gave up that status to heed the call to fight. There are many tales of woe among them, particularly those drawn from the Thornwood. They have lost mates, children, and parents, and they find life between battles a reminder that they are the last of proud bloodlines. To ready for their next conflict, they draw on the strength of their brothers in arms, inspire hope in all their kin, and stride fearlessly to embrace their fates. Each champion knows he will die in bloodshed, but he intends to bring as many enemies with him as his weapons can reach.

> *Brotherhood is forged in battle, and by brotherhood we will stand where others fall.*
>
> —Champion Torush Fennborn

KITHKAR					CMD 9
SPD	STR	MAT	RAT	DEF	ARM
5	8	8	4	12	17

CHAMPION					CMD 7
SPD	STR	MAT	RAT	DEF	ARM
5	8	7	4	12	17

HAND WEAPON		
SPECIAL	POW	P+S
—	4	12

HAND WEAPON		
SPECIAL	POW	P+S
—	4	12

KITHKAR DAMAGE	10
CHAMPION DAMAGE	8
FIELD ALLOWANCE	2
VICTORY POINTS	3
LEADER AND 4 TROOPS	106
BASE SIZE	MEDIUM

Kithkar
Leader

Unit
Brothers in Arms - Any Trollkin Champion in base-to-base contact with another model in his unit gains +2 DEF against melee attacks.

Concert - A Trollkin Champion gains +1 cumulative bonus to melee attack and melee damage rolls for each other model in his unit that has made a successful melee attack against an enemy model this turn.

Fearless - A Trollkin Champion never flees.

Tough - When a Trollkin Champion suffers sufficient damage to be destroyed, his controller rolls a d6. On a 5 or 6, the Trollkin Champion is knocked down instead of being destroyed. If a Trollkin Champion is not destroyed, he is reduced to one wound.

Trollkin Scattergunners

Trollblood Trollkin Unit

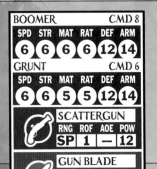

BOOMER					CMD 8	
SPD	STR	MAT	RAT	DEF	ARM	
6	6	6	6	12	14	

GRUNT					CMD 6	
SPD	STR	MAT	RAT	DEF	ARM	
6	6	5	5	12	14	

SCATTERGUN			
RNG	ROF	AOE	POW
SP	1	—	12

GUN BLADE		
SPECIAL	POW	P+S
—	3	9

FIELD ALLOWANCE	2
VICTORY POINTS	2
LEADER AND 5 TROOPS	77
UP TO 4 ADDITIONAL TROOPS	12ea
BASE SIZE	MEDIUM

Boomer
Leader

Slaughterfest (Order) - Every Scattergunner that received this order may charge an eligible target or run. When a Scattergunner damages a target with a charge attack, it may immediately make a POW 12 damage roll against the target. This additional damage roll is caused by the scattergun.

Unit

Tough - When a Scattergunner suffers sufficient damage to be destroyed, his controller rolls a d6. On a 5 or 6, the Scattergunner is knocked down instead of being destroyed.

They charged from the underbrush and cut us down with a spray of shrapnel before slamming into our line. Half my pack fell before we could raise our spears.

—Korlash Cloudeye, Huntsman of the Wolves of Orboros

Tough as boiled leather, the dedicated scattergunners are soldiers equal to any kingdom army and twice as hardy. Increasingly, trollkin warriors following the old ways are seeing the effectiveness of modern weapons in the hands of the rugged kriels on the eastern front. They made these firearms uniquely their own; the enormous booming guns can shred whole enemy formations to tatters.

Even in the wilds trollkin have been using firearms for centuries. They have been scavenging many of the weapons and adapting them since the 242 AR uprisings, but acquiring blasting power has always been a problem. The Trollblood received a massive infusion of the low-grade powder after Chief Ironhide's negotiations with King Leto. Ironhide was also equipped with a number of small cannons intended for fixed position defenses. Instead of using these cannons in their intended role, the trollkin strapped stocks on them, attached enormous axe-blades to the front of the barrels, and stuffed them with powder and scrap metal to turn them into the scatterguns. They are weapons well suited to the trollkin requiring their combination of strength and stamina to wield. The short range matters little to the toughened scattergunners. They do not fear charging forward against the enemy while firing a spray of debris that tears flesh to ribbons.

Each shot of these tremendous guns consumes an obscene quantity of blasting powder, which has engendered ongoing raids to gather more kegs of powder. The scatterguns can be loaded with an assortment of scrap metal, chain links, or iron nails. If enemies make the mistake of standing too close together, these guns can rip several men to shreds with a single blast. Scattergunners also fight just as ruthlessly when the enemy closes by swinging the hefty axe blades attached to the ends of their guns.

The brave males and females of the scattered kriels form the core of the trollblood forces. Life in a wilderness kriel is difficult—all able bodied mature trollkin must learn how to fight and hunt. They are sorted by aptitude, and the strongest youths are given axes, hammers, or swords, strapped with the best armor their kriel can produce, and expected to defend their people.

Warriors gather and spend a short time learning to fight well together and in the company of a chosen shaman of Dhunia. To ensure they are ready for battle, the warriors endure a grueling cycle of abuse to learn discipline and to trust in their ancient instincts and recuperative powers—the birthright of all Trollbloods. This trial would be deemed barbaric by human standards. They are pushed near death and often incur maiming injuries while sparring with tribal champions. It is not uncommon for the victor to sever a foe's fingers, a hand, or even an arm or leg. With enough food and time, a trollkin can recover from these injuries and will

The humans have fouled Dhunia's lands long enough. Fight bravely and remember our kriel, our kin. Our sacrifice ensures their safety!

—Jata Lorgosh, war shaman of Dhunia

not make the same mistake twice. They also learn to fight among their savage distant cousins, the pureblood trolls. A trollkin learns not to be complacent around these thick-skulled "allies," particularly when the trolls are wounded and hungry.

Most of these warriors have already seen time in battle serving as the front line against the myriad of enemies faced by the trollkin villages. Their leadership is entrusted to accomplished Dhunian priests, and these war shamans lend wisdom to the group as well as infuse them with the power of Dhunia's wrath. Usually the same shaman who trained them will lead them to war, for the camaraderie and loyalty of these tight-knit groups provide resolve against the difficult fights to come.

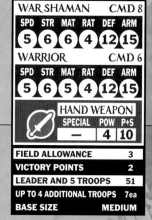

WAR SHAMAN					CMD 8
SPD	STR	MAT	RAT	DEF	ARM
5	6	6	4	12	15

WARRIOR					CMD 6
SPD	STR	MAT	RAT	DEF	ARM
5	6	5	4	12	15

HAND WEAPON		
SPECIAL	POW	P+S
—	4	10

FIELD ALLOWANCE	3
VICTORY POINTS	2
LEADER AND 5 TROOPS	51
UP TO 4 ADDITIONAL TROOPS	7ea
BASE SIZE	MEDIUM

War Shaman
Leader

Prayers of Dhunia - The War Shaman may recite one of the following prayers each turn during his activation. Every model in his unit, including himself, gains the listed benefits for one round:

- Potency: Gain +2 STR.
- Quick Strike: Make an additional melee attack.
- Swift Foot: Gain +2" of movement.

Unit

Combined Melee Attack - Instead of making melee attacks separately, two or more Kriel Warriors in melee range of the same target may combine their attacks. In order to participate in a combined melee attack, a Kriel Warrior must be able to declare a melee attack against the intended target. The Kriel Warrior with the highest MAT in the attacking group makes one melee attack roll for the group and gains +1 to the attack and damage rolls for each Kriel Warrior, including himself, participating in the attack.

Tough - When a Kriel Warrior suffers sufficient damage to be destroyed, his controller rolls a d6. On a 5 or 6, the Kriel Warrior is knocked down instead of being destroyed.

Pyg Bushwhackers

Trollblood Pygmy Troll Unit

BOOMER					CMD 7	
SPD	STR	MAT	RAT	DEF	ARM	
6	5	5	5	13	12	

BUSHWHACKER					CMD 5	
SPD	STR	MAT	RAT	DEF	ARM	
6	5	4	4	13	12	

RIFLE			
RNG	ROF	AOE	POW
10	1	—	10

SWORD		
SPECIAL	POW	P+S
—	3	8

FIELD ALLOWANCE	2
VICTORY POINTS	2
LEADER AND 5 TROOPS	64
UP TO 4 ADDITIONAL TROOPS	10ea
BASE SIZE	SMALL

We were taking fire from both sides of the Bramblerut, and I thought there were dozens of them, but it turned out to be a handful of those damned pygmies! When we hacked through the brush they were long gone.

—Cygnaran reinforcement making his way to the war front

Boomer

Leader

Unit

Advance Deployment - Place Pyg Bushwhackers after normal deployment, up to 12" beyond the established deployment zone.

Bushwhack - Pyg Bushwhackers may make a ranged attack before moving. After attacking, Pyg Bushwhackers may advance normally but cannot perform actions afterwards.

Combined Ranged Attack - Instead of making ranged attacks separately, two or more Pyg Bushwhackers may combine their attacks against the same target. In order to participate in a combined ranged attack, a Pyg Bushwhacker must be able to declare a ranged attack against the intended target and be in a single open formation group with the other participants. The Pyg Bushwhacker with the highest RAT in the attacking group makes one ranged attack roll for the group and gains +1 to the attack and damage rolls for each Pyg Bushwhacker, including himself, participating in the attack.

Pathfinder - Pyg Bushwhackers ignore movement penalties from rough terrain and obstacles. Pyg Bushwhackers may charge across rough terrain.

Tough - When a Pyg Bushwhacker suffers sufficient damage to be destroyed, his controller rolls a d6. On a 5 or 6, the Pyg Bushwhacker is knocked down instead of being destroyed.

Pygmy trolls and trollkin have not always been friendly, but recent turmoil in the Thornwood has brought them together, for the ongoing war in the region has decimated the generally complacent pygs. As both groups were seeking safer sites in which to settle, the pygmies sought the trollkin and asked for aid. The gathered kriels agreed on the condition that the pygs join the fight and prove they could hold their own. The impressive number of kills racked up in recent months by bushwhackers has earned more advocates among the kriels, and they have since become an indispensable part of the Trollblood forces.

Though not noted for sophisticated culture or aptitude for crafts, pygs are quite intelligent and nimble. They are cunning creatures capable of laying complex ambushes and working together to bring down larger prey. Over time the pygs have increasingly emulated the trollkin living in their proximity. The spoils of war have landed a number of firearms in their hands, and it did not take them long to start employing these weapons with surprising effectiveness.

After witnessing the pygs in action, Chief Ironhide saw their potential and decided to organize and arm them, using some of the militia rifles and powder given to him by Cygnar. With a little modification to the stock and trigger mechanisms, these weapons became perfectly suited to the diminutive pygs. Madrak's unconventional plan met with skepticism, but the pygs have proven to be deadly shots. What the pygs lack in discipline, they more than make up in tenacity and enthusiasm, adopting improvised calls and hand signals to coordinate in the bush. Bushwhackers move ahead of Trollblood forces, keeping lookout with stolen spyglasses to scout and watch for the best places to set up ambushes.

KRIELSTONE BEARER & STONE SCRIBES

TROLLBLOOD TROLLKIN UNIT

Krielstones are sacred monuments of the trollkin, and the great carved rocks are covered with carefully inscribed Molgur runes immortalizing heroism over the ages. The largest krielstones are placed at sites of importance to Dhunia or noted ancient battlegrounds and are often near or part of shrines to the Ravaged Mother. Through the prayers of generations, they become replete with spiritual power, and miracles have long been associated with them. Most stones are too great and heavy to move, but a tradition has arisen over the centuries whereby kith carve smaller krielstones with the specific intent of carrying them to battle. These are reservoirs capable of preserving the strength warlocks draw from their beasts. Empowered by their runes, the stones can radiate powerful protection to the brave warriors fighting in their proximity.

It is customary for the strongest trollkin of a kith to pit themselves against the stones, working throughout

When you can lift this stone, then you are ready.

— Krielstone Bearer Bontur Irongullet
speaking to his nephew

adolescence to bulk up and master the raw power to lift one and carry it into battle. The strength of these specialized trollkin is enormous, and they can gain reputations across various kriels for their prowess. Each attempts to outdo the others in the size of the stone he can carry.

Stone scribes accompany the bearers to witness and immortalize brave deeds in battle. They will carve the next krielstones for future generations based on the deeds of the present. Scribes train in the art of capturing the sacred power of krielstones onto ceremonially prepared scrolls created from rubbings on the stone surfaces. Scribes have enormous reverence for the stones and those who bear them and gladly volunteer for battle to help defend them. This bond is so strong they will sacrifice their lives to preserve the bearer from injury.

KRIELSTONE BEARER CMD 9					
SPD	STR	MAT	RAT	DEF	ARM
5	8	6	4	12	13

STONE SCRIBE CMD 7					
SPD	STR	MAT	RAT	DEF	ARM
5	7	6	4	12	13

BATTLE AXE		
SPECIAL	POW	P+S
—	4	11

FIELD ALLOWANCE	1
VICTORY POINTS	2
LEADER AND 3 TROOPS	34
UP TO 2 ADDITIONAL TROOPS	8ea
BASE SIZE	MEDIUM

Krielstone Bearer

Fury Vault - A friendly Trollblood warlock may place fury points on a Krielstone Bearer in his control area instead of discarding them during his activation. A Krielstone Bearer may have up to one fury point for each model currently in the unit including himself. When a Stone Scribe is destroyed or removed from play, immediately remove fury points from the Krielstone Bearer in excess of the number of models in the unit. While the Krielstone Bearer is within a friendly Trollblood warlock's control area, that warlock may leach fury from the Krielstone Bearer during his controller's Control Phase.

Leader

Protective Aura (★Action) - As a special action, the Krielstone Bearer may spend a fury point to generate a Protective Aura for one round. During this round, friendly models gain +2 ARM while within 4" of the Krielstone Bearer +1" per fury point on the Krielstone Bearer. This bonus is not cumulative with itself.

Stone Scribes

Self Sacrifice - When the Krielstone Bearer takes sufficient damage to be destroyed and the destruction is not prevented by a successful Tough roll, the Krielstone Bearer's controller may choose a Stone Scribe in the Krielstone Bearer's unit within 3" to be destroyed instead.

Unit

Fearless - The Krielstone Bearer and Stone Scribes never flee.

Tough - When a Krielstone Bearer or Stone Scribe suffers sufficient damage to be destroyed, his controller rolls a d6. On a 5 or 6, the model is knocked down instead of being destroyed.

FELL CALLER

TROLLBLOOD TROLLKIN SOLO

FELL CALLER				CMD 8	
SPD	STR	MAT	RAT	DEF	ARM
6	7	7	4	13	15

SONIC BLAST			
RNG	ROF	AOE	POW
SP	1	—	12

SWORD		
SPECIAL	POW	P+S
—	3	10

SWORD		
SPECIAL	POW	P+S
—	3	10

DAMAGE	8
FIELD ALLOWANCE	2
VICTORY POINTS	1
POINT COST	35
BASE SIZE	MEDIUM

The fell callers on those raids were terrors. Their booming calls shook the ground, rallied the other trollkin, and worked them into a state of battle frenzy.

—Vlasin Kostok, fromer scout for the Khadoran Free Mercenaries

The sons and daughters of Bragg—the legendary father of the fell caller bloodline—are viewed as incarnations of trollkin culture and pride. Their powerful booming voices raised in chant can do more than rally their brethren; they can also rally nearby trollkin to heroic efforts or by a singular sonic attack shatter bone and flesh. Few trollkin warlocks are willing to take to the field without the support of a son or daughter of Bragg. In addition, only the kithkar of the champions can challenge their weapon supremacy as they lunge forward with a sword in each hand to deal lethal blows.

There are occasional problems caused by these wild and irrepressible crooners however. They are an arrogant, self-assured breed, and sometimes they have difficulty following orders. They are also a hardy bunch who enjoy living the good life even in these difficult and troublesome times. They are prone to excessive drinking—even by trollkin standards—and inspiring wild revelries at inappropriate times. Traveling fell callers can be a source of friction to visiting kriels, particularly when they begin seducing local mates or the daughters of influential chiefs. Most sons of Bragg feel an almost irresistible urge to spread their seed far and wide to pass their legacy to the next generation. This habit is also found in the rare female fell callers who are just as ardent as their male counterparts.

Despite these disruptive habits, fell callers remain a welcome presence among Trollblood warriors. By their presence alone they have served as rallying points to hold the line and have prevented the rout of beleaguered armies. As powerful as their fell calls are, each is a singular warrior of proven ability capable of shredding through lesser enemies. They lead by both bellow and deed, and few can resist the call to follow when a fell caller drives deep into the enemy, heedless of the odds.

Fell Caller

Inspire - After the Fell Caller successfully charges an enemy model, friendly Trollblood warrior models/units currently within 6" of him gain +2 to attack rolls this turn.

Rallying Point - Friendly Trollblood models/units within a number of inches equal to the Fell Caller's CMD, including himself, never flee. Fleeing friendly Trollblood models/units move toward the nearest friendly Fell Caller and immediately rally when within a number of inches equal to the Fell Caller's CMD.

Tough - When the Fell Caller suffers sufficient damage to be destroyed, his controller rolls a d6. On a 5 or 6, the Fell Caller is knocked down instead of being destroyed. If the Fell Caller is not destroyed, he is reduced to one wound.

Victory Howl - When the Fell Caller destroys an enemy model with a melee attack, enemy models/units within 6" of him must pass a command check or flee. Victory Howl may be used once per turn.

Weapon Master - The Fell Caller rolls an additional die on his melee damage rolls.

Fell Calls

As a special action, the Fell Caller may make one of the following calls during his activation. A friendly Trollbllod model/unit can only be targeted by one Fell Call each turn.

• **Open Road** (★Action) - Target friendly Trollblood warrior model/unit within 6" of the Fell Caller gains Pathfinder this turn. Models with Pathfinder ignore movement penalties from rough terrain and obstacles. Models with Pathfinder may charge across rough terrain.

• **Reveille** (★Action) - Friendly knocked down Trollblood models within 6" of the Fell Caller immediatley stand up. Models immediately stand up even if they were knocked down this turn.

• **War Cry** (★Action) - Target friendly Trollblood warrior model/unit within 6" of the Fell Caller gains +2 to melee and ranged attack rolls.

Circle Orboros

THE CIRCLE ORBOROS

Kaya the Wildborne crouched and peered through the trees to survey the ruins of a nameless Khadoran village on the western shore of Blindwater Lake. She could read its history by the silvery light of the full moon—a fishing village with rugged but simple inhabitants working their nets from dawn until dusk before retiring to their rustic homes. The only excitement they might expect required a trek across the great lake to visit the city of Skirov.

Now the empty despoiled houses stood silent, and the only sound heard in the once lively village was the meaty tear of flesh and the crunching of bones sucked for marrow. The village put up a fight against the blind serpentine creatures descending on them, but it fell rapidly. Arrows had picked off the outer sentries, and the small shredders descended on the unsuspecting township to feast.

Kaya watched the aftermath with a clinical eye and felt only slight empathy for the slain. She reached out with her mind to the argus accompanying her. The two-headed hounds were creeping quietly in a wide arc toward the nearest of the dragonspawn. Though blind, the shredders had a keen awareness, so it was difficult to surprise them. The only emotion Kaya felt as she watched them feast was loathing; dragonspawn registered to her awareness as a dark stain. She had honed her mind to connect with animals of the wild, and it was clear from the first that these creatures were entirely unnatural. Whatever superficial resemblance they bore to living things was a perversion—a blighted mockery. They were hollow shells, and their minds were filled with a keening noise like glass scraping steel.

All your power is mine if I wish it.

Moving along the perimeter with an argus named Lodis, Kaya sought the blighted archers who had eliminated the sentries. She found them at the dirt road leading from the fishing pier to the town's square. She cloaked Lodis in mist and sent him against the archers while she unleashed the rest of her pack on the feasting shredders in the town square behind her.

The pack beset the foe from multiple directions and filled the air with distinctive piercing barks. Kaya reached across the distance to Lodis, feeling its soul and the sound of its heartbeat. She wrenched on that connection, vanished, and reappeared next to one of the surprised archers who was nocking an arrow to his bow. She swept her staff around in a crushing delivery that splintered the archer's bow before cracking his skull. In another sweep of blurred wood she toppled the blighted elf next to him and ended his life. By Lodis' fangs and her staff, the archers fell quickly, but she sensed something amiss in the battle behind her.

More shredders than she had anticipated scurried from the surrounding homes and hemmed in her pack. Even with two heads her loyal argus could not fend off all the snapping creatures. Kaya knew she should abandon them, yet she felt a hot surge of anger in her heart. She pulled rage from Lodis as she told him to charge and then yanked herself by spirit door into the midst of her pack with her staff held high.

Suddenly there was a gale of wind behind her and the crackling of thunder. Lightning exploded from the most wounded argus and crackled with white fire into the shredders around it. A vortex of solid air tore past Kaya, lifted a shredder, and sent it hurling through the wall of a nearby house with an explosion of wood and dust. Kaya turned to see the slender form of Krueger the Stormwrath. His body was lit by inner power as a howling wind swirled his black robes. For a moment she forgot her customary resentment as she felt a flood of relief, yet she frowned in annoyance as she sensed him siphoning all the fury from her pack to himself as if to tell her without speaking the words, *all your power is mine if I wish it.*

They dispatched the shredders and checked the bloodied ruins for stragglers. Krueger finally condescended to speak to her. "You fight well," he allowed, "but you were distracted from the main tendril. Follow me."

"Where is Baldur?" She asked.

A strange grimace touched Krueger's lips and his expression became blank. "He is being… initiated into the mysteries. We won't require him for this."

Another time Kaya might have made some quip, but the memory of Krueger arriving in time to save her pack was still fresh. For once prudence tempered her tongue, and she followed in silence with her pack of argus fanning out protectively to either side.

An Unending Cycle

Autumn 606 AR, Omnipotent Lortus of the Wyrmwall, Watcher of Blighterghast

Some believe we exist to sow chaos and reap destruction, but this is not true. We all know the power of nature's fury and the strength of storm and flood. It is not our goal to unleash these powers blindly upon the world to the detriment of the natural order. We are the conscious and enlightened extensions of nature on the face of Caen. We do not serve this power; we bend it to *our* will.

To understand our Circle, one must grasp the nature of Orboros. Just as a man may have several titles representing his role, it is even truer of those beings recognized as gods. Names have power, and each title given to a god describes one aspect of its nature while its true name encompasses its entire essence. Orboros is not a god but something greater. Orboros and Dhunia share a special onus as the primal fonts of creation, and their essence is tied inextricably into the world. We of the Circle do not deny the existence of the Devourer Wurm, but this title embodies only a single aspect of Orboros. The Devourer Wurm is the ravenous hunger, the conscious awareness of Orboros, and the embodiment of His will.

There is an ancient and unending rivalry between the Devourer and Menoth, the creator of mankind. Since the dawn of time the Devourer has embodied the wild and ravenous forces of nature while Menoth represents a civilizing and organizing force carving pockets of order from the wilds. Man arose from Menoth's shadow to conduct this work, instinctively sheltering together around the warmth of fire, building lasting monuments, and fighting off the beasts that would eat his flesh. In time Menoth retreated to Urcaen to build the city that would protect the souls devoted to Him. The Devourer chased after, and its consciousness in the living world faded. Priests of the Devourer commune with the God of Feasts, call on His power across that divide, and give Him offerings and services. They have promised their souls to the Beast of All Shapes.

Those who devote themselves fully to the Devourer Wurm do not realize Orboros is still here, on Caen, inextricably bound into the living world. While the will of Orboros is in Urcaen battling Menoth as the Devourer, His essence is tied into and pervades our world. Menoth can never win in His battle as long as the Devourer replenishes Himself from the wellspring of power on Caen. Orboros has no need for the souls of worshipers for His power. He only requires the untamed wilderness: flowing rivers, storm clouds, and the raging ocean. Only our Circle can access this strength unfettered.

Dhunians speak of the ravaging of their goddess by the Wurm as if this were a single act of procreation at the dawn of time. It is ongoing: every season, every storm, and each drop of rain link Orboros to Dhunia. The seed of Orboros gives rise to every predator, and His shifting bones sunk deep into the rocks and mountains of the world cause the ripples of earthquakes. Orboros' pumping heart-blood powers the ocean tide like the flooding of a river swollen by rain. His tongue is lightning and fire, and His breath is the hurricane wind. This is not allegory but literal truth.

Though the majority of humanity is obsessed with taming the wild, building walls, and planting fields, there have been those born with an innate connection to the untamable chaos since the earliest times. We of the Circle were born touched by Orboros, and we draw strength from the font of creation. When this power awakens in us in childhood it is mistaken for madness or even possession. We call it the *wilding* when a child hears voices on the wind or perceives lines of power thrumming below the soil and along rivers.

Our progenitors founded our fellowship after the fall of the Molgur tribes and the rise of the Menite priest-kings. Golivant and Khardovic embodied a drastic shift in the nature of humanity, one which we knew would constrict and strangle the natural power of the world. Ultimately the efforts of our order are a mirror of the battles in Urcaen between the Devourer and Menoth. By watching the rise of the new cities of man, we witnessed the stifling of natural forces that are the lifeblood of Orboros. Each city built on a crucial natural nexus weakens Orboros and makes the Devourer's battles in Urcaen more difficult.

We swore pacts in those ancient days to work against the rise of these cities. This has sometimes required culling populations, breaking dams, toppling walls, and burning fields all in the name of Orboros. It is a tightrope we walk, for our power relies on the strength of Orboros but also on His distraction. If the Devourer ever won His war against His rival, the Wurm would return in full force from Urcaen to topple mountains with earthquakes, set loose tsunamis, and erase humanity from the face of Caen. Far better for us to be the ones to pick and choose nature's wrath. It is a delicate balance, but increasingly the works of man have advanced and left our course clear.

To keep the Devourer in Urcaen, we must ensure that Menoth's focus stays on the afterlife, so He does not watch Caen. The more attention paid to this world by the patron of man, the greater the chance the Devourer will arouse Himself here. By working as we do and following our old pacts, we hope to keep Orboros strong in His battles against Menoth, freeing up His energy and by consequence strengthening our own power over the wilds.

Ultimately this is a struggle we are doomed to fail. We are few against the teeming masses. Eventually the works of mankind will clog the arteries of Orboros, and the Devourer will return to bring ruin and annihilation. If man's cities ever grow too strong, the Beast will return to obliterate them personally and thereby redouble His strength.

The masses do not understand our struggle, nor would they embrace it if they knew.

The masses do not understand our struggle, nor would they embrace it if they knew. The sons and daughters of Menoth mistakenly believe their gods can protect them.

In the time of the Molgur there was no need for our efforts. Mankind was nomadic and had not taken up the commandments of Menoth. In this age the worship of the Devourer was open and widespread. Remember that priests and cultists of the Wurm are not our peers. Our relationship with Orboros is intimate, not worshipful. Minions of the Devourer have long been our pawns, eager to heed our suggestions. Do not lower yourself to treat them as equals. They can be useful, even powerful allies, but ours must always be the guiding hand.

Our membership learned to hide our nature after the breaking of the Molgur, and we began to implement subtle plans. We brought the power of nature by flood and earthquake to slow the spread of civilization. It was by our efforts that neither Golivant's empire nor Khardovic's avoided their deaths, but the roots of what would become Caspia sunk too deep for us to pull that tooth loose. The City of Walls continues to vex our fellowship, immune to all efforts to bring it to ruin.

Despite the spread of Menoth's word, the Thousand Cities era was good for us. Mankind remained fractured and divided as countless petty fiefdoms and city-states vied for dominance, and we did everything in our power to maintain this situation. Where necessary we destroyed cities without repercussions. Under the city of Ceryl, hidden below mud and tons of earth, rest the ruins of a dozen townships destroyed by our hand. Other ruins spotted the landscape, blamed on freak floods, terrible fire, earthquake, or plague—all our work.

The first major setback in our endless war was the rise of the Khardic Empire. This did not happen as the result of one incident, but rather it stemmed from a long process of calcification whereby tribes banded together under strong lords. We could not prevent this, only slow the process. Some of our order used murder and assassination, but such crude attacks rarely succeed, often backfire, and create martyrs. Disease has been a more effective tool in some times and places as we have sowed plague to create chaos and destroy large populations. Removing individual leaders rarely helps; they arise by factors beyond their ken. When we remove one, another rises in his place.

There were other forces at play with the northern empire. Amid the tedious struggles of the Kossite, Skirov, and Khardic tribes, a strange figure arose to confound even the most learned of our fellowship. The immortal Zevanna Agha, sometimes called the Old Witch of Khador, is a power who, acting alone, has sometimes thwarted the plans of our entire order. She protects the northern tribes and their lands for her own reasons; her agenda is indiscernible to us. At one time she walked in our midst, for her power seemed similar to the *wilding*, yet ultimately she betrayed our Circle and used our lore against us. Her ability to draw on the vitality of the land is near to ours, yet she also draws on the vast strength of the people themselves. All attempts to unravel her power or even understand it have failed.

We have clashed with her many times in our effort to weaken the Khardic Empire and more recently to thwart the Khadorans who inherited their legacy, but she has vexed our efforts. Her crows leave nothing but the bones of those who try to tear her down, so our best tactics against her have involved misdirection and avoidance of direct engagement. Recent events have forced us to send our order into the north to fight the blighted threat. I know she will confront us soon enough. My hope is to convince her that our purposes on this matter are not at odds, for the rise of the blighted has put her people at risk as well.

On the subject of the blighted, let me speak of the arrival of Lord Toruk to the Scharde Islands and our vigil on the dragons. Even

before His exodus from the mainland, we watched His movements and those of His progeny. Our agents observed as Toruk destroyed Gaulvang and consumed his athanc in 1387 BR, and an omnipotent witnessed first hand the struggle between Toruk and His progeny that rent the skies with fire and left a blizzard of caustic ash to flutter to the earth. Dragons fascinate our order since their destructive power approaches that of the Devourer yet arises from some wholly tainted and unnatural source.

It is not uncommon for the ignorant to link dragons to the Wurm, but dragons are a perverse mockery of true life entirely outside the natural order. They share no commonality with any living thing that walks and spawns on Caen nor any part of the cycle shared by Orboros and Dhunia. Where they walk, the blight follows. Blight is anathema to our power, sapping our sacred connection to Orboros and interfering with our mastery of the elements. Since the rise of Toruk's island empire, we have come to believe dragons represent a larger and more imminent threat than the civilizations of mankind.

The Scharde Islands were once a bastion for our order. Many druids found the western islands amenable to their designs, laced with latent power and wild species well suited to beast mastery. We established strong ties on several islands, encouraged blood magic, and fostered increased *wilding* among the scattered descendents of the Molgur. Our plans were unraveled in the presence of Toruk's blight.

The Circle suffered one of its greatest betrayals when the mightiest druid of the Scharde Islands became enamored with Toruk's unholy majesty. We do not speak this druid's name, for he violated all we hold sacrosanct when he offered himself to Toruk. We must always be wary of the seductive call of these creatures. Serving the dragons is an utter betrayal of all we have sworn to fight. Toruk and other dragons have found it amusing to pervert others of the *wilding*, including the Satyxis reaver-witches. Their magic is not druidic, but it bears a similarity drawn from our influence in ancient days and shares the life power found in blood.

The Orgoth understood this power of blood and fought to capture our loci of nature power, our stone rings and sacred mounds, particularly those linked to rituals of sacrifice. However, their techniques were not of clean rites linked to predation and natural consumption like those among our discipline. Instead the Orgoth twisted this power with death-magic to imprison and consume souls. One of the most powerful examples was an ancient site of sacrifice named Garrodh, a site we had recovered in centuries past from the kingdom of Morrdh. Morrdh's black altars rest below our stones there, but now there sits an enormous blackened Orgoth temple. It is a place where the barrier between Caen and Urcaen was thin and the strength of Orboros flowed like a torrent. The Orgoth captured this sacred place from us and corrupted its energies, but in the end of the rebellion we managed to sink it into the earth to shield its malignant energies. Recently the lich who was the unnamed druid of the Scharde Islands who betrayed us long ago unearthed this site for his own unholy rites. This place is too powerful for the minions of dragons. We may need to sink it again far enough below the earth it can never be recovered.

We had victories against the Orgoth particularly through the disease called Rip Lung—a gift of Orboros. It decimated the Orgoth and led to their fall. No one would believe a simple ailment could topple an empire, but the plague spread back to the Orgoth homeland and reinforcement ships stopped arriving. It is true that many Immorese also died of this disease, but we can never place too much weight on individual lives. Were every major city in western Immoren to fall to plague and flood, there would still be too many humans leeching life from the body of Orboros.

Recovering from the blows dealt by the Orgoth has been a gradual process over the last four centuries. Our ability to recuperate from disasters is hindered by the slow rate at which the *wilding* manifests. In recent decades we have seen a sudden upswing of such births, and I attribute them to a natural response to the dangerous fact that Menoth has turned His attention back to Caen. The presence of the Menite Harbinger is a dangerous portent, and it indicates a need to renew battle against the Menites.

The foremost imperative of our order is to locate and retrieve humans born with the *wilding* before their potential is ruined. Through our awareness of certain portents, we have learned how to predict the manifestation of our brethren accurately. A mentor is sent to recover them and bring them into their new life, and it has engendered wild stories. We are called the corruptors of youth, and some believe we sacrifice the young, but by our guidance these children learn to control primal energy and put their past behind them.

Though our connection to Orboros is innate, mastery is a lifelong pursuit. We afford great freedom to our number once they are inculcated in the basic mysteries and come to grips with the nature of their calling. Each wilder must find his own way, learn to control what he can grasp, and become a power unto himself.

In time we renew those old bonds. Wilders become warders trusted with more difficult tasks. As a druid's power grows, the Circle will call on him and grant him greater responsibility. We organize in small groups with considerable secrecy to preserve our fellowship in dark times. The Menites are eager for our deaths, and we must not reveal our nature to those who would undo our work.

Many druids spend their entire lives as warders, and there is no shame in this. They are the backbone of our Circle. Those few who can approach mastery and prove capable by trial become overseers granted with even greater responsibility. These proven druids inherit territories to patrol and sacred sites to protect and are sent to coordinate plans abroad. A chosen few are initiated into the deepest mysteries and elevated to potent. Potents watch vast regions, are trusted with executing plans sometimes requiring years to unfold, and are given the careful oversight of dozens of subordinates as well as minions outside the order.

The potents maintain the relationships with groups who owe us favors or disparate Devourer worshiping cabals eager to fight in our wars and thereby earn bloody glory. Each of these groups is an asset carefully nurtured and expended only as required. While our numbers and strength are far greater than most city people could imagine, they are not infinite. At the head of the order stand the omnipotents, always three in number, who lead and know the inner secrets and the deepest enigmas of Orboros.

Each druid works to master one of the great core aspects of Orboros. Earth shapers learn the strength in stone and trees—the bones, sinews and blood of Orboros—and how to breathe life into the inanimate. Elemental constructs are not just the guardians of our places of power; they are much more. They serve as an extension of the strength of Orboros and fight in our stead wherever our battles take us. The power of earth and stone is one of the slowest powers to master, but it is also vital to our strength. Noted masters of this path can provoke earthquakes and cause sections of cities to be swallowed whole. Some druids choose instead to shape storm, wind, and flood—the breath and fangs of Orboros. They invoke the lightning tongue of the serpent to smite enemies with the wildest power of nature's wrath, and a master of storm can awaken Orboros on Caen to cause unequalled devastation. Another of the great paths is the transformative power of beasts; the predators stalking the wilderness serve as fangs, claws, eyes, and ears of Orboros. By our connection to these beasts we can draw supernatural strength into our limbs, transform into other forms, and defeat entire armies by summoning packs drawn to the call of the wild.

No aspect of Orboros is inherently superior to another, and in time we must learn them all. If you aspire to omnipotent, you will be expected to master every weapon at our disposal. However, even as we hone our ability, we must remember that this power has a purpose. We cannot be reluctant to act. Our habit in the past has been to wait until the right convergence of the seasons, conjunction of the stars, or gathered reinforcements. Ahead is a time of crisis. The era of scheming is over.

I fear the ultimate battle is upon us. Even now Orboros stirs, and we must draw on that power openly to bring every weapon to bear against our enemies. Warfare consumes the kingdoms, and this is the time to strike—while the nations are distracted and locked in mortal toil. We are not the only ones sensing this opportune time to act. Invaders from the east have arrived from the Marches and seek to impose their own empire. They are the least of our concerns.

No current difficulty can compare to what may be the direst event in recent history: the awakening of Everblight. This dragon is capable of bold strides and unexpected imagination unlike the rest of its kind. The dragon has demonstrated an ability to spread its influence and blight in a fashion never before witnessed in Toruk's spawn, for the blight itself seems to spread like a virulent disease not rooted in the dragon's body. It may be that by refusing to take flesh, Everblight has managed to exceed the potential of any of his siblings.

Minions of the dragon have annihilated the homelands of the Nyss in northern Khador. Many of the Nyss—perhaps the majority—have been corrupted and brought into willing service of the dragon. Their bodies are strangely twisted and changed in a more deliberate fashion than we have ever seen before. It is as though Everblight has taken their forms and found ways to "improve" on the natural, at least according to his narrow purpose: sowing death and destruction. Our highest priority and the focus of all our assets must be Everblight's immediate destruction, yet even as we fight this battle we must expend our resources wisely. Let others take the fall; the lives of our peers are a precious commodity.

Our fellowship has been too slow to react to events and not subtle enough in recent machinations. Pride has blinded us. We became too self-assured in our mastery of primitive species, and we have had great success in influencing disenfranchised species in the wilds such as the Dhunians. Until just recently we counted the trollkin among our allies, and a most potent ally they might have been. We had worked over many generations of slow effort to gain their trust, yet by a grave miscalculation we have undone those plans and earned ourselves an enemy instead of what could have been our greatest weapon. This happened when my predecessor Ergonus underestimated the nature of a chieftain of the Thornwood named Madrak Ironhide who had begun to unite his people. Ergonus attempted to enlist his help directly in the fight against Everblight, but we were too absorbed in our own struggle to recognize the Thornwood trollkin were in the midst of their own battles.

> **Even now Orboros stirs, and we must draw on that power openly to bring every weapon to bear against our enemies.**

Rather than finding another way to convince him, or even loaning aid to his people, Ergonus decided to have Ironhide killed. As I said before, such simple assassinations invariably backfire. Not only is Madrak Ironhide still alive, but trying to slay him also earned us the wrath of all trollkin from the Scarsfell Forest to the Gnarls. Worse, Omnipotent Ergonus was slain at a time when we could have used his strength. This is not how I had hoped to assume the mantle of leadership. The trollkin are our bitter enemies now. They stand as a barrier to our progress and have sought to undermine our strength by attacking our territories. We have no choice but to quash them lest they interfere with the timing of crucial events. We must remember always the larger enemy and our greater purpose.

In the days to come we will call on your strength and loyalty. Our numbers are few, but we channel the primal forces of nature as we enter a battle that may destroy us. This is the end of days. Let us show our enemies what it means to invoke the wrath of the masters of Orboros.

Kaya the Wildborne
Circle Orboros Warlock Character

Kaya and her pack are one. The spirit of the Wurm fills her when she stalks the forest.

—Kund, Huntsman of the Wolves of Orboros

Kaya has plunged herself into the minds of beasts with an abandon unequalled among her peers. She is only complete when she fights alongside her pack and enters the flow of battle as a true predator. While riding this tide she is a ruthless and savage creature who tirelessly stalks her prey day or night. Joined with her pack, Kaya casts humanity aside to embrace her primal essence. When she enters this battle trance there is no future and no past, only the infinite present and the sweet promise of blood.

Her willingness to submerge so deeply into the consciousness of her pack worries her mentor Baldur the Stonecleaver, yet it seems inseparable from her nature. Older druids have tried to teach her patience, but she chafes at their lack of imagination and inability to see her strengths. For Kaya more than any druid in recent memory, the *wilding* was no struggle but an awakening of her true self. She throws herself into battles with ardent courage without worrying about her own preservation. This irrepressible spirit has led to victory after victory and provided unexpected windfalls to the Circle Orboros.

Kaya no longer remembers her life before the Circle, but she was born in eastern Ord within sight of the dark Thornwood Forest. She felt the *wilding* as an infant and disturbed her parents in the middle of the night on Calder's full moon by shrieking out her window. Even more alarming were the answering howls of wolves. Perhaps it was with relief that they handed their peculiar daughter to the hulking blackclad stranger who came knocking on their door, and Baldur has been her mentor and father ever since. Though her path has taken her away from Baldur's instruction, she always returns for advice, and he remains the only ranking druid she trusts implicitly. He alone has never dismissed her for her youth or uttered snide insults disguised as instruction.

On several occasions Kaya has stormed out of meetings with superior druids and shown flagrant insubordination, for she rarely agrees with many of the decisions made by Circle leaders and believes they are needlessly manipulative. She has no ability to govern her tongue, and she has spoken grave insults to many of her peers without even knowing she has caused

offense. It may come as a result of so much time spent in the minds of beasts who do not dissemble, lie, or understand tact, and she has no idea how often Baldur has had to intervene to prevent punitive measures from falling on her head due to these outbursts. Recently Baldur promoted her to overseer despite the protests of several of his peers. Kaya is aware of the criticism he has endured on her behalf and has tried to curb her temper, but she finds it difficult to admit mistakes or apologize. She prefers to let her actions speak for her as she strikes even harder against the enemies of the Circle, and her recent effectiveness in numerous engagements against Everblight's Legion has won her some latitude.

Kaya does not participate in the schemes and plots for which the druids are famed, for she finds the motivations of beasts to be much simpler. They require only food, shelter, and a strong voice of leadership. She wishes people were similarly transparent, and she is frustrated when they are not. Though capable of sacrificing them if the need is great, Kaya has a tight bond with her beasts and is able to inspire in them remarkable efforts. Subsequently, their loyalty to her is genuine. With piercing eyes that contain the cold hard stare of a battlefield veteran twice her age, she conveys with the merest glance that she has experienced more than her share of horrors and intends to do her part to end them.

SPECIAL RULES

Feat: Wild Mastery - The *wilding* removes a druid from the rest of humanity, opens a primeval conduit to forgotten powers, and enables communion with beasts. Kaya the Wildborne endured a *wilding* so intense it has left her with unrivaled mastery of her feral warbeasts. She can unleash a surge of rage in any nearby warbeast and siphon this ferocity to lend the bestial strength to her own power.

Kaya may place up to three fury points on each friendly Circle warbeast in her control area. She may then leach up to her current FURY stat from any friendly Circle warbeasts in her control area.

KAYA

Calm - Friendly Circle warbeasts in Kaya's control area make threshold checks at +1 THR.

Pack Hunters - While in the Kaya's control area, each friendly Circle warbeast gains a +1 cumulative bonus to its melee attack and melee damage rolls for each other friendly Circle warbeast in her control area that has made a successful melee attack against the same enemy model this turn.

KAYA					CMD 8
SPD	STR	MAT	RAT	DEF	ARM
6	5	6	4	16	13

SPLINTER		
SPECIAL	POW	P+S
Multi	6	11

FURY	6
DAMAGE	16
FIELD ALLOWANCE	C
VICTORY POINTS	5
POINT COST	59
BASE SIZE	SMALL

Pathfinder - Kaya ignores movement penalties from rough terrain and obstacles. Kaya may charge across rough terrain.

SPLINTER

Critical Knockdown - On a critical hit, target model is knocked down.

Reach - 2" melee range.

SPELL	COST	RNG	AOE	POW	UP	OFF
Cloak Of Mists	2	6	-	-	X	

Target friendly Circle model/unit gains Stealth. Attacks against a model with Stealth from greater than 5" away automatically miss. If a model with Stealth is greater than 5" away from an attacker, it does not count as an intervening model. Cloak of Mists immediately expires if an affected model runs or makes an attack.

SPELL	COST	RNG	AOE	POW	UP	OFF
Rager	2	6	-	-		X

Target friendly Circle warbeast may make a power attack and then attack with each of its melee attacks during its activation this turn without being forced. The warbeast may be forced to make additional attacks. An affected warbeast cannot charge and make power attacks during the same activation.

SPELL	COST	RNG	AOE	POW	UP	OFF
Spirit Door	3	CTRL	-	-		

Spirit Door may target Kaya or a friendly Circle warbeast in her control area regardless of LOS. If Spirit Door targets Kaya, immediately place her within 2" of a friendly Circle warbeast in her control area at the time the spell is cast. If the spell was cast on a warbeast, immediately place the model within 2" of Kaya. There must be room for the moved model's base in the new location. A model affected by Spirit Door cannot be targeted by free strikes during this movement. A model cannot move after being targeted by Spirit Door this turn. Spirit Door may be cast once per turn.

SPELL	COST	RNG	AOE	POW	UP	OFF
Spirit Fang	2	10	-	11		X

Target model damaged by Spirit Fang suffers –2 SPD and DEF for one round.

Baldur the Stonecleaver

CIRCLE ORBOROS WARLOCK CHARACTER

I eagerly endorse Baldur's elevation to potent. He is the Rock of Orboros. Let him be the force that crushes the plague-blight.

—Omnipotent Dahlekov

A bastion of strength and resolve noted for his steadfast loyalty, Baldur Stonecleaver is described by other druidic leaders as the Rock of Orboros. Some of his peers jest that he has spent too long communing with mountains, for he is calm and serene compared to his more passionate peers. In battle, however, he becomes a different man. When his temper is finally aroused, he is an unstoppable juggernaut made flesh.

Baldur shrugs off questions about his past by joking he was born in a bear cave near Boarsgate, but there is a Khardic flavor to his features and hulking frame. He carries his mass with deceptive ease, and strength flows into him from the earth. When he unlimbers his massive stone sword, it sings through the air in his fingers and shatters anything it encounters. No other man has ever even been able to lift this blade let alone wield it in battle. Baldur asserts this ability has nothing to do with strength of limb and that the sword is as much a part of him as his arms.

He has overseen numerous territories in his tenure among the Circle and is older than he looks. Baldur also has friends in unusual places; he has shared lore with dwarven stonemasons and has decades ago conducted terse exchanges with the guardians of Ios. Caring nothing for the politics of man, Baldur reserves his philosophy to the shaping of stone. His recent promotion to potent continues his slow and gradual rise through the ranks, and he has been trusted with the deeper mysteries of his order.

The Stonecleaver is a paragon of the earth-shaping path of druidic magic; he has a deep understanding of stone, earth, and the forest. He mastered the shaping of all forms of woldwardens and their ilk, and he is capable of infusing primal

power into the scored runes covering each piece of stone. His thick fingers possess the skill and artistry of a sculptor, but his masterpieces spring to life and stride onto the battlefield to tear walls and beasts asunder. Baldur's magic allows forests to spring to life even in blighted places, and with these trees he can cross enormous distances to flank his enemies, attack from unexpected directions, and cleave them in two with his unstoppable sword.

The menace of Everblight's Legion weighs heavily on Baldur's mind even with his proven ability and new authority. Their unnatural blight warps all it touches and leeches away vital energies essential to druidic power. Since the rise of this threat, he has had difficulty sleeping more than a few hours at a time. He wakes each morning before sunrise either to work on a warden or muster for battle on the front line. He has spent considerable time patrolling the wilds of northern Khador, slicing into the forward tendrils of the encroaching Legion.

Baldur is also concerned with the disappointing rift with the trollkin. In better days he was a welcome guest among kriels of the Thornwood and the Scarsfell, but now they are bitter foes. The pragmatic Stonecleaver knows they cannot leave their flanks vulnerable and must protect centers of power from troll retaliatory strikes. Somehow despite all dire omens, Baldur remains at heart optimistic about the future. He stands as a beacon of energy and vitality among the doomsayers of his fellowship and insists no fight is lost until all will is lost.

SPECIAL RULES

Feat: Broken Earth - For Baldur earth and stone are living things—the skin and bones of Orboros. Boulders spring from the ground, crevices pull apart, and rumbling earth makes every footstep perilous. No enemy can take a single step in his direction when the earth moves to intercede.

Enemy models cannot move into Baldur's control area during their controller's turn. During their controller's turn, enemy models currently in Baldur's control area cannot end their movement closer to Baldur than they started. Broken Earth lasts for one round.

BALDUR

Elemental Mastery - Friendly Elemental Constructs in Baldur's control area may charge or perform power attacks without being forced. Baldur may heal Elemental Constructs.

Forest Walker - While completely within a forest, Baldur may forfeit his movement to use Forest Walker. Remove Baldur from the forest and place him in a new location completely within a forest. Baldur's new location must have been completely within his control area prior to forfeiting his movement. There must be room for Baldur's base in the new location. Baldur cannot be targeted by free strikes while forest walking.

Pathfinder - Baldur ignores movement penalties from rough terrain and obstacles. Baldur may charge across rough terrain.

TRITUS

Weight of Stone - Models damaged by Tritus suffer –3 DEF, and their base SPD is reduced to 1 for one round.

BALDUR				CMD 8	
SPD	STR	MAT	RAT	DEF	ARM
5	7	7	4	14	16

	TRITUS		
	SPECIAL	POW	P+S
Weight		7	14

FURY	6
DAMAGE	17
FIELD ALLOWANCE	C
VICTORY POINTS	5
POINT COST	65
BASE SIZE	SMALL

SPELL	COST	RNG	AOE	POW	UP	OFF
EARTH'S BLESSING	2	6	-	-		X

Target friendly Circle model/unit cannot be knocked down and gains Pathfinder. Models with Pathfinder ignore movement penalties from rough terrain and obstacles. Models with Pathfinder may charge, slam, and trample across rough terrain.

SPELL	COST	RNG	AOE	POW	UP	OFF
EARTH SPIKES	3	10	3	13		X

When making Earth Spike attacks, ignore cover and elevation. On a critical hit, models in the AOE are knocked down.

SPELL	COST	RNG	AOE	POW	UP	OFF
RAPID GROWTH	2	CTRL	5	-		X

Place a 5" AOE template anywhere completely within Baldur's control area but not touching a model's base, an obstacle, or an obstruction. This template is a forest that stays on the table as long as upkeep is paid.

SPELL	COST	RNG	AOE	POW	UP	OFF
STONE SKIN	2	6	-	-		X

Target friendly Circle model/unit gains +2 STR and ARM but suffers -1 SPD and DEF.

Krueger the Stormwrath

CIRCLE ORBOROS WARLOCK CHARACTER

To understand Krueger you must think of him not as a man but as a force of nature. He is the raging hurricane, the wild tornado obliterating anything in its path and leaving others to pick up the pieces.

—Omnipotent Lortus of the Wyrmwall Mountains, Watcher of Blighterghast

Krueger earned his namesake after a challenge made by one of his pupils who doubted the stories of druids culling the populations of man throughout history. Krueger went atop the highest of the Watcher Peaks, called down storm and thunder, and unleashed a deluge so powerful it raised the waters of Lake Rimmocksdale and did lasting damage to the city of Orven. His pupil clung to a tree in horror as the lightning danced around Krueger's mad face, and the Stormwrath laughed into the howling winds. His student never doubted his stories again.

Universally feared and respected—but not liked—within the Circle hierarchy, Krueger counts no man as friend and no druid his equal. He was the only witness to the death of Omnipotent Ergonus, and Krueger seethes at the decision to have Lortus elevated to replace him. Convinced that being passed up for promotion was a rebuke for surviving the fight that took Ergonus' life, Krueger longs to reach the pinnacle of authority so he can bring the druids back to the right path. They have been too soft and accommodating and must return to the old days of plague and fire.

Born in a small village north of Sul, Krueger is one of the rare few to have survived a *wilding* in the Protectorate of Menoth. His father was a priest of Menoth, and when Krueger began behaving strangely, this priest recognized the corruption of the Wurm. Proclaiming him a spawn of the Devourer, Krueger's father tied his first born to a stake and prepared to burn him alive. Druids of the Circle intervened, descended on the village with bloody efficiency, and slayed any who interfered. After rescuing the boy the druids took him to a hidden dwelling near the ruins of Acrennia. It was the home of one of the harshest masters of the Circle renowned for teaching the power of desert and ocean by cruel example. He once stripped Krueger and abandoned him in the desert hills east of Acrennia where he had to return on his own strength and cunning.

Krueger delights in bringing suffering to the hive masses of city dwellers whom he considers maggots on the face of Caen. He would shatter the walls of Sul and Caspia and flood the inhabitants of both cities out into the Gulf to drown. He has a particular scorn for Menites and hopes to wipe all traces of the despicable religion from the face of Caen. Striking against the outer patrols of the Protectorate, he has baptized his spear in the blood of Menites. By his arts this great weapon contains the tongue of the Wurm, an endless lightning storm captive in the heart of its wooden shaft.

More than his peers, Krueger revels in the Devourer and believes the distinction between this title and Orboros is meaningless. Krueger has attended the savage rites of the Tharn and other berserker tribes on the fringes of humanity, offering human sacrifices on druid stones and standing awash in blood to gnaw on the hearts of the slain. Krueger fully embraces the destructive energies he has learned to unleash.

Omnipotent Ergonus was the only druid Krueger considered his superior, and it shook him deeply when the trollkin killed this legend. This has prompted a deep and unshakable hatred for trollkin, and Krueger has sworn to crush them and spill their blood on a ring of stones to feed the Wurm. The Stormwrath rides a constant wave of barely restrained fury visible to any brave enough to look into his eyes. His deep and unquenchable rage will only be satisfied when every institution of civilized man lies broken, burned, and scattered at his feet.

SPECIAL RULES

Feat: Storm Ravager - This is the Stormwrath. All despair when the sky shouts its verdict of thunderous doom and death by lightning's spear.

Place three 3" AOEs anywhere completely within Krueger's control area. Krueger may make a magic attack against each enemy model in one or more of the AOEs, ignoring Camouflage, concealmen, cover, elevation, Invisibiity, LOS, screening, and Stealth. Models hits suffer a boostable POW 10 damage roll. During each of his Maintenance Phases, Krueger's controller removes one of the Storm Ravager AOEs from the table. He may then move the remaining AOEs in his control area up to 6". AOEs must end this movement completely within Krueger's control area. Enemy models touched by one or more moving AOEs suffer an unboostable POW 10 damage roll after all the AOEs have moved. An enemy model moving into or ending its activation in one or more Storm Ravager AOEs suffers an unboostable POW 10 damage roll. An enemy warbeast in one or more AOEs during its controller's Maintenance Phase must pass a threshold check or frenzy.

KRUEGER					CMD 8
SPD	STR	MAT	RAT	DEF	ARM
6	5	5	6	15	14

LIGHTNING			
RNG	ROF	AOE	POW
10	1	—	13

LIGHTNING SPEAR		
SPECIAL	POW	P+S
Multi	7	12

FURY	7
DAMAGE	16
FIELD ALLOWANCE	C
VICTORY POINTS	5
POINT COST	61
BASE SIZE	SMALL

KRUEGER

Pathfinder - Krueger ignores movement penalties from rough terrain and obstacles. Krueger may charge across rough terrain.

LIGHTNING SPEAR

Reach - 2" melee range.

Sustained Attack – Once Krueger hits a target with the Lightning Spear, additional attacks with it against the same target this turn automatically hit. No additional attack rolls are necessary.

SPELL	COST	RNG	AOE	POW	UP	OFF
FORKED LIGHTNING	3	10	-	12		X

Lightning arcs from target model to d3 additional models. The lightning arcs and automatically hits the nearest enemy model within 4" of the last model hit, but it cannot strike the same model more than once. Each additional model hit suffers a POW 12 damage roll.

LIGHTNING TENDRILS	2	6	-			X

Increase the range of target model/unit's melee weapons by 2".

SKY BORNE	2	SELF	-	-		

Krueger gains +2 DEF and +2" of movement and ignores movement penalties from rough terrain and obstacles. Krueger may move through other models if he has enough movement to move completely past the model's base. Krueger may charge across rough terrain, over obstacles, or through other models. Krueger cannot be targeted by free strikes. Sky Borne lasts for one round.

TORNADO	4	10	-	13		X

Target model hit by Tornado is thrown d6" directly away from the spell's point of origin and suffers a POW 13 damage roll. Do not make a deviation roll when determining the thrown model's point of impact. If the thrown model collides with another model with a smaller or equal-sized base, that model suffers a POW 13 collateral damage roll.

WIND STORM	3	SELF	CTRL	-		

While in Krueger's control area this round, friendly models gain +2 ARM and DEF vs. ranged attacks. Cloud effects within Krueger's control area expire when Wind Storm is cast.

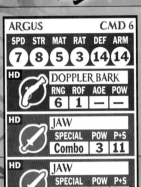

Argus

CIRCLE ORBOROS LIGHT WARBEAST

ARGUS				CMD 6	
SPD	STR	MAT	RAT	DEF	ARM
7	8	5	3	14	14

HD	DOPPLER BARK			
	RNG	ROF	AOE	POW
	6	1	—	—

HD	JAW		
	SPECIAL	POW	P+S
	Combo	3	11

HD	JAW		
	SPECIAL	POW	P+S
	Combo	3	11

FURY	3
THRESHOLD	9
FIELD ALLOWANCE	U
VICTORY POINTS	2
POINT COST	54
BASE SIZE	MEDIUM

Argus

Circular Vision - The Argus has no back arc, and its front arc extends 360°.

Doppler Bark

Paralysis - Doppler Bark attacks do no damage. A model hit by Doppler Bark suffers Paralysis. A model suffering Paralysis must forfeit either its movement or action during its next activation.

Jaws

Combo Bite (★Attack) - The Argus' heads bite a target simultaneously for a devastating attack. It may make normal Jaw attacks separately, or it may make a special attack to bite with both Jaws at the same time. Make one attack roll for the Combo Bite. Add the Argus' STR once and the POW of both Jaws to the damage roll.

I require a living specimen. I have several experiments in mind. First I will expose their larynxes, and second I will open their skulls to test if their brains are actually independent.

—Lord Tyrant Hexaris of the Skorne Empire

These huge and ferocious two-headed canines are beasts of thick muscle, solid bone, and sharp teeth. The druids have spent centuries taming, breeding, and training them for battle and employ the hounds as guardians. The breed used by the Circle is far larger and more vicious than the breed tamed with some difficulty in northern Khador. In recent battles the argus have been increasingly fielded to harass enemies with their crippling bone-rending bite. They pack a surprising punch in battle for their size, but they are doubly valued for the power of their paralyzing bark. It is capable of rendering even the mightiest warbeast powerless, and it allows the druids to strike when and where they choose.

The argus are virtually impossible to surprise. Each head constantly scans the surroundings, and its eyes are particularly sensitive to the slightest movement. Warlocks can call on the fast reflexes of an argus to spring instantly on any who harm their pack. This pack instinct is irrepressible; after bonding as pups they will eagerly sacrifice their lives to protect their master. Famed for endurance, the argus can run at a rapid pace

ANIMUS	COST	RNG	AOE	POW	UP	OFF
REFLEX	3	SELF	-	-		

WHEN AN ENEMY ATTACK DESTROYS OR REMOVES FROM PLAY ONE OR MORE FRIENDLY CIRCLE MODELS WITHIN 3" OF THE MODEL USING THIS ANIMUS, IT MAY IMMEDIATELY MOVE UP TO ITS CURRENT SPD IN INCHES AND MAKE ONE MELEE ATTACK, AFTER WHICH THIS ANIMUS EXPIRES. REFLEX LASTS FOR ONE ROUND.

for an extended period of time. The combination of endurance and their almost supernaturally keen senses make them ideal hunters, and the druids use them to track prey—two footed or otherwise. Argus are surprisingly intelligent, and druids who know their argus well can, after some effort, train them to understand complex orders.

In addition to a crippling combined bite, the argus has developed a signature sonic attack able to funnel its bark into an ear-shattering and painful punch of sound. Those struck by the impact of this solid wave find themselves disoriented, dazed, and unable to do more than shake off the pain. Argus hunting together as a pack will coordinate with one Argus paralyzing a foe with its bark while the others leap in for the kill.

ANIMUS	COST	RNG	AOE	POW	UP	OFF
VIGILANCE	2	6	-	-		

TARGET FRIENDLY CIRCLE MODEL MAY MOVE UP TO 2" AND MAKE A MELEE ATTACK AGAINST AN ENEMY MODEL THAT MOVES AND ENDS ITS MOVEMENT WITHIN 2" OF THE TARGET MODEL AFTER WHICH THIS ANIMUS EXPIRES. RESOLVE THIS MELEE ATTACK IMMEDIATELY AFTER MOVEMENT ENDS. THE TARGET MODEL MAY MAKE ONE ATTACK WITH A SINGLE MELEE WEAPON AND GAINS +2 TO THE ATTACK ROLL. IF THE ATTACK SUCCEEDS, ROLL AN ADDITIONAL DAMAGE DIE. THE ATTACK AND DAMAGE ROLLS CANNOT BE BOOSTED. VIGILANCE LASTS FOR ONE ROUND.

A pair of woldwatchers sent ahead will serve as pillars of protection to cover your advance through the forest. Let them receive the blows meant for you.

—Lortus, the Watcher of Blighterghast

WOLDWATCHER CMD –

SPD	STR	MAT	RAT	DEF	ARM
5	8	5	5	10	17

ELEMENTAL STRIKE			
RNG	ROF	AOE	POW
10	1	—	12

LFT
CLAW		
SPECIAL	POW	P+S
Fertilizer	4	12

RT
CLAW		
SPECIAL	POW	P+S
Fertilizer	4	12

FURY	2
THRESHOLD	–
FIELD ALLOWANCE	U
VICTORY POINTS	2
POINT COST	72
BASE SIZE	MEDIUM

Woldwatchers draw on the strength of rock, soil, tree, and stone and are enlisted to defend sacred groves and screen advancing armies led by the Circle. It is impossible for one to doubt their power after witnessing enemies overcome with a blast of elemental energy that tears bodies asunder and showers blood down on the hungry earth. Those felled by this power fertilize the ground with blood, for each drop is imbued with the raw power of blood sacrifice. From this spray erupts a sudden grove of trees growing up and through the still-twitching body, tearing it apart in a plume of gore.

Rolled up into tight piles of easily overlooked stone, the woldwatchers are often placed to protect key territories in the forest. Triggered by the tread of intruders, they spring to action, show their true form, and call on the power of earth to neutralize interlopers and turn them into fertilizer. Druids following the path of earth can build them from any strong stone and a variety of materials cobbled and lashed together by ropes that have tasted blood. They then inscribe ancient runes into the stones in a particular ritual designed to imbue them with a mirrored imprint of their creator. This animates them with a semblance of life. Many druids prefer these versatile elemental constructs to their larger counterparts, for they are considerably quicker to assemble and can fulfill a variety of roles on the battlefield.

In ancient days the blood of victims was a more integral part of the creation of the wold-watchers, for their ropes were wound from vines watered by the blood of sacrifices. They still draw great power from life essence though, and they are able to cause a short-lived but dramatic explosion in plant growth. From the power imbued in them they have a particularly strong connection to the earth, and by standing still they can become nearly impervious to harm.

Woldwatcher

Advance Deployment - Place the Woldwatcher after normal deployment, up to 12" beyond the established deployment zone.

All Terrain - The Woldwatcher ignores movement penalties from rough terrain and obstacles. The Woldwatcher may charge or slam across rough terrain.

Elemental Construct - The Woldwatcher is not a living model. The Woldwatcher never makes threshold checks, automatically passes command checks, and never frenzies or goes wild. The Woldwatcher cannot run or be healed.

Stone Form (★Action) - The Woldwatcher gains +4 ARM and can only be moved by its controlling player for one round. While affected by Stone Form, the Woldwatcher's base DEF is reduced to 5, and it is automatically hit by melee attacks. A model screened by the Woldwatcher in Stone Form gains an additional +2 DEF. Attacks that ignore screening also ignore this bonus. This bonus is not cumulative with itself. Stone Form lasts for one round or until the Woldwatcher moves.

Elemental Strike & Claws

Fertilizer - If a model is destroyed by Elemental Strike or a Claw attack, center a 3" AOE template on the model and then remove the model from play. The template is a forest that remains on the table for one round.

Gorax

CIRCLE ORBOROS LIGHT WARBEAST

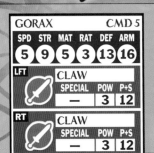

GORAX				CMD 5	
SPD	STR	MAT	RAT	DEF	ARM
5	9	5	3	13	16

LFT	CLAW		
	SPECIAL	POW	P+S
	—	3	12

RT	CLAW		
	SPECIAL	POW	P+S
	—	3	12

FURY	4
THRESHOLD	9
FIELD ALLOWANCE	U
VICTORY POINTS	2
POINT COST	57
BASE SIZE	MEDIUM

Gorax

Pain Response - While all of its aspects are damaged, the Gorax gains +2 to melee damage rolls.

I'd seen one of dem ugly cusses afore, but that 'un was starved an' mangy. This'un was big an' mean as a hungry troll. It grabbed Lars an' used 'is skull to break a tree in two!

—Trollkin warrior

Classified somewhere between beast and man, gorax are hulking primitives with broad and massively muscular torsos that boast extremely long arms ending with oversized claws. Their jaws protrude from ugly faces and are filled with hardened fangs designed for tearing off flesh and sinew for their carnivorous diet. There are few creatures that better embody the primal rage and uncontrollable fury of a warbeast. The most terrible aspect of the gorax is their reaction to pain. They become even more dangerous when injured, and the pain drives them to lash out with fearsome strength.

Gorax are no strangers to fighting at the behest of others. For centuries they have been captured, enslaved, and trained for battle. In the Thousand Cities era, warlords used them as front-line shock troops where they were flung into frenzied melee by the hundreds and often killed by their own masters when their blood lust became too great to control. They appreciate the taste of human flesh and some prefer it above all other fare. Their tendency to attack friend and foe alike quickly diminished their use in the wars of man, but the druids have drawn them forth again to terrorize western Immoren.

Despite their fearsome guise, they are smarter than animals. They have a guttural approximation of speech and can learn to follow instructions. The druids have pulled them from their wilderness lairs and bribed them with food and mates, for they are very receptive to training and do not require any armament to fight

ANIMUS	COST	RNG	AOE	POW	UP	OFF
PRIMAL	2	6	-	-		

TARGET FRIENDLY CIRCLE WARBEAST GAINS +2 STR AND MAT FOR ONE ROUND BUT AUTOMATICALLY FRENZIES DURING ITS CONTROLLER'S NEXT CONTROL PHASE. THIS SPELL CANNOT TARGET ELEMENTAL CONSTRUCTS.

effectively. The Circle sees them as an answer to the pure-blood trolls sent against them by the Trollbloods, brawn for brawn. Druids can tap into the primal chaos seething deep within the maddened minds of gorax, and they can hurl that raw strength into other warbeasts to transform untapped aggression into bestial destruction.

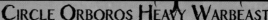

ANIMUS	COST	RNG	AOE	POW	UP	OFF
BAYING OF CHAOS	2	SELF	*	-		

ENEMY MODELS/UNITS WITHIN 5" OF THE MODEL USING THIS ANIMUS MUST PASS A COMMAND CHECK OR FLEE. THE WARPWOLF'S CONTROLLER MAY PLACE ONE FURY POINT ON OR REMOVE ONE FURY POINT FROM EACH ENEMY WARBEAST THAT FAILS THE COMMAND CHECK.

Warpwolves arose from a deranged cult seeking to connect more directly to the Beast of All Shapes. The original cult unlocked a potent mystical elixir which tapped into the bestial essence in man and was linked to the madness of the shifting moons. By drinking this elixir a man or woman would become a hulking, bipedal lupine monster when distressed or injured. The afflicted transform into a predatory embodiment of the Devourer Wurm filled with the urge to slaughter and feast. A cabal within the Circle hierarchy has long maintained watch on these creatures and has frequently unleashed them as weapons on the cities of man.

The traumatic transformation from human to warpwolf prompts irreversible shifts in the body's tissues that allow them to reproduce when in warpwolf form. Offspring conceived in this manner are born with the ability to transform and do not need the special elixir. Officially Circle druids are instructed only to utilize

I do not know if it is right for us to use them; they are unnatural and I fear tainted. But at this point I am beyond caring. I am glad to have their wild and raw strength.

—Kaya the Wildborne, Overseer of the Circle

warpwolves born to this condition, but some among the order know how to brew the elixir and have used it secretly to recruit more of these fearsome monsters. Since the rise of Everblight and the unexpected feud with the trollkin, the Omnipotents have turned a blind eye to this practice, neither sanctioning nor forbidding it.

Few warpwolves retain their human sanity, and even when they revert to human form they are nervous, tense, and prone to lashing out in violent rages. They enjoy any excuse to unleash their predatory nature, and in battle their bodies constantly shift and warp. Muscles and tendons thicken on legs or arms to provide bursts of speed or power to their rending claws, and tooth-like spurs erupt to protect vulnerable areas of flesh. Wounds quickly close on their bodies as skin wriggles, ripples, and reforms over an injury to erase it entirely.

There are few more blood-curdling sounds than the triumphant howling of a warpwolf on the hunt.

WARPWOLF				CMD	7
SPD	STR	MAT	RAT	DEF	ARM
6	10	6	3	14	16

LFT	CLAW		
	SPECIAL	POW	P+S
	–	4	14

RT	CLAW		
	SPECIAL	POW	P+S
	–	4	14

FURY	4
THRESHOLD	10
FIELD ALLOWANCE	U
VICTORY POINTS	3
POINT COST	108
BASE SIZE	LARGE

Warpwolf

Chain Attack – Throat Ripper - If the Warpwolf hits with both of its initial Claw attacks against the same warjack or warbeast in the same activation, after resolving the attacks it may immediately make an additional melee attack against the target. If the attack succeeds against a warjack, the target suffers one damage point to the first available box of each system including its Hull and is knocked down. If the attack succeeds against a warbeast , the target suffers one damage point to the first available circle of each branch and is knocked down.

Controlled Warping - At the beginning of the Warpwolf's activation, its controller may choose one of the following warp effects. Warp effects last for one round.
• The Warpwolf gains +2 STR.
• The Warpwolf gains +2" of movement.
• The Warpwolf gains +2 ARM.

Reactive Warping - When the Warpwolf suffers damage, its controller always chooses which branch takes the damage.

Regeneration [d3] - The Warpwolf may be forced to remove d3 damage points from anywhere on its life spiral once per activation. The Warpwolf cannot regenerate during an activation it runs.

Woldwarden
Circle Orboros Heavy Warbeast

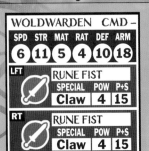

WOLDWARDEN CMD -					
SPD	STR	MAT	RAT	DEF	ARM
6	11	5	4	10	18

LFT	RUNE FIST		
	SPECIAL	POW	P+S
	Claw	4	15

RT	RUNE FIST		
	SPECIAL	POW	P+S
	Claw	4	15

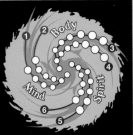

FURY	3
THRESHOLD	—
FIELD ALLOWANCE	U
VICTORY POINTS	3
POINT COST	116
BASE SIZE	LARGE

I will gladly pit my woldwardens against any of those noisy, smoke-belching warjacks. I have already destroyed several which made the mistake of blundering into my territory.

—Baldur the Stonecleaver, Potent of the Circle

The woldwarden's solid frame is inscribed with an intricate lattice of runes that glow when infused with raw natural power. They combine the permanence of stone and wood with the chaos of living entropy. With mighty stone fists strengthened by nature's wrath, the towering constructs can deliver an onslaught of fearsome blows.

A woldwarden's greatest asset stems from a mystic harmony forged with its controlling druid. This bond allows the woldwarden to act as a vessel for the druid's arcane might, which is fueled by the power of the earth rather than the druid's own energy. The woldwarden can unleash potent offensive magic allowing its controlling druid to attack from two places at once. More than a mere weapon, the woldwarden is an extension of its druid's will and embodies his absolute power within his territory.

Woldwarden

All Terrain - The Woldwarden ignores movement penalties from rough terrain and obstacles. The Woldwarden may charge, slam, or trample across rough terrain.

Chain Attack – Druid's Wrath - If the Woldwarden hits the same target with both its initial Rune Fist attacks during the same activation, after resolving the attacks it may immediately make an additional melee attack against the target. If the attack succeeds, the target is slammed d6" directly away from the Woldwarden with the same effect as a slam power attack.

Elemental Construct - The Woldwarden is not a living model. The Woldwarden never makes threshold checks, automatically passes command checks, and never frenzies or goes wild. The Woldwarden cannot run or be healed.

Spell Strike (★Attack) – While within the control area of a friendly Circle warlock, the Woldwarden may cast one of the warlock's offensive spells with a fury point cost of three or less without being forced or spending fury points. The Woldwarden uses the warlock's FURY stat to resolve all effects of the spell including attack rolls. The Woldwarden may be forced to boost magic attack and magic damage rolls. The warlock whose spell was cast may spend fury points to upkeep spells cast by the Woldwarden.

Rune Fists

Claw - The Woldwarden's Rune Fists have the abilities of Claws.

ANIMUS	COST	RNG	AOE	POW	UP	OFF
UNDERGROWTH	2	SELF	*	-		

WHILE WITHIN 3" OF THE MODEL USING THIS ANIMUS, FRIENDLY CIRCLE MODELS, INCLUDING THE MODEL USING THIS ANIMUS, GAIN CONCEALMENT. WHILE WITHIN 3" OF THE MODEL USING THIS ANIMUS, ENEMY MODELS TREAT OPEN TERRAIN AS ROUGH TERRAIN AND SUFFER −2 DEF. UNDERGROWTH LASTS FOR ONE ROUND.

Crafted from huge blocks of stone and inscribed with countless runes of power, the woldwarden is created from a slow process that imbues it with the will of its creator. In times of quiet the woldwardens guard the most heavily defended sacred sites of the Circle Orboros, but in the current crisis they have been brought forth from those groves to contest directly with the Circle's enemies.

Some druids, particularly those who follow the path of earth, consider them far superior and infinitely more reliable than the wild beasts others struggle to tame. Woldwardens are able to charge unimpeded through any terrain and are capable of enduring tremendous punishment in battle. Through their natural power they can cause thorny vines and gnarled bushes to erupt around them to hinder enemies attempting to engage them.

There have always been those willing to offer strength of arms to the wilderness prophets, and the Circle has made use of such men and women to guard their territories and serve as agents in towns and villages on the wilderness fringes. Families in the dark forests and isolated hills have passed this tradition down to sons and daughters initiated into a secret cabal that brings together rugged folk serving as guardians of the druids. These are the wolves of Orboros—hunting packs marching against the enemies of the druidic order they promised to serve.

In exchange for this fealty, the druids vow to watch over their lands and families—a significant gesture in the brutal regions beyond civilization. Druids select these family lines because a greater than average number of their children undergo the *wilding*. The Circle shelters and protects such families as a precious commodity. Due to the pressure of recent battles, the Circle has recently turned to employing more mercenaries among their number, hardy and grim-faced men and women

I heard the drums at night and saw them marching into the fog, spears in hand. There were hundreds of them ready for war. Seeing them chilled my blood as trolls have not.

—Dragho Vozc, former Winter Guard and troll hunter of the Scarsfell Forest of Khador

HUNTSMAN				CMD	8
SPD	STR	MAT	RAT	DEF	ARM
6	5	7	4	13	13

WOLF				CMD	6
SPD	STR	MAT	RAT	DEF	ARM
6	5	6	4	13	13

CLEFT SPEAR		
SPECIAL	POW	P+S
Multi	4	9

FIELD ALLOWANCE	3
VICTORY POINTS	2
LEADER AND 5 TROOPS	51
UP TO 4 ADDITIONAL TROOPS	8ea
BASE SIZE	SMALL

possessed of pragmatic survival skills as well as a willingness to serve. Some cannot explain why they serve, only that it feels right to do so. Being coerced or intimidated into joining the brotherhood is not unheard of, but the Circle knows such behavior breeds resentment and can lead to problems, so they prefer voluntary recruits.

Each wolf trains to master the cleft-bladed spear, a powerful piercing weapon designed to punch through thick hides and armor. They must prove their skill with this weapon and the ability to survive in the wilds to pass the initiation ritual and earn the wolf pelt marking them as a brother or sister.

Huntsman
Leader

Unit
Combined Melee Attack - Instead of making melee attacks separately, two or more Wolves of Orboros in melee range of the same target may combine their attacks. In order to participate in a combined melee attack, a Wolf must be able to declare a melee attack against the intended target. The Wolf of Orboros with the highest MAT in the attacking group makes one melee attack roll for the group and gains +1 to the attack and damage rolls for each Wolf of Orboros, including himself, participating in the attack.

Pathfinder - Wolves of Orboros ignore movement penalties from rough terrain and obstacles. Wolves of Orboros may charge across rough terrain.

Cleft Spear
Powerful Charge - When making a charge attack, a Wolf of Orboros gains +2 to his attack roll.

Reach - 2" melee range.

Druids of Oboros

CIRCLE ORBOROS UNIT

WARDER					CMD 8	
SPD	STR	MAT	RAT	DEF	ARM	
6	6	6	4	14	13	

WILDER					CMD 6	
SPD	STR	MAT	RAT	DEF	ARM	
6	6	5	4	14	13	

VOULGE			
	SPECIAL	POW	P+S
	Reach	4	10

FIELD ALLOWANCE	2
VICTORY POINTS	2
LEADER AND 5 TROOPS	84
BASE SIZE	SMALL

To preserve natural order, we must be prepared to harness primordial forces to hold the predations of the civilized world at bay.

—Krueger the Stormwrath,
Potent of the Circle

Called "blackclads" by outsiders, druids are discussed in whispers and dread rumors. They are seen as heralds of doom, dark cultists, and reminders of when mankind feared the howls of the wilderness. They are known to take care of their own and invoke brutal reprisal on any who interfere with their plans. Watching multiple druids emerge from the foggy mist of a dark and shadowed forest can be enough to unnerve even veteran soldiers. The *wilding* is fresh in their blood, and gathered together they become a channel for enormous natural power over the earth, making the ground itself betray the enemy and swallow them whole.

Druids wield mighty voulges, but their true power is mastery over primal forces, enabling them to work in conjunction to obliterate the enemy. They are suffused with the spirit of Orboros, and the earth responds to their call. With a wave of their hands they can uproot enormous rocks to hurl through the air with tremendous force to break the bones of foes and topple them down embankments. Wreathed in storm, they confound their enemies with wind and mist. The druids can draw on the chaotic energies of Orboros to disrupt and unravel magic formulae brought to bear in their vicinity to undo the works of arcanists, warlocks, or priests.

The druids of Orboros are trained in diversion and ambush, and they seldom fight in the open. Dense forests part to make way for their advance and then shroud them in protective cover. They prefer to keep to the trees, move among marshy swamps, or attack from the vantage of cliffs. Though sending these precious druids into battle is a risk, the Circle believes strength requires conflict and the worthy will rise to power while the weak are culled.

Warder

The Devouring (Order) - Instead of making magic attacks separately, every Wilder who received this order and is in an open formation group with the Warder may combine his attack with the Warder against the same target. The Warder cannot make The Devouring attack by himself. The Devouring is a RNG 10, POW 10 magic attack. The Devouring has an AOE based on the number of Druids of Orboros participating in the attack. If 2-3 Druids of Orboros participate, place a 3" AOE. If 4-5 Druids participate, place a 4" AOE. If all 6 Druids participate, place a 5" AOE. Make one magic attack roll using the Warder's Magic Ability score of 7, gaining +1 to the attack and damage roll for each Druid of Orboros participating in the attack, including the Warder. On a critical hit, models in the AOE are knocked down. The Devouring cannot target a model in melee.

Leader

Unit

Camouflage - A Druid of Orboros gains an additional +2 DEF when benefiting from concealment or cover.

Pathfinder - Druids of Orboros ignore movement penalties from rough terrain and obstacles. Druids of Orboros may charge across rough terrain.

Magic Ability

A Druid of Orboros may cast one of the following spells as a special action or special attack. To resolve a magic attack, roll 2d6 and add the Druid of Orboros's Magic Ability score of 7. If the roll is equal to or exceeds the target's DEF, the attack hits.

- **Counter Magic (★Action)** - Instead of performing separate special actions, all models in the unit may combine their actions to cast this spell. Enemy models within 1" of a Druid of Orboros +1" per Druid of Orboros in the unit cannot cast spells. Friendly models within 1" of a Druid of Orboros +1" per Druid of Orboros in the unit cannot be targeted by enemy spells. Counter Magic lasts for one round.

- **Elemental Bolt (★Attack)** - Earth Attack is a RNG 8, POW 10 magic attack. On a critical hit, target model is knocked down.

- **Summon Vortex (★Action)** - Center a 3" AOE cloud effect on the Druid of Orboros. Enemy models in the cloud suffer –2 to attack rolls. This cloud effect remains on the table for one round.

Voulge

Reach - 2" melee range.

Among the Tharn it is not the men alone who heed the call of the Circle Orboros; women in this tribe are equally bloodthirsty and savage. Experts in tracking both beast and man, they live to hunt. Bloodtrackers are a remnant of ancient ways—a people of a darker time—and their choice of weapons reflects this. They prefer to pierce foes at a distance with weighted javelins, but they also wield spiked bucklers like claws to impale those who close with them in melee. Bloodtrackers rarely allow the enemy to get so close, however. Their lean forms are barely seen shadows among the depths of the forest. Keeping in constant motion, they hurl javelins and dart away to strike from a different direction.

Those who have faced them learn to fear the bloodtrackers for the frenetic savagery with which they conduct their attacks. Though bloodtrackers do not adopt the hulking forms of the ravagers, they do call the Wurm to imbue them with bestial aspects that emulate the animals that strike with lightning swiftness. Bloodtrackers have a hyperactive awareness enhanced well beyond human sensitivity. These stalkers slice enemy forces to ribbons with savage relentlessness. Once they have chosen a target for their hunt, they

Once the hunt is called there is no escape or trail we cannot follow. We are the serpent in the grass, the falcon which strikes unseen from on high.

—Ksana Stagheart, Bloodtracker Huntress

will track them to extinction without remorse before selecting new prey.

Few have ever seen a bloodtracker clearly, and those who have faced them say they draw shadows like cloaks. It is a myth, but without question their ability to hide and blend into the environment is nearly supernatural as is their tremendous speed and mobility in even the densest underbrush.

HUNTRESS				CMD	8
SPD	STR	MAT	RAT	DEF	ARM
7	6	6	6	14	11

BLOODTRACKER				CMD	6
SPD	STR	MAT	RAT	DEF	ARM
7	6	5	5	14	11

THROWN JAVELIN			
RNG	ROF	AOE	POW
7	1	—	3

FIGHTING CLAWS		
SPECIAL	POW	P+S
—	3	9

FIELD ALLOWANCE	1
VICTORY POINTS	2
LEADER AND 5 TROOPS	60
UP TO 4 ADDITIONAL TROOPS	9ea
BASE SIZE	SMALL

Huntress

Ambuscade (Order) - Each Tharn Bloodtracker that received this order may advance SPD +3" directly toward a target model, throwing her javelin as she closes. The target model must be an eligible target for ranged attacks. After all models in the unit have completed their movement, each Tharn Bloodtracker participating in the Ambuscade makes a thrown javelin ranged attack against her target, gaining +2 to the attack roll. A Tharn Bloodtracker is not considered to be in melee when making the thrown javelin ranged attack, nor is the target considered to be in melee with her. Tharn Bloodtrackers that moved at least 3" gain boosted damage on successful thrown javelin ranged attacks.

Leader

Unit

Advance Deployment - Place Tharn Bloodtrackers after normal deployment, up to 12" beyond the established deployment zone.

Bushwhack - Tharn Bloodtrackers may make a ranged attack before moving. After attacking, Tharn Bloodtrackers may advance normally but cannot perform actions afterwards.

Pathfinder - Tharn Bloodtrackers ignore movement penalties from rough terrain and obstacles. Tharn Bloodtrackers may charge across rough terrain.

Prey - Before the start of the game, the Tharn Bloodtrackers' controller declares an enemy model/unit to be the unit's prey. A Tharn Bloodtracker beginning her activation within 10" of the prey gains +2 of movement. Models in the unit also gain +2 to attack and damage rolls targeting their prey. When the prey has been destroyed or removed from play, the Tharn Bloodtrackers' controller may immediately select another model/unit as their prey.

Stealth - Attacks against a Tharn Bloodtracker from greater than 5" away automatically miss. If a Tharn Bloodtracker is greater than 5" away from an attacker, she does not count as an intervening model.

Thrown Javelin

Thrown - Add the Tharn Bloodtracker's current STR to the POW of thrown javelin attacks.

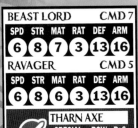

Tharn Ravagers
Circle Orboros Tharn Unit

BEAST LORD				CMD	7
SPD	STR	MAT	RAT	DEF	ARM
6	8	7	3	13	16

RAVAGER				CMD	5
SPD	STR	MAT	RAT	DEF	ARM
6	8	6	3	13	16

THARN AXE		
SPECIAL	POW	P+S
Multi	5	13

BEAST LORD DAMAGE	8
RAVAGER DAMAGE	5
FIELD ALLOWANCE	2
VICTORY POINTS	3
LEADER AND 3 TROOPS	76
UP TO 2 ADDITIONAL TROOPS	17ea
BASE SIZE	MEDIUM

Beast Lord
Leader

Unit
Camouflage - Tharn Ravagers gain an additional +2 DEF when benefiting from concealment or cover.

Fearless - Tharn Ravagers never flee.

Heart Eater - A Tharn Ravager gains a heart token each time he destroys a living model with a melee attack. The Tharn Ravager may only have one heart token at any time. A Tharn Ravager may spend a heart token to boost an attack or damage roll or to make an additional melee attack.

Pathfinder - Tharn Ravagers ignore movement penalties from rough terrain and obstacles. Tharn Ravagers may charge across rough terrain.

Tree Walker - A Tharn Ravager's LOS is never blocked by forests. While within a forest, a Tharn Ravager gains +2 DEF against melee attacks and may move through obstructions and other models if he has enough movement to move completely past the obstruction or the model's base.

Tharn Axe
Powerful Charge - When making a charge attack, a Tharn Ravager gains +2 to his attack roll.

Reach - 2" melee range.

They yet revel in the old ways, feasting on the hearts of the fallen and quenching their thirst in warm blood drawn from still living flesh.

—Krueger the Stormwrath, Potent of the Circle Orboros

The Tharn have always been able to channel the savage power of the Devourer Wurm. Within their villages, the Tharn look similar to savage Khadorans, but they are never seen on the warpath in this form. Before battle they bellow a call to the Wurm and they enter a chaos frenzy whereby their bodies are transformed—muscle mass expands and thickens, skin hardens, and teeth grow to terrible fangs. Their senses become as keen as the beasts they revere, and they feel the urge to feast. Legends of inhuman deprivations among the ravagers are true; they hunger to tear out and eat the hearts of their prey. These acts of frenzied cannibalism let them deliver grievous attacks while their eyes glow with berserk madness.

Just three centuries ago, the Tharn were one of the largest barbarian tribes and numbered in the tens of thousands across the northern Thornwood. Used as pawns by a Khadoran queen against Cygnar, most were slaughtered while the rest fell to a curse which withered their numbers. Decades ago the leaders of the Circle Orboros were secretly able to unravel this curse and restore the Tharn's numbers, and they have grown strong again. The work of the blackclads has engendered their complete and absolute loyalty, and they are eager to repay the debt.

The druids have encouraged the ravagers to come forth, led by their beast lords to provide much needed strength and ferocity to the battles being waged by the Circle Orboros. Few allies are as eager as the ravagers to engage in brutal carnage and charge forth from the depths of the forest to hack apart foes with their long-handled axes. Their trail of mutilated bodies is a reminder of the dark age when humans embraced the Menite priest-kings to save them from these savage tribes.

Trollkin are proud of their krielstones, but they have only the crudest reckoning of the true power of stone explored and mastered by the Circle Orboros. For many centuries the druids have marked their territories with intricate columns carved with runes of power. The ignorant believe shifting stones to be simple warning markers delimiting the druid's territories, but they are actually fulcrums of natural power tapping into the pervading essences of Orboros gathering in certain nexus points. Below the soil across Caen are numerous ley lines serving as the capillaries and arteries within the "body" of Orboros.

When activated by the power of the druids of Orboros, the top sections of shifting stones slide open to reveal glowing runes of power capable of unleashing energies gathered over time to alter the flow of battle radically. The stones can bathe nearby allies in raw life essence, prompt tissues to knit together rapidly, and repair internal organs to regenerate even the most grievous wounds. The stones also have other mysterious powers linked to the inner mysteries of Orboros. Through their connection with the ley lines, the stones can sink quickly

We have not even begun to exhaust the mysteries of earth and rock.

—Baldur the Stonecleaver,
Potent of the Circle

SHIFTING STONE CMD –					
SPD	STR	MAT	RAT	DEF	ARM
0	0	0	0	5	18
DAMAGE					5
FIELD ALLOWANCE					2
VICTORY POINTS					2
POINT COST FOR 3 STONES					21
BASE SIZE					SMALL

into the earth and rise again wherever they are most needed by the order. By a similarly enigmatic process, all three stones can unleash a single burst of power to send another creature to a completely different area of the battlefield.

Some of the greatest stones are rumored to be able to send messages across tremendous distances, and other powers may also be attributed to them that require major blood sacrifices or certain conjunctions of the stars and seasons. Being able to call upon these stones is one reason the movements of the druids of the Circle Orboros are so difficult to track or anticipate, and it allows them to spring unexpected reinforcements on the enemy.

Shifting Stones

Advance Deployment - Place the Shifting Stones after normal deployment, up to 12" beyond the established deployment zone.

Inanimate - A Shifting Stone is not a living model, has no back arc, and its front arc extends 360°. A Shifting Stone never flees. A Shifting Stone has no melee range and cannot engage or be engaged. A Shifting Stone is automatically hit by melee attacks. A Shifting Stone cannot move, be moved, or be knocked down.

Made of Stone - A ranged attack must have a POW of at least 14 to damage a Shifting Stone, but AOE attacks and attacks that cause fire or corrosion do full damage.

Shifting Powers

A Shifting Stone may perform one of the following actions during the unit's activation:

- **Restoration (★Action)** - Friendly Circle models within 1" of the Shifting Stone may remove d3 damage points from themselves. Roll separately for each model. A model may only benefit from Revivification once per turn.

- **Shifting (★Action)** - The Shifting Stone may be placed up to 8" away from its current location. There must be room for the Shifting Stone's base. The Shifting Stone must be in formation after all Stones have completed their actions.

- **Teleportation (★Action)** - Instead of performing separate special actions, all three Shifting Stones may combine their actions to teleport one friendly Circle model whose base is at least partially in the triangular area between all three Shifting Stones. Place the model up to 8" away from its current location. There must be room for the teleported model's base. A model cannot move this turn after being teleported.

Lord of the Feast

CIRCLE ORBOROS SOLO

LORD OF THE FEAST				CMD	10
SPD	STR	MAT	RAT	DEF	ARM
4	8	7	5	12	17

RAVEN			
RNG	ROF	AOE	POW
10	1	—	—

WURMBLADE		
SPECIAL	POW	P+S
Multi	5	13

DAMAGE	10
FIELD ALLOWANCE	C
VICTORY POINTS	1
POINT COST	33
BASE SIZE	SMALL

We called the Feast Lord to slaughter in the time of the Orgoth. He stalked those places stolen from us and littered the forest floor with their bones.

—Omnipotent Dahlekov

A walking horror of prehistory, the Lord of the Feast feeds the ravenous hunger of the Devourer Wurm. Reeking of innumerable slaughters, it lurks in shadow and falls upon those doomed to cross its path. From each victim it takes bloody trophies by rending flesh to claim the viscera and vital organs within. The Feast Lord then prepares its offering of a mighty blood sacrifice to the Beast of All Shapes and is rewarded with a wave of savage power that reinvigorates all who serve the Wurm's cause. Bathed in this spirit of predation, they rise in a murderous tide to feed the Devourer's gluttony further. Upon the completion of his work, the Lord of the Feast transforms into ravens that linger to consume the eyes of the slain.

The Circle seldom intentionally draws the attention of the Devourer, for they prefer to tap into the mindless power of Orboros lingering in the world. Dark times however often require dark measures, and the druids have preserved the forgotten lore once known only to the highest priests of the Molgur tribes. In this hour they have turned to these black rites and called forth an avatar of the Unsleeping One clothed in flesh on Caen and unleashed upon the living. The Lord of the Feast is a towering, utterly savage incarnation of the God of Feasts who descends on the battlefield to glut on destruction and death.

The Feast Lord's only companion is a raven joining him to descend on fields of carnage. Ranging ahead of its master, the raven summons its lord to fresh victims where he emerges like a shadow in their midst ready to reap blood and meat. His long blade blurs like a storm of steel as he carves into enemy flesh.

Lord of the Feast

Advance Deployment - Place the Lord of the Feast after normal deployment, up to 12" beyond the established deployment zone.

Carrion Feast - When the Lord of the Feast destroys an enemy living model with a melee attack, mark one of the five (5) Carrion circles on its card.

The Offering (★Action) - After all five (5) Carrion circles have been marked, as a special action the Lord of the Feast may make an offering to the Devourer Wurm. Friendly Circle models/units currently within 5" of the Lord of the Feast may be activated again at the end of this turn after all friendly models have completed their normal activations. Remove the Lord of the Feast from play immediately after he performs The Offering. Victory points are not awarded for the Lord of the Feast if he makes The Offering special action.

Pathfinder - The Lord of the Feast ignores movement penalties from rough terrain and obstacles. The Lord of the Feast may charge across rough terrain.

Stealth - Attacks against the Lord of the Feast from greater than 5" away automatically miss. If the Lord of the Feast is greater than 5" away from an attacker, he does not count as an intervening model.

Terror – Enemy models/units in melee range of the Lord of the Feast and enemy models/units with the Lord of the Feast in their melee range must pass a command check or flee.

Raven

Shifter - Raven attacks do no damage. If the attack hits an enemy model, immediately place the Lord of the Feast in base-to-base contact with the model. There must be room for the Lord of the Feast's base. After being placed, the Lord of the Feast may make melee attacks.

Wurmblade

Flying Steel - The Lord of the Feast may make d3 Wurmblade attacks each activation.

Reach - 2" melee range.

SKORNE

THE SKORNE

Archdomina Makeda of House Balaash stood in her full regalia and looked over her army with the eyes of a bird of prey. It was the first and perhaps last time they would gather together pristine and unspoiled. Their lines were perfect and they stood like rank and file statues in a gathering never equaled in all the history of her ancestors.

Makeda stood before them with her hands resting on the hilts of her great ancestral blades and felt a powerful pride blow through her like a desert wind. In fact the muted howl of that wind could be heard through the walls. They were at the center of the largest hall ever constructed by the slaves and master architects of the Skorne Empire. In any other fortress or castle this would have been an open-air courtyard, but the Stormlands allowed no such exposure, and even here the wind tried to seek them out. Above them countless carefully set stones supported a great dome, already considered a wonder of the empire, that kept the raging lightning storms and flesh-burning rain at bay.

This was *her* army. The Army of the Western Reaches was both massive and impressive with its long lines of armored Praetorians, leading ranks of elite Cataphracts—both Cetrati and Arcuarii—and Venators and paingivers standing just behind. Towering above all these ranks were the great armored beasts enslaved for war: titans, helmeted cyclopes, and hulking basilisks all wearing the red and gold of the western army. With this army she could conquer a world.

The army was divided into cohorts, each a mixed division that had drilled together incessantly since arriving at the fortress. The ranking tyrant stood in front of each cohort. As her eyes fell on them, each bowed deeply to her with arms crossed before their chests and hands open and outward. She sensed hesitation from Lord Tyrant Hexeris before he performed this genuflection. She pursed her lips, but it was only the briefest pause.

There was a clash of discordant horns and *konyis* metal-sheet drums, and she turned smartly on her heels toward the stairway rising into the higher palace of the great fortress. The Conqueror stepped forth onto his dais decked in intricately detailed armor of skorne design, yet his foreign nature was clear by the mane of black hair falling to his shoulders shot through with grey. This sight always startled Makeda—she had ceased to think of him as anything but skorne, and the image reminded her of his origin. She forced the thought away. He was reborn, flesh inconsequential.

There was another clash of the *konyis* drums like a sound of thunder. As if part of one giant organism, the entire army bowed with Makeda in perfect synchronicity, prostrating themselves before Supreme Archdominar Vinter Raelthorne. He let them stay this way for several long heartbeats before horns sounded and they rose.

As Makeda stood she felt a shock of surprise to see a great stone figure brought up next to Vinter. The exquisitely carved piece of obsidian towered over him, and several hooded extollers in ceremonial robes stood near the massive statue with their chained arms folded. Her soldiers were too well disciplined to break formation or speak at a time like this, but she could feel their tension.

The most ornately dressed extoller stepped forward and pulled back his hood to reveal his single eye; the other had been plucked out and replaced with a translucent orb. This orb glowed with a silver light—a sign that a great ancestor spoke through him. His voice boomed to reach the furthest ranks of the army. "Kotormo, Archdominar of the Lykus dynasty, stands before you. Your ancestors bless this conquest and stand by those who command you." Makeda felt tears rise to her eyes as the intensity of this statement fell like a hammer on the army. Kotormo was one of their mightiest ancestors tied by blood to her own house, and he was now here before them in a sacral tomb of obsidian speaking his blessing through the extoller.

They watched as several chained cyclopes carried dozens of smaller but still impressive dark statues on platforms from behind Vinter. They represented powerful sacred weapons—each a guardian containing an exalted warrior. None were as distinguished as Kotormo, but they were still revered. They were crafted at considerable expense and carried empty sacral stones ready to receive the fallen. With their inclusion the soldiers knew they could earn the rare opportunity to be exalted in death. The effect on the army was electric. Every soldier there would have fallen on his sword for Vinter in that moment if asked.

Vinter raised his own gauntleted hand and looked directly at Makeda. "Go now Archdomina, and bring victory!"

WEIGHT OF ANCESTORS

From the recent annals of Sohexol, extoller and elder historian of House Balaash, Halaak, Spring 606 AR.

It has been my honor to compile a brief overview of the history of our people, ordered at the behest of Supreme Archdominar Vinter, hereafter referred to as the Conqueror or the Reborn. This will serve as a point of reference for outsiders brought under our dominion to learn their place. Praise to House Balaash. I invoke the guidance and steady resolve of our ancestors to guide my hand. I invoke by my blood Sokost, my father's great grandfather.

We did not begin recording our history in stone until after we became a settled people, long after we had learned to preserve the spirits of our ancestors. Because the houses horde our holy ancient texts and sharing this information is uncommon, piecing together an accurate portrait of the ancient times is difficult even for those of us indulged with expending our lives in this pursuit.

The examination of the past is aided by calling on the voices of our ancestors. Through sacral internment rites, the essences of our most esteemed ancestors are crystallized and preserved, becoming exalted. There are many formalities and liturgies required before a house Aptimus Extoller grants permission to interact with exalted, so we do not undertake this lightly. Through these techniques we have recreated documents stretching back to the first exalted of our race.

For most of our ancient past we were a nomadic people ranging with unfettered freedom across the southern reaches of eastern Immoren—what we call *Scindor Solum*. To the north stretched the Lyoss Empire, a vast realm controlled by a species western outlanders call elves. These soft and pathetic lowlanders regarded us as barbarians. Pampered by their gods, they lived long lives of lush excess in fertile valleys and plains. Even then we reviled them, having chosen a harder and nobler path.

We preyed upon Lyoss as predators will feed on a herd grown fat and torpid. Our war bands struck any place they left vulnerable. We occupied the worst badlands and lived free without need for cities. It was a tough but challenging life among the desolate scrub, barren steppes, buttes, dusty flats, and the occasional sheltered mountain retreat. Lyoss loathed us and saw in our lean faces a rugged determination they could not fathom. They called us many things: "the godless," "faithless," and the "shunned." They did not understand that we accepted the term "godless" with pride. Those

we exalt arise from our own blood—those heroes who earn immortality through brave deeds, battle triumph, or sacrifice. We have no need for gods.

An ancient master named Voskune introduced the fundamentals of exaltation. Voskune was a philosopher and ascetic whose life predated written history. After decades mortifying his flesh and fasting in the desert, Voskune worked to understand the connection between the body and essence—the spirit. He dissected the living and the dead to understand this fundamental connection. He plucked out his own eye to learn its complex structure of fluids and fleshy tissues, and he replaced the ruined orb with a smooth crystal which allowed him to perceive vital essence, vivid in moments of anguish or when the body lingers near death.

> We preyed upon Lyoss as predators will feed on a herd grown fat and torpid. Our war bands struck any place they left vulnerable.

Voskune was lost to us, but his pupils carried the work forward. Ten generations passed before two skorne named Ishoul and Kaleed worked together to achieve a breakthrough. Ishoul discovered that cutting and polishing certain stones will pull at a spirit, drawing one as water is absorbed into a sponge. Ishoul and Kaleed spent their life working with these stones. The two duplicated the sacrifice of their eyes to perceive spirits, and since that time all extollers have done likewise. It is a small price to pay to perceive life's essence.

The dominar of their house, a venerable warlord named Vuxoris, became the First Exalted through their ministrations. This revered ancestor invented the code of battle known as *hoksune*, still followed today, and asked Ishoul to preserve his spirit so his lore would not fade. They captured Vuxoris' essence in a great polished piece of obsidian and watched as the stone transformed with a lattice of powerful energy. Vuxoris could be contacted, albeit with difficulty, and was preserved and immortal. Kaleed was astonished to realize the stone now emanated great power and manifested strange phenomena. It would be many more generations before we learned how to harness this power and call on the ancestors to aid us.

This stone became a treasured relic of our people. Countless wars and the slaughter of thousands erupted over ownership of the First Exalted. With this stone we learned that smaller pieces carved from a sacral stone could be incorporated into weapons and armor, thereby imbuing those items with some shadow of ancestral power. This was done sparingly to preserve the integrity of the original stone, yet over time some ancient stones were slowly carved away piece by piece. In the ages to come this first stone was lost, perhaps divided too many times, but it is part of the inevitable destruction brought by the passage of time.

> **By tapping into the power of the dying or suffering, a skorne can be sustained on almost no nourishment or water and live regardless of injuries.**

The process of preservation to exalted is a complex and difficult ritual requiring much preparation. Only the most honorable within a given house are deemed worthy. Poor houses lacking extollers have no choice but to endure their leaders expiring and passing into the void to suffer endless torment.

Another great ancestor arose twelve generations before the destruction of Lyoss. He was a philosopher-warrior named Morkaash. He focused on learning anatomy and the infliction of pain and agony. Morkaash believed sublime enlightenment was a result of suffering, and he sought to understand the mechanisms by which living bodies function. Morkaash tested himself against the great beasts of the badlands by conquering them in battle, taming them, and bending them to his will. His philosophy carried on after his death, and his followers improved their techniques over many lifetimes, eventually giving rise to paingivers and chirurgeons.

Both paingivers and chirurgeons study nerves, blood vessels, tendons, and other living tissues. They do not dwell on philosophy or mysticism. Chirurgeons seek mastery of anatomy to provide aid to the wounded in battle and assist members of their house in recovery from injury. They learn to set bones and sew lacerations as well as conduct ritual scarification. Chirurgeons also learn alchemy to create balms and purgatives. There is no glory in this pursuit, and the caste is not highly respected, but dominars and tyrants both have been saved from death by their ministrations.

Paingivers are the other side of this discipline, learning to apply agony to root out traitors or question enemies for vital information. This is a necessary art in the complex intrigues between and within the houses. There are always those seeking greater power, and it is through the paingivers that the overly ambitious are discovered. Dominars also task paingivers with keeping and training the great warbeasts required for war, and they comply by bending their skill to train and condition the creatures' behavior. Only a fool marches to war with soldiers alone. Though individual paingivers work for a house, they do not belong to them. Paingivers give up their house loyalties when initiated into their art, for only by divorcing themselves from inter-house struggles can paingivers dispassionately execute their duties.

In the centuries following the death and exaltation of Voskune and Morkaash, some continued to devote themselves to deeper mysteries. These were often extollers not content merely to undertake funerary rites and see to the treasured ancestral stones. This gave rise to mortitheurgy, now a fundamental art underlying all of our arcane power. The fundamentals of mortitheurgy arose from the awareness that there is great power released by the flesh as it undergoes transition and that blood and sacrifice have innate potency.

Mortitheurgy provides an enormous advantage in battle because through mystical effort a warrior can be forced to fight well past the limits of his flesh. By tapping into the power of the dying or suffering, a skorne can be sustained on almost no nourishment or water and live regardless of injuries. This is a short reprieve and there is a price to pay for such efforts, however. The warrior fighting past the limits of his flesh will still die often in great agony, yet those extra moments in battle could mean victory instead of defeat. Paingivers achieve similar ends from the use of certain stimulants, extracted toxins, and alchemical substances. Through mortitheurgy one can draw on the fundamental energies of life, death, and the strength of will.

All who expect to lead a house or become heirs must learn to utilize these energies. They become indispensable tools in the domination of the will of their subjects. From these bonds a warlord may force even reluctant vassals to fight or tap into the strength of enslaved beasts, and he uses them as extensions of himself in battle. This art

allows a warlord to have the strength of a titan and shed injuries that would fell an entire cohort.

Some few skorne take these studies further. Master mortitheurges draw on the infinite energy contained in every immortal essence of living beings—the spirit. This must be done with care, however, for those who delve too deeply into these arts can exceed their limits and become stretched to a point from which there is no return. Annihilation in this fashion is utterly permanent and beyond even the art of the extollers.

Our ancestors remain our most treasured relics, and it is no wonder the houses have battled over their keeping. It is the goal of every skorne to prove worthy and earn the reward of exaltation. Those who pass avoid the ceaseless torments of the void, and we are inspired to fight more fiercely in the hopes of earning this honor. Battle has always been the surest path to exaltation; we who engage in scholarly pursuits know we will not be chosen. I have steeled myself against the knowledge that my essence will be lost when I die, and I hope my words will serve as a legacy.

The Lyoss Empire knew none of our philosophies and never attempted to understand our ways. It was impossible for them to comprehend that a nomadic people could master power over death. All their strength, luxury, and prosperity sprang from their gods, and as a result they were complacent like babes refusing to be weaned from the milk of their mothers.

Our dominars celebrated the day Lyoss was obliterated. The sun exploded in the sky over their greatest cities and sent sheets of flame and molten rock across all they had built. The wave of destruction was awesome to behold—a catastrophe so powerful it rippled the earth like cloth stirred by the wind. We lost many lives in the following tumult of savage winds, unremitting storms, and ceaseless lightning, yet we, having already honed our strength, stood firm while they panicked and died. Our tribes harassed the survivors as they fled the ruined empire in a long column of dispirited refugees wailing and scattering into the west. We came upon them like reapers at harvest, beheading those too slow to flee and taking whatever they dropped. All the legacy of their peerless civilization had come to ashes, and what little survived fell into our hands.

The Lyoss Empire fell nearly two hundred and fifty generations ago. Exalted ancestors who survived this period passed down descriptions of the fall, but it was only in the fullness of time that we realized the benefits of the destruction of Lyoss. It happened in a time of calamity, disaster, and upheaval, and a long dark age followed as the continent was sundered by the unnatural powers released in that onslaught of destruction. The Abyss opened to swallow the capital of Lyoss as unquenchable fire consumed the outer cities.

One result of the aftermath was a transformation of our society away from its nomadic roots. It became imperative to build permanent shelters against unpredictably intense windstorms, dust gales, and flooding. Our ancestors learned the crafts of masonry, engineering, and city building, but there were some who resisted this inevitable transformation. They believed it moved us away from our austere heritage, but our society has retained its core values over the years.

The fractured houses continued to vie and war with one another for temporary dominance and crucial resources like stone quarries, isolated plots of fertile soil, untainted wells, underground streams, and access to difficult hunting grounds. In this period life became short and cruel; death waited at every turn. A great house could be wiped from existence in a few short days, leaving no trace of its passage except spoils plucked by those who pillaged its carcass.

With perseverance we made progress. Slowly the storms receded, the weather became more predictable, and the flooding became a distant memory. Our cities stabilized and prospered, the glorious eternal war of houses continued with renewed passion, and our philosophies and traditions were restored. Still, much was lost, including many sacral ancestral stones.

Some of the exalted were released when their stones were broken. Such an event is an ill tiding bringing plague, misfortune, and the wrath of that ancestor, for without a sacral stone their essence becomes twisted. The strongest ancestral spirits can endure this indignity, and in very rare cases they can be reborn. More often they become what we call *Kovaas*, or "rage ghosts," possessed of endless fury. The destruction of a sacral stone can breed insanity in these spirits and turn them into mindless wrathful beings with endless reserves of energy. Mortitheurges and extollers consider it imperative to banish tormented *Kovaas*. On some occasions an extoller can re-inter them in a new stone, but this rarely brings good fortune. Sacral stones of the *Kovaas* are buried or sealed away to prevent them from bringing harm to the living.

On the fringes of Lyoss, the unquenched fire retreated, and we were able to occupy those lands and gain useful stone and other salvage. Much of that region is still hostile to life, but over thousands of years the wake of the cataclysm offers forgotten treasures and mysteries. There is merit to the salvage of their metals and stone, but great and powerful beasts roam the periphery of those ruins.

There has never been a period when there was not warfare between our houses. It is natural for warlords to vie against one another, to test their strength, and to ensure the mighty arise and cast down the weak. Others who do not lead serve. Our master paingivers and chirurgeons have improved countless beasts of war. In some cases it takes patient effort and generations of experimentation to bend these creatures into weapons, but in other cases the transformation is a matter of bringing out native qualities. We have learned that while forged weapons have their place, flesh is stronger and more malleable than stone or metal.

Under the watchful eye of the Conqueror, archdominars are stronger and more unified now than they ever were in any period of our history. He has done much to reform our society and create a unified government. By his decree, our empire has been divided into distinct regions across which an archdomina or archdominar has absolute authority. Before the Conqueror's arrival, this title was only taken when one dominar had defeated and subjugated at least three other houses and forced their leaders to bend the knee. This was rare since most houses would refuse to submit, and the victor was forced to crush and absorb them. Wards of war would begin as slaves and only through successive generations earned rights of membership in the house.

One of the most recent warlords at this level of power before the Reborn came was Vaactash, a legendary leader of my own house. By slaughter and careful politics he carved out a territory north of Halaak. His rule outlasted any archdominar in record, and he rooted out numerous attempts by his subordinates to assassinate him. He is now exalted and preserved in a place of honor among his ancestors. The ruling of his house went first to his son, who did not endure, then to his grandson, and finally to his granddaughter Archdomina Makeda who leads the Army of the Western Reaches for the Conqueror. When the western lands lay defeated and under skorne rule, our house will reap its rewards.

Ongoing house wars forged our strength for two hundred and fifty generations after the fall of Lyoss and the start of our settled period. I will not relate an unending series of tales from this time; our culture has not changed significantly. Great houses rose and fell, and heroic ancestors distinguished themselves to earn the right to be exalted. Our people spread from the badlands to occupy any lands where the fires of Lyoss were extinguished and growth began again. Lesser species fell under our yoke, including many tribes of cyclops savages from the desert. Through our history we never abandoned the principles that life is struggle and the nature of this struggle defines us. Through conflict and war we are stronger, and our houses benefit.

Though some traitors whisper that we have abandoned that path, it is my belief we have been preparing for the arrival of the Reborn—the one who would unite us. With a new land to pillage and dominate, it is destined we would follow a supreme archdominar. I do not see this as a contradiction in our philosophies. Enormous wealth in slaves and resources await our taking. The decadent west lays open for our soldiers to cull the weak and enslave the strong.

The Reborn emerged from beyond the Stormlands twelve years ago, battered yet strong. Those who discovered him attempted to kill the foreigner and failed; they were slaughtered to the last. It became clear that this was no mere foreigner, for his talent with a blade was peerless. Hundreds of skilled warriors engaged him, but all fell. There were whispers he was a blood-mad messiah, and some believed he was a vengeful *Kovaas* spirit and not flesh at all. Soon those he approached bowed to him and joined his cause. He fought his way to our largest city, Halaak, gathering a following from the outlying houses and defeating all champions who challenged him.

The greatest conflict against Vinter during his First Unification was outside the great fortress of my house, Balaash. Domina Makeda battled him with all the resources of our house in a clash that we who witnessed it will never forget. We lost the strength of a generation that day. In the end the struggle came down to Conqueror versus Domina Makeda crossing blades while the fight raged around them. My mistress called on her strength over beasts to fortify her, and even with this power she could not gain an advantage. When the last of her titans died, she was defeated. In this defeat my mistress realized the truth. She saw that this Conqueror was Reborn. He was clearly the essence of one of our great ancestors despite his flesh, perhaps one whose sacral stone was destroyed in the wake of the fall of Lyoss. I too have accepted this realization, as have many who serve the Conqueror. While encased in outlander flesh, his essence is skorne.

Three years ago there was a shameful period when the fickle dominars turned their back on the Conqueror. It occurred after he ventured into the west on a scouting expedition. We had been a fractured people so long that it was inevitable we would divide without his stern hand to guide us. The dominars seized power for themselves, confident the Reborn would die in the west. The Conqueror returned and fell on the betrayers, capturing all base-born pretenders to endure torment beyond imagination at the hands of his personal paingiver. The Conqueror had them slaughtered and refused them the rites of the extollers as a lesson to their heirs.

> **Through our history we never abandoned the principles that life is struggle and the nature of this struggle defines us.**

Only our house, Balaash, stayed true to the Reborn. Archdomina Makeda weathered assassination attempts, retreated into our fortress compound during the strife in Halaak, and fought all who tried to crush us for staying true to the Reborn. After months of siege the Reborn arrived in wrath and broke through to my mistress. For her loyalty, the Reborn bestowed on Makeda the dominion of the western empire and tasked her to lead her army into the fertile lands beyond the Stormlands to dominate and subjugate all who oppose the Conqueror.

The Conqueror has built a mighty fortress-bridge crossing the Abyss of the Stormlands, and it is there where our army musters and trains for the battles to come. It was built on the labor of thousands of slaves taken among the houses of the betrayers. The Conqueror sits unassailable on his throne, and his many vassals and agents ensure the myriad houses stay loyal and do not seek to betray him. We of house Balaash, those not sent west for war, work to this end. We have sworn to provide the Reborn every weapon, beast, and tool he requires to unite the continent. Behind us stands the weight and strength of our ancestors, and we will not fail them.

Master Tormentor Morghoul

Skorne Warlock Character

I have learned to feed on treachery like meat and savor loyalty like rare wine. The terror you inspire in the ranks will serve in the place of true fidelity.

—Vinter Raelthorne the Conqueror to Master Tormentor Morghoul

Masked and sheathed in the armor of a paingiver, Master Tormentor Morghoul is a terror on the battlefield. By drawing on the strength of beasts, he transforms himself into a whirlwind of bladed death while nimbly evading injury. In a heartbeat he can strike a dozen times to nick arteries, pierce hearts, and sever tendons. Morghoul knows the intricate byways of living bodies with surpassing precision, so each organ and blood vessel becomes an opportunity to inflict pain or death. He has lost count of the bodies that have fallen under his knife, methodically stripped of their innermost secrets, for spirit and flesh alike bend to his ministrations.

After rising in reputation plying his cruel trade for a dozen houses, Morghoul was enlisted by House Vokuul in the great city of Halaak. Tasked to unravel plots against their domina, he systematically tortured his way through her house. Later the flayed skin of the domina's own children were left drying on the house gates, and by the end of Morghoul's work the Vokuul domina was forced to choose a new heir but had attained absolute obedience within her house.

The Vokuul joined the skorne defenders when Vinter Raelthorne first beset Halaak, but Morghoul watched the battles silently. Though the domina ordered him to engage, the master tormentor coldly informed her that his services had come to an end and left her to her fate. After the Conqueror crushed House Vokuul and its domina along with the rest at Halaak, Morghoul approached Vinter and offered his services knowing he would gain ample opportunity to practice his craft.

As Vinter went into the west, Morghoul stayed to watch the capital. Stalking the servitors of the dominars, he uncovered the plot to overthrow the Conqueror. He became the Walking Death in Halaak, using his mastery of the city's subterranean tunnels to traverse unseen while he captured and slayed any he felt might have useful information. Terrible noises echoed from below ground as Morghoul played exposed nerves like an instrument. Nearly a hundred fell during Morghoul's terror campaign against the traitors. The dominars went into seclusion and unleashed their own agents to track him down, but none sent to engage him returned. They would surface from waterways or across rooftops, drained of blood and wearing faces twisted into expressions of unrecognizable agony.

Morghoul ceased his efforts on word of Vinter's return from the western fringes. Traveling to meet his chosen lord, Morghoul revealed the information he had painstakingly gathered, including the whereabouts of every secret passage and poorly guarded sector of the capital. Morghoul had laid the groundwork for Vinter's rapid and bloody Second Unification. Vinter gathered an army of his surviving loyalists and assaulted the gates of Halaak. This served as a distraction for Morghoul to slip into the city and capture the heads of the largest houses. The remaining betrayers Morghoul had not yet captured were undone by their own retainers who offered their masters to the Conqueror while pleading for their lives.

A month long festival of agony followed the capture of the betrayers. Silence was enforced on pain of death in the capital with the only sound being their inarticulate screams—the music of Morghoul unleashing the full imagination of his horrible arts. The citizens of the capital learned exactly what depths of pain one with the power of mortitheurgy and the lore of a paingiver was capable of inflicting.

Having risen to the top of his form, Morghoul dreams of ruling his own house and knows service to Vinter may allow him to exceed his caste. Makeda's army is terrified of the master tormentor, so Vinter tasked him to ensure that no treachery in the ranks disrupts the invasion and to keep a close eye on the warlords. Where he walks, silence follows.

SPECIAL RULES

Feat: Pain & Agony - A virtuoso of the paingiver arts, Master Tormentor Morghoul inflicts unrelenting agony without even touching his victims. By unleashing an explosion of torment, he severs the intimate connection between warlocks and their warbeasts to drown out all thoughts but survival.

While within Morghoul's control area this round, enemy warbeasts cannot be forced or have damage transferred to them.

MORGHOUL

Anatomical Precision - If Morghoul's melee damage roll fails to exceed target living model's ARM, the target automatically suffers one damage point.

Inflict Pain - Anytime Morghoul hits a warbeast with a melee attack, he may place one fury point on or remove one fury point from the target warbeast.

Perfect Balance - Morghoul cannot be targeted by combined melee attacks, combined ranged attacks, or free strikes. Perfect Balance negates back strike bonuses against Morghoul. When knocked down, Morghoul may stand up during his activation without forfeiting his movement or action.

MORGHOUL				CMD 8	
SPD	STR	MAT	RAT	DEF	ARM
7	6	8	4	17	13

RIPPER			
	SPECIAL	POW	P+S
	Double	3	9

RIPPER			
	SPECIAL	POW	P+S
	Double	3	9

FURY	5
DAMAGE	15
FIELD ALLOWANCE	C
VICTORY POINTS	5
POINT COST	57
BASE SIZE	SMALL

RIPPERS

Double Strike - Morghoul may make one melee attack with each Ripper when he spends a fury point for an additional attack.

SPELL	COST	RNG	AOE	POW	UP	OFF
ABUSE	2	8	-	-		

Target friendly warbeast gains +2" of movement and +2 STR for one round and immediately suffers d3 damage points.

| TORMENT | 2 | 10 | - | 12 | | X |

Target model damaged by Torment loses Regenerate and Tough for one round. Damage from Torment cannot be transferred.

| UNRELENTING | 2 | 6 | - | - | | X |

Anytime target friendly model suffers damage from an enemy attack, it may immediately move up to its SPD in inches if it is not stationary. Target model cannot be targeted by free strikes during this movement.

Archdomina Makeda

Skorne Warlock Character

Were she not willing to serve another, I would count her my equal.

—Vinter Raelthorne IV, Supreme Archdominar of the Skorne Empire

As archdomina of the Western Reaches and leader of the skorne army, Makeda is the Conqueror's sword. The success or failure of the invasion rests on her capable and ruthless shoulders. Vinter made the difficult decision to stay at his fortress in the Stormlands to maintain iron control over the Skorne Empire, chose Makeda to lead in his stead, and sent her west against the nations of mankind.

During the First Unification after the fall of Halaak, the Conqueror marched north on House Balaash. Even enormously outnumbered, Makeda stood steadfast against him determined to fight to the last. Three times she rallied her army, cutting swaths from his ranks before Vinter forced her back. Her iron resolve refused to wane, and she pushed her soldiers beyond the limits of death. The domina decided her only chance was to slay the Conqueror and force his army to rout. She charged and broke through his line with her greatest war-bred titans and basilisks and her remaining cataphracts. She urged them forward and forced them into a frenzy of bloodshed.

The Conqueror and Makeda met in the center of battle in an epic clash of blades. Vinter had never fought an adversary so strong, and he did not yet comprehend the nature of the domina's link to her enslaved beasts. The blood they spilled turned the desert's baked earth to mud. Makeda withstood a rain of lethal blows by shunting the damage to nearby titans and basilisks instead. Fueled by powers over life and death, Makeda gave Vinter pause, and he almost faltered. She too was amazed, having never expended herself so completely against a foe without crushing him. She could not understand how he could boast such skill and mad resolve drawn only from an invincible wellspring of his being. At last Vinter disarmed Makeda. All of her beasts had been slain and her soldiers brought to ruin. It was at this moment Makeda had the realization that this man must be

Reborn, his vital spirit some ancient ancestor brought to test her while cloaked in strange flesh.

Broken and exhausted but not crushed, the domina stood calmly and awaited the death blow. To the astonishment of his army, the Conqueror walked away after speaking the words that would give her renewed purpose: "Another day and it would be me at your blade. Pick up your swords and fight in my name."

Makeda spent the years of Vinter's first reign rebuilding the strength of her house. When he took his probing expedition in 602 AR to capture Corvis, he left Makeda in Halaak to coordinate and organize the massive army that was to follow and serve as reinforcements for his drive on Caspia. Vinter had tasked all of the house leaders to muster these forces and to work on the great bridge-fortress that he intended would provide a permanent crossing of the Abyss. Unfortunately the Conqueror had not anticipated that his dominars were plotting for his overthrow. They were awaiting his departure to spring to action, hoping to return Halaak to its old ways and break apart the unified government.

The betrayers occupied the skorne capital and targeted Makeda for assassination. She gathered her loyal vassals and fought her way to her northern stronghold and sealed the gates. The siege of House Balaash was a test of her skill that required her to maximize her limited resources and continually fend off a besieging army vastly outnumbering her own. She endured against impossible odds until Vinter returned to break the siege.

Now Makeda serves the Conqueror by leading his invasion. Fused into her heavy armor and twin ancestral blades, the souls of her most revered House Balaash ancestors loan her strength. She leads an army larger than has ever been gathered together by the skorne and she will unleash them in a multi-pronged attack against the human lands. She will create permanent strongholds for the eventual occupation of all of western Immoren. With each step she takes, she expands the border of the Skorne Empire.

SPECIAL RULES

Feat: Walking Death - In service of the Archdomina, even death does not release a soldier from his obligations. Makeda can force the living spirit to linger and fight even after the heart has ceased to beat and the lungs can no longer breath.

Friendly Skorne troopers destroyed in Makeda's control area this round return to play during her controller's next Maintenance Phase if Makeda has not been destroyed or removed from play. A returned model must be placed in her control area within 3" of another model in its original unit. A model cannot be returned to play if all models in its original unit have been destroyed or removed from play. A returned model cannot move during its activation this turn. A returned model causes its unit to lose benefits or effects that it received from the original destruction of the returned model. A model returned to play is reduced to one wound.

MAKEDA					CMD 9
SPD	STR	MAT	RAT	DEF	ARM
6	7	7	4	15	16

SWORD OF BAALASH		
SPECIAL	POW	P+S
—	5	12

SWORD OF BAALASH		
SPECIAL	POW	P+S
—	5	12

FURY	6
DAMAGE	16
FIELD ALLOWANCE	C
VICTORY POINTS	5
POINT COST	64
BASE SIZE	SMALL

Dauntless Aura - Friendly Skorne models/units in Makeda's command range never flee and immediately rally.

Vivisection - Makeda gains a +1 cumulative bonus to melee damage rolls each time she makes a successful melee attack roll targeting an enemy model this turn, including the first.

MAKEDA

Command Authority - Makeda may issue any order to a unit that its original leader or officer could issue.

SPELL	COST	RNG	AOE	POW	UP	OFF
CARNAGE	3	SELF	CTRL	-		

Friendly Skorne models attacking enemy models in Makeda's control area gain +2 to melee attack rolls. Carnage lasts for one round.

DEFENDER'S WARD	2	6	-	-		X

Models in target friendly Skorne unit gain +1 DEF and ARM. While in tight formation, models in the affected unit instead gain +2 DEF and ARM.

SAVAGERY	2	6	-	-		X

Target friendly Skorne non-warlock model/unit may run without being ordered or forced to do so. Affected models may also make melee attacks after running.

THE LASH	3	10	3	13		X

Models/units damaged by The Lash suffer –2 CMD and THR for one round.

Lord Tyrant Hexeris
Skorne Warlock Character

Though peerless in the arts of death, he is a danger. His eyes reflect not but annihilation.

—Archdomina Makeda of House Balaash

A master mortitheurge, Hexeris is unrivaled in his manipulations of life and death. He has long lost the ability to empathize with the living and sees them as simple machines with precisely analyzed thresholds for potential, injury, and pain. Those who speak to him leave feeling violated and tainted, for his eyes can pierce through to the immortal essence. Only the truly courageous can endure his company long.

Hexeris was born to the Kurshon, an influential house of Halaak. A strong-framed and massive skorne, he could have qualified to join the elite cataphracts, and he did spend some time training among them. In the end, his exceptional mind opened other doors as he was not destined for the simple life of a soldier. His house has long valued occult power, and his dominar encouraged his studies of mortitheurgy. Hexeris was obsessed with this sepulchral research which he saw as the key to his rise to eventual domination of the house.

Dominar Lokoda led House Kurshon at this time. On the Conqueror's arrival the dominar shrewdly joined his cause rather than risk weakening his house. However, he made the fatal mistake eight years later of joining the betrayers. A practiced occultist, Lokoda's divinations in blood and entrails led him to conclude Vinter would fail, and he emboldened the other dominars in their conspiracy.

When Vinter returned, Dominar Lokoda sealed his house, desperate to avoid Morghoul's murderous reach, but Hexeris foresaw a far greater destiny waiting in the shadow of the Conqueror. Tracking almost imperceptible hints of death energies left behind by the master tormentor, Hexeris met with

Morghoul. He offered Morghoul free entrance to House Kurshon in exchange for a place in the Conqueror's host. With this betrayal, Kurshon was undone and Dominar Lokoda was captured alive despite all his precautions. He was tortured for days in the great public excruciation and executions.

Vinter accepted Hexeris among his vassals and put his considerable powers to use. Hexeris has since risen in the ranks to become one of the most formidable tyrants, and he was recently placed in charge of the largest single cohort of the Army of the Western Reaches. Every soldier in this cohort marches with perfect discipline and silence, and there is a pervasive sense of dread in their ranks, for all know their master will sacrifice them instantly should it serve his agenda. To Hexeris these soldiers are nothing more than expendable resources.

His bladed pole-arm Gulgalta is his own design and laced with power woven into its length. Upon his chest sits the sacral stone containing the honored soul of his own great-grandfather, the legendary mortitheurge Javekk Kurshon. Hexeris is a secret dabbler in the extoller craft, and through communication with this ancestor he has gained forgotten secrets including hints of the location of several lost sacral stones of special potency. As his power and lore has grown, Hexeris has become convinced that Vinter is not a Reborn skorne, but he has not yet informed Makeda about his suspicion. He knows she would not believe him and schemes to find a use for this revelation. Increasingly his ancestor Javekk speaks to him and guides his studies by unlocking powers never before combined in a single mortitheurge.

Hexeris' interactions with Archdomina Makeda are laced with wary undertones. The lack of trust does not concern Hexeris, for he knows she could not comprehend his work. Recently Hexeris has been leading the northernmost skorne assault, waging war against the stalwart trollkin east of Corvis. Setbacks have aroused his cruel anger, but he is fascinated by their species and their unnatural resiliency. Hexeris is eager to capture as many trollkin and troll slaves as possible and dissect them after exposing them to the full brunt of his dark powers.

SPECIAL RULES

Feat: Dark Dominion - To Hexeris the process of dying is just another strategic mechanism, for he can insinuate his will onto a body as its spirit slips away. Invoking the most potent of his powers, he can reach across the battlefield and turn his enemies into his puppets when they die, their flesh pulled by strings of his will.

When a non-stationary enemy model is destroyed in Hexeris' control area, Hexeris' controller may immediately move the model up to its SPD in inches and make one melee attack, after which it is removed from play. The model cannot be targeted by free strikes during this movement. The model may move out of formation during this movement. During this movement and attack, the model is a friendly Skorne model. The model cannot be forced. Ignore the effects of lost warbeast aspects during this attack. Dark Dominion lasts for one turn.

HEXERIS

Vampiric Reaving - Hexeris may reave fury points from enemy warbeasts destroyed in his control area if he is closer to the warbeast when it is destroyed than other warlocks that could reave its fury.

HEXERIS					CMD 8	
SPD	STR	MAT	RAT	DEF	ARM	
6	8	6	4	15	16	

GULGALTA			
SPECIAL	POW	P+S	
Multi	6	14	

FURY	7
DAMAGE	17
FIELD ALLOWANCE	C
VICTORY POINTS	5
POINT COST	67
BASE SIZE	SMALL

GULGALTA

Beat Back - Target model hit by a Gulgalta attack may be pushed 1" directly away from Hexeris immediately after the attack is resolved. A pushed model moves at half rate in rough terrain and stops if it comes in contact with an obstacle, obstruction, or a model with an equal or larger-sized base. The pushed model cannot be targeted by free strikes during this movement. Immediately after the target model is moved, Hexeris may move up to 1" directly toward the center of the pushed model. Hexeris may be targeted by free strikes during this movement. Hexeris may make melee attacks after following up.

Life Drinker - When Hexeris destroys a living model with a Gulgalta attack, he may remove one damage point from himself.

Reach - 2" melee range.

SPELL	COST	RNG	AOE	POW	UP	OFF
DEATHBRINGER	3	8	*	*		X

Models within 3" of the target model suffer a damage roll with a POW equal to the STR of the target model. The target model then takes d3 damage points for each model destroyed by Deathbringer.

| **DEATH MARCH** | 3 | 6 | - | - | | X |

Target living friendly model/unit can briefly serve Hexeris after death. When an affected non-stationary model is destroyed by an enemy attack, it may immediately move up to its SPD in inches and make one melee attack with automatically boosted attack and damage rolls, after which it is removed from play. Ignore the effects of lost warbeast aspects during this attack. The model cannot be targted by free strikes and may move out of formation during this movement.

| **SOUL SLAVE** | 2 | 6 | - | - | | X |

Hexeris utterly dominates target friendly warbeast, transforming it into an instrument of his will. Hexeris may force, leach, or reave from the affected warbeast even if it is outside his control area. The affected warbeast never makes threshold checks.

| **SPIRIT LEACH** | 3 | 10 | - | 13 | | X |

If Spirit Leach damages a warbeast, Hexeris may transfer a fury point from it to himself.

| **THE SUFFERING** | 2 | 8 | - | - | X | X |

Target warbeast suffers –2 THR and must pass a threshold check or frenzy during its controller's Control Phase whether it has fury points or not.

CYCLOPS SAVAGE

SKORNE LIGHT WARBEAST

CYCLOPS SAVAGE				CMD 6	
SPD	STR	MAT	RAT	DEF	ARM
6	8	6	3	13	17

—	FALCHION		
	SPECIAL	POW	P+S
	Reach	5	13

FURY	3
THRESHOLD	9
FIELD ALLOWANCE	U
VICTORY POINTS	2
POINT COST	62
BASE SIZE	MEDIUM

Cyclops Savage

Future Sight - The Cyclops Savage may boost attack and damage rolls after making the rolls.

Falchion

Reach - 2" melee range.

'Twas like it toyed with me. Ignored my feint, stepped aside my best cut, then nearly clove me in two before the impaler ran 'em through.

—Champion Horthol of the Thornwood Kriel

The cyclopes are a brutish carnivorous species from eastern Immoren that live to hunt and kill. They drew the notice of the skorne through feats of battle prowess surprising for creatures of such primitive and dim intelligence. The skorne learned these creatures had the singular ability to sense the future, and they have enslaved the cyclopes for centuries to refine techniques for enhancing and exploiting this ability.

Captured at youth, cyclops savages receive years of training and conditioning whereby they learn to obey orders without hesitation. Unlike some beasts, they do not require much encouragement—they are bloodthirsty and welcome any excuse to fight. They are so prone to violence that the paingivers sedate them with narcotics between battles. Experienced beast handlers are cautious when moving among the cyclops savages, for the creatures can kill even a veteran with a single blow. In the wild they improvise crude clubs from bones or gnarled wood, but the skorne have outfitted their savages with oversized curved blades sharpened to a keen edge.

Over the centuries the skorne paingivers and chirurgeons have subjected them to extensive experimentation. By refining strategic sections of their brains, they have developed techniques to amplify all of the cyclopes' most formidable instincts and reinforce their love of battle and cruelty. The

ANIMUS	COST	RNG	AOE	POW	UP	OFF
PRESCIENCE	2	6	-	-		

TARGET FRIENDLY SKORNE MODEL MAY BOOST ATTACK AND DAMAGE ROLLS AFTER MAKING THE ROLLS THIS ROUND.

cyclopes have a limited ability to see into the future, which is the key to their amazing intuition in battle. Their complex and sensitive single eye demonstrates unusual perceptiveness, and these flashes of future events give them an edge. They can see exactly how to evade blows or adjust their movements to penetrate a foe's defenses. To help protect this valued ability, the skorne outfit the cyclopes with enclosed steel helmets and also gear them in extensive plated armor to the point where they resemble towering soldiers marching amid the skorne ranks.

BASILISK KREA
SKORNE LIGHT WARBEAST

ANIMUS	COST	RNG	AOE	POW	UP	OFF
PARALYTIC FIELD	3	8	-	-		X

TARGET MODEL MOVES AT HALF RATE AND SUFFERS −3 DEF. WHILE WITHIN 2" OF TARGET MODEL, ENEMY MODELS ALSO MOVE AT HALF RATE AND SUFFER −3 DEF. PARALYTIC FIELD LASTS FOR ONE ROUND.

The ability to unleash the full potential of the basilisk kreas was a triumph of the beast handlers, for these creatures contain tremendous mystical powers even greater than their male counterparts. The skorne unleashed cruel chirurgery to sew their eyes shut and focus their power. Implementing surgical modifications not only made the kreas more manageable, but it also unlocked additional abilities. When blinded in this fashion a krea's other senses become unnaturally sensitive and enable her to detect her surroundings. When prompted to rage and denied the ability to focus her sealed eyes, a krea builds to a critical threshold until powerful energy radiates from her flesh. This strange field is distinctly different from the disruptive blast that once poured from her eyes. It saps strength and slows the movements of anything nearby as if those afflicted were passing through a thick fluid. This can almost halt projectiles launched at the krea and forms a powerful defense.

Further experimentation and training has enabled the krea to direct this power against specific foes. She can catch them in a vortex where a similar resistance

Blinded, their powers are focused, turned inward, and intensified.

—Lord Tyrant Hexaris

slows movement and makes defending against attacks extremely difficult. Tyrants in the field use this effect to cripple the most dangerous enemies and pick them apart. "Blinded" kreas can likewise inflict a spiritual paralysis that disrupts the natural synergy between enemy warlocks and warbeasts.

For centuries the skorne did not bring female basilisks to battle; they used them only for breeding drakes. They are foul-tempered and violent creatures prone to lashing out against their handlers. The unusual energies focused in their reptilian bodies are strongly amplified for several years after they give birth. Handlers suspect the great power of the kreas derives from a defense mechanism in the wild to protect their young from the predators prowling the badlands. Whatever the origins of their powers, basilisk kreas are now a favored warbeast of many and are capable of completely turning the tide of battle.

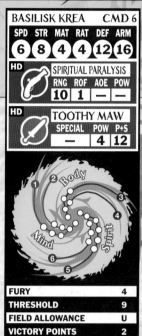

BASILISK KREA				CMD	6
SPD	STR	MAT	RAT	DEF	ARM
6	8	4	4	12	16

HD — SPIRITUAL PARALYSIS

RNG	ROF	AOE	POW
10	1	—	—

HD — TOOTHY MAW

SPECIAL	POW	P+S
—	4	12

FURY	4
THRESHOLD	9
FIELD ALLOWANCE	U
VICTORY POINTS	2
POINT COST	64
BASE SIZE	MEDIUM

Basilisk Krea

Eyeless Sight - The Basilisk Krea ignores Camouflage, cloud effects, concealment, forests, Invisibility, and Stealth when declaring charges or slams or making attacks.

Magic Sensitivity - The Basilisk Krea gains +3 to magic attack rolls.

Paralytic Aura - During its activation, the Basilisk Krea may be forced to activate Paralytic Aura. Enemy models within 2" of the Basilisk Krea move at half rate and suffer −3 DEF. Friendly models within 2" of the Basilisk Krea, including the Basilisk Krea, gain +2 DEF and ARM against ranged attacks. The effects of Paralytic Aura and Paralytic Field are not cumulative. Paralytic Aura lasts for one round.

Spiritual Paralysis

Spirit Lock - A successful Spiritual Paralysis attack causes no damage. A warlock cannot leach fury from a warbeast hit by Spiritual Paralysis for one round.

Basilisk Drake

Skorne Light Warbeast

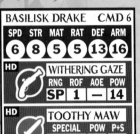

BASILISK DRAKE				CMD 6	
SPD	STR	MAT	RAT	DEF	ARM
6	8	5	5	13	16

HD	WITHERING GAZE			
	RNG	ROF	AOE	POW
	SP	1	—	14

HD	TOOTHY MAW		
	SPECIAL	POW	P+S
	—	4	12

FURY	3
THRESHOLD	9
FIELD ALLOWANCE	U
VICTORY POINTS	2
POINT COST	67
BASE SIZE	MEDIUM

It looked upon me and my skin felt like I'd leapt into a blazing fire. I longed for death until I managed the strength to turn away.

—Kaya the Wildborne, Overseer of the Circle Orboros

Basilisk Drake

Stud - While within 3" of a Basilisk Drake, a Basilisk Krea gains boosted melee attack and melee damage rolls.

Withering Gaze

Gaze - A model damaged by a Withering Gaze attack must immediately turn so that the Basilisk Drake is no longer within its LOS if possible.

Few creatures can withstand the withering gaze of the basilisk drake, one of the most dreadful attacks of any creature inhabiting the badlands surrounding the Skorne Empire. When their eyes focus with deadly intent on a foe, it unleashes a wave of power causing the air to ripple and shimmer as if turned into a flow of heavy liquid. This wholly unnatural wave of entropic energy causes living creatures to suffer indescribable pain as skin sloughs from the bone and muscle tissues fall apart as if roasted. This energy can grind stone to dust, and iron in its path is melted and sheared, twisting and tearing apart with rending screeches of protest. This energy severs the fundamental connections binding solid matter together. Those struck are unable to face the source of the gaze and must turn away.

Taming basilisks has always been a costly proposition resulting in the gruesome deaths of many beast handlers, but there was never any question the skorne would find a way to turn them into weapons in their ongoing house wars. When captured young and properly trained, drakes are receptive

ANIMUS	COST	RNG	AOE	POW	UP	OFF
IMPACT	2	6	-	-		

MODELS DIRECTLY HIT BY RANGED ATTACKS MADE BY TARGET FRIENDLY SKORNE MODEL/UNIT ARE PUSHED D3" DIRECTLY AWAY FROM THE ORIGIN OF THE ATTACK. IMPACT LASTS FOR ONE TURN.

to commands and can be handled with a reasonable assurance of control. Paingivers attach hooks to the sides of their mouths and upper lips to provide a means of wresting their gaze away when necessary. They are trained only to unleash their gaze on command. In addition, handlers have discovered the basilisk females fight with even greater fervor in the presence of a drake, so they are often brought together to be pitted against the foe.

Though its terrible gaze earns it notoriety and makes it a terror to the predators in eastern Immoren, the basilisk is also capable of inflicting gruesome biting wounds with its powerfully muscled and toothy maws. Their claws, however, are utilized exclusively for burrowing, as they prefer to lair underground during the evening and emerge to bask in the heat of the day.

TITAN GLADIATOR

SKORNE HEAVY WARBEAST

ANIMUS	COST	RNG	AOE	POW	UP	OFF
SUBDUE	2	SELF	*		-	

ENEMY MODELS/UNITS BEGINNING THEIR ACTIVATION WITHIN 5" OF THE MODEL USING THIS ANIMUS CANNOT CHARGE, MAKE SPECIAL ATTACKS, OR GIVE OR RECEIVE ORDERS THIS ROUND.

Titans are solid walls of muscle and flesh. The extremely strong bipedal and four-armed pachyderms have served the skorne for thousands of years as their favored beasts of war, for they have the stamina to endure brutal punishment and the strength to rip most any creature apart. Titan nervous systems are well charted and understood, and beast handlers create a variety of barbed hooks to keep imbedded in their skin at sensitive locations to goad titans to the threshold of rampaging madness before battle. By the time it is unleashed, a titan is ready to slaughter anything in its way. A titan gladiator's entire armored body is a weapon it slams into foes to send them flying. When an enemy is pierced and pinned by both of its bladed war-gauntlets, the gladiator can grasp it with its extra pair of arms, seize its weapons, or throw it across the battlefield to land in a quivering lump of shattered bones or broken steel.

Titans congregate in herds where they are occasionally beset by pack hunters grown desperate from hunger. The hunters rarely come out ahead in these engagements, however, and are usually torn to shreds by a titan's tusks or flattened underfoot. They are normally relatively docile unless threatened, but the skorne have made every effort to change that by inflicting a cruel assortment of torments to goad them. Warlocks can tap into their suffering to inflict spiritual pain on others that saps the will to fight or even move.

The earth shakes as they come, and I doubt any creature alive can withstand the full impact of their weight. I pray they do not have many of them.

—Chief Madrak Ironhide after his first engagement with the skorne invaders

TITAN GLADIATOR			CMD 7		
SPD	STR	MAT	RAT	DEF	ARM
4	12	5	3	12	19

LFT WAR GAUNTLET

	SPECIAL	POW	P+S
	Claw	4	16

RT WAR GAUNTLET

	SPECIAL	POW	P+S
	Claw	4	16

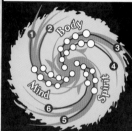

FURY	4
THRESHOLD	10
FIELD ALLOWANCE	U
VICTORY POINTS	3
POINT COST	109
BASE SIZE	LARGE

Titan Gladiator

Bull-Headed - When the Titan Gladiator frenzies, if it would charge a model, it slams that model instead. If the Titan Gladiator cannot slam that model, it frenzies normally.

Chain Attack – Grab & Smash - If the Titan Gladiator hits with both of its initial War Gauntlet attacks against the same target in the same activation, after resolving the attacks it may immediately make a double-hand throw, head-butt, head/weapon lock, push, or throw attack against the target without being forced.

Grand Slam - The Titan Gladiator may slam without being forced. The Titan Gladiator does not suffer the normal attack roll penalty for making a slam attack. Models slammed by the Titan Gladiator are moved an additional 2".

Massive Tusks - The Titan Gladiator gains +3 to slam damage rolls.

War Gauntlets

Claw - The Titan Gladiator's War Gauntlets have the abilities of Claws.

TITAN CANNONEER

SKORNE HEAVY WARBEAST

CANNONEER				CMD	7
SPD	STR	MAT	RAT	DEF	ARM
4	11	5	4	12	18

RT	SIEGE GUN			
	RNG	ROF	AOE	POW
	12	1	3	15

LFT	WAR MACE		
	SPECIAL	POW	P+S
	—	4	15

FURY	4
THRESHOLD	10
FIELD ALLOWANCE	U
VICTORY POINTS	3
POINT COST	115
BASE SIZE	LARGE

Cannoneer

Bull-Headed - When the Titan Cannoneer frenzies, if it would charge a model, it slams that model instead. If the Titan Cannoneer cannot slam the selected model, it frenzies normally.

Massive Tusks - The Titan Cannoneer gains +3 to slam damage rolls.

Siege Gun

Batter - Double the number of damage points a structure takes from the Siege Gun.

I know Corvis fought them off before, but they didn't bring the titans that time. If those cannoneers reach Corvis, the walls will fall in a matter of hours.

—Alten Ashley, monster hunter of Ternon Crag

The skorne have employed titans to carry and fire cannons for almost two hundred years. Their tremendous strength allows them to maneuver with these massive weapons in a fashion no lesser creature could imitate. This enables the skorne to field its most physically imposing warbeast together with a powerful siege weapon. It is a brutal combination.

Skorne warrior codes, the cost of manufacture, and the extensive time required to train the titans have all combined to make them rare assets deployed only by the most wealthy houses. In the wars between the skorne, the cannons served to blast down the walls and gateways of fortified strongholds, allowing soldiers to charge through the breach and decimate defenders. Only in the last few decades have house fortresses been built with sufficiently thick and sloped walls to endure this type of siege weapon.

ANIMUS	COST	RNG	AOE	POW	UP	OFF
DIMINISH	2	SELF	-	-		

WHILE WITHIN 3" OF THE MODEL USING THIS ANIMUS, ENEMY MODELS SUFFER –3 STR THIS ROUND.

Under the consolidation of the Conqueror and his formation of the Army of the Western Reaches, all wealthy houses were forced to relinquish cannoneers to Archdomina Makeda. Some dominars whisper that Vinter's purpose in assembling them is to prevent another rebellion and any chance of lesser houses laying siege to his fortress in the Stormlands.

Titans demonstrate phenomenal dexterity in the complex three-armed juggling act required to operate these weapons, however this task is a strain on their limited intelligence. Although they are trained and conditioned, the supervision of a warlock is usually required for a cannoneer to perform these maneuvers repeatedly. In addition to its potent cannon, the titan cannoneer wields an oversized war mace allowing it to batter opponents in melee. If driven to frenzy, the cannoneer will revert to wild instincts where it prefers to slam an opponent and rend it apart with its metal-tipped tusks.

Recognized by their distinctive two weapon fighting style, the Praetorians represent one of the most ancient traditions of skorne warfare. In the harsh skorne society, all able-bodied adults are required to learn to fight. They must carve their place in society at a blade's edge, and their status is earned by blood. The Praetorians form the backbone of all house armies as well as the Army of the Western Marches.

Praetorians must undergo endless drills and training to refine their natural ability and learn to fight with precision in the twin bladed fighting style, obeying the ancient warrior code of *hoksune*. A Praetorian's only hope of glory is to fight well and survive. There is no early return for wounded nor any reprieve for the weary. Tyrants ensure they fight as long as their flesh and sinew holds their bones together, and the Praetorians are eager to capture slaves and territory to prove themselves worthy for elevation in the ranks.

All seem identical to me—individuality drilled out of them. I sense no joy, no passion, nothing but grim purpose and obedience to orders.

—Kaya Wildborne, Overseer of the Circle

When Vinter Raelthorne moved to his Abyss fortress, he ordered the dominars to send to him their best swordsmen. For those who passed the muster, Archdomina Makeda offered welcome into the fortress and inclusion in the great conquest to come. Those deemed inferior returned to their houses in shame. Even the least of Makeda's Praetorians are thus the best their houses could offer and are therefore rightfully proud of their abilities and standing. Accustomed to linking their honor with their houses, these soldiers have transferred that pride to their cohort, and there is considerable competition between the various Praetorian cohorts to outdo one another for glory and spoils.

Praetorians wear expertly crafted and flexible plated armor, and their swords are crafted from the finest materials. In the capable trained hands of a Praetorian, each keen-edged blade can penetrate the thickest hides or armor.

DAKAR				CMD	8
SPD	STR	MAT	RAT	DEF	ARM
6	6	7	4	13	14

PRAETOR				CMD	6
SPD	STR	MAT	RAT	DEF	ARM
6	6	6	4	13	14

SWORD			
	SPECIAL	POW	P+S
	Combo	3	9

SWORD			
	SPECIAL	POW	P+S
	Combo	3	9

FIELD ALLOWANCE	3
VICTORY POINTS	2
LEADER AND 5 TROOPS	53
UP TO 4 ADDITIONAL TROOPS	8ea
BASE SIZE	SMALL

Dakar
Leader

Unit
Penetrating Strike - After a successful attack against a warjack or warbeast, a Praetorian may automatically inflict one damage point instead of making a damage roll.

Swords
Combo Strike (★Attack) - A Praetorian can make sword attacks separately, or he may make a special attack to strike with both swords simultaneously. Make one attack roll for the Combo Strike. Add the Praetorian's STR once and the POW of both swords to the damage roll.

Venators

Skorne Unit

DAKAR					CMD 8
SPD	STR	MAT	RAT	DEF	ARM
6	5	6	6	13	13

ARMIGER					CMD 6
SPD	STR	MAT	RAT	DEF	ARM
6	5	6	5	13	13

REIVER			
RNG	ROF	AOE	POW
12	1	—	10

SWORD		
SPECIAL	POW	P+S
—	3	8

FIELD ALLOWANCE	3
VICTORY POINTS	2
LEADER AND 5 TROOPS	70
UP TO 4 ADDITIONAL TROOPS	11ea
BASE SIZE	SMALL

Dakar
Leader

Unit
Combined Ranged Attack - Instead of making ranged attacks separately, two or more Venators may combine their attacks against the same target. In order to participate in a combined ranged attack, a Venator must be able to declare a ranged attack against the intended target and be in a single open formation group with the other participants. The Venator with the highest RAT in the attacking group makes one ranged attack roll for the group and gains +1 to the attack and damage rolls for each Venator, including himself, participating in the attack.

Reiver
Needle Burst - A Venator gains +1 to damage rolls against medium-based models and +2 against large-based models.

Put aside the teachings of your hoksune masters. It will be your reivers that carry the day. I promise your ancestors will see and remember.

—Vinter Raelthorne to the assembled Venators at the training field of his Abyss fortress

Traditionally skorne military tactics have revolved around closing with the enemy and butchering them in melee. Their large and clumsy ranged weapons were designed to provide covering fire, bring down the walls of rival houses, and slay oversized beasts. These applications have changed in the last century as skorne weapons have been refined and tyrants began to learn the power of combined arms. Vinter Raelthorne knew these lessons and has encouraged the recruiting and training of large numbers of Venators for his invading army.

Mastering the heavy gas-driven reivers requires more skill and finesse than other soldiers sometimes realize. They have always been deemed a lesser caste than the Praetorians, but these disciplined combatants have begun to earn respect. Announcing their presence on the battlefield with a hail of iron needles, the Venators are the scourge of both man and beast. Reivers unleash bursts at tremendous velocity that disintegrate flesh, rend metal, and leave their targets strung across the field begging for a release from their agony. With a lethal swarm of concentrated fire, the Venators tear into the most imposing targets by covering their bulk with razor sharp projectiles.

The lowest ranking Venators are termed armigers and organized in "taberna," a small group named after those who share the same tent, led by a Dakar. They must train extensively in swordplay in addition to accurate operation of their reivers. The reiver itself is driven by cylinders of explosive gas and is somewhat less complicated to reload than western firearms. With the trigger's pull, the gas ignites to propel the needles out of the spinning cone with a burst of flame. The sound of firing reivers is unlike any western firearm. It creates an eerie and loud metallic buzzing caused by the cone's internal mechanisms. Each reiver cone stores hundreds of needles that are fired in clustered bursts, and the Venators carry several cones and gas canisters for reloading.

Cataphract Arcuarii

Skorne Cataphract Unit

These imposing warriors are encased in extremely thick lacquered armor capable of withstanding an onslaught of punishment that renders them almost impervious to normal attacks. Fighting effectively in this heavy layered shell requires a lifetime of training and both exceptional strength and endurance. Arcuarii wield great hooked harpoons that can be wielded in close quarters or fired across the battlefield to impale enemies and drag them close. Though individually masters with the arcus, the Arcuarii are trained to act in concert to bring down the mightiest prey. Arcuarii are deployed alongside the beast handlers and help bring fresh supplies of wild titans to be broken and trained for war.

Not all skorne can aspire to become a Cataphract, for it requires exceptional height, bulk, strength, and unflagging endurance. Nor does every house boast Cataphracts among their warriors as only the most esteemed and wealthy can field even a small number of these heavily armored combatants. When Vinter assembled the Western Army for Archdomina Makeda, he drew on the gathered Cataphracts of multiple houses and brought them under one banner.

There is nothing living that cannot be felled.

—Motto of the Cataphract Arcuarii

Archdomina Makeda has ensured that the ranking primus of each unit is a loyal veteran of House Balaash to keep mixed house units in line.

In past millennia the arcus was a simpler hurled weapon attached to a tether. They were refined by the construction of small but extremely strong crossbow mechanisms integrated into each weapon's shaft. This enables the heavy bladed head of the harpoon to be fired at tremendous force and surprising range, and it reels out a length of chain. The harpoon sinks deeply into an adversary who can then be drawn in and set upon. Few beasts can stand against the Arcuarii when they are grouped as a unit, and they are skilled and efficient killers capable of defeating almost any lesser enemy infantry one on one.

PRIMUS						CMD 9
SPD	STR	MAT	RAT	DEF	ARM	
5	7	8	6	12	15	

CATAPHRACT						CMD 7
SPD	STR	MAT	RAT	DEF	ARM	
5	7	7	5	12	15	

HARPOON			
RNG	ROF	AOE	P
8	1	—	12

ARCUS		
SPECIAL	POW	P+S
Reach	5	12

PRIMUS DAMAGE	8
CATAPHRACT DAMAGE	5
FIELD ALLOWANCE	2
VICTORY POINTS	3
LEADER AND 3 TROOPS	87
UP TO 2 ADDITIONAL TROOPS	20ea
BASE SIZE	MEDIUM

Primus
Leader

Unit

Fearless - A Cataphract Arcuarius never flees.

Weapon Master - A Cataphract Arcuarius rolls an additional die on his melee damage rolls.

Harpoon

Chains - If the Harpoon damages a target model with a small- or medium-sized base, the model may be dragged any distance directly toward the Cataphract Arcuarius. The model stops if it contacts another model, an obstacle, or an obstruction. During this movement the model cannot be targeted by free strikes.

Hog Tie - When three or more Cataphract Arcuarii hit a target large-based model with Harpoons in the same turn, the model suffers Hog Tie. Hog Tie is a continuous effect that reduces the affected model's base SPD to 1 and base DEF to 7. Hog Tie expires in the model's controller's Maintenance Phase on a d6 roll of 1 or 2.

Arcus

Reach - 2" melee range.

CATAPHRACT CETRATI

SKORNE CATAPHRACT UNIT

PRIMUS					CMD 9	
SPD	STR	MAT	RAT	DEF	ARM	
5	7	8	4	12	16	

CATAPHRACT					CMD 7	
SPD	STR	MAT	RAT	DEF	ARM	
5	7	7	4	12	16	

WAR SPEAR			
	SPECIAL	POW	P+S
	Multi	5	12

PRIMUS DAMAGE	8
CATAPHRACT DAMAGE	5
FIELD ALLOWANCE	2
VICTORY POINTS	3
LEADER AND 3 TROOPS	64
UP TO 2 ADDITIONAL TROOPS	14ea
BASE SIZE	MEDIUM

They endured the charge like rocks the waves break upon. We could not move them.

—Golund Stonefist, trollkin shaman

The Cataphract Cetrati form the hard center of the skorne army. They are the front line of the vanguard expected to meet the foe first and be the last to fall. Wielding wicked pole-arms and locking shields as they enter battle, the Cetrati embody perfect skorne discipline and fearless tenacity. A wall of Cetrati charging across the field in their massive armor can inflict terrible wounds and crush through lines of unprepared infantry. They will occupy strategic ground and then lock into formation, setting their sharp-pointed halberds to impale any who charge to engage.

Among the skorne, combat is more than a means to an end—it has intrinsic meaning. The grueling discipline and training required to become a Cetrati is welcomed not as a travail to be overcome, but a transformative process to be relished. The Cetrati spend years in intensive training as a formation mastering the difficult fighting maneuvers of their caste. They are expected to fight together as a seamless machine, each only part of a larger whole. There is an awareness held by each Cetratus that he is part of an esteemed tradition stretching back for millennia and that many of the greatest exalted ancestors were once members of this caste.

The sheer weight of equipment borne by the Cetrati is difficult to fathom, for they stand almost entirely engulfed in the massive overlapping armor plating which would seem too heavy to allow them to move. When considered with the heavy thickness of their curved shields and the length of a halberd, it is no wonder why only a special breed of the strongest skorne can fill these ranks.

Primus
Leader

Shield Wall (Order) - Every Cataphract Cetratus that received the order who is in tight formation with the Primus at the end of the unit's movement gains +4 ARM. If the Primus is no longer on the table, the largest tight formation group forms the shield wall. If there is more than one group with the largest number of troopers, the unit's controller decides which group forms the shield wall. A trooper that did not receive the order cannot join the shield wall. This bonus does not apply to damage originating in the model's back arc. Models that do not end their movement in tight formation do not benefit from the shield wall. This bonus lasts for one round.

Unit
Combined Melee Attack - Instead of making melee attacks separately, two or more Cataphract Cetrati in melee range of the same target may combine their attacks. In order to participate in a combined melee attack, a Cetratus must be able to declare a melee attack against the intended target. The Cataphract Cetratus with the highest MAT in the attacking group makes one melee attack roll for the group and gains +1 to the attack and damage rolls for each Cataphract Cetratus, including himself, participating in the attack.

Fearless - A Cataphract Cetratus never flees.

War Spear
Brutal Charge - A Cataphract Cetratus gains +2 to charge attack damage rolls.

Reach - 2" melee range.

PAINGIVER BEAST HANDLERS

On the path to mastery, paingivers must learn not only the anatomy of fellow skorne, but also that of the warbeasts the skorne use to wage battle. Beast handlers are a specially trained class of paingivers that can evoke tremendous effort from the beasts under their charge, enraging them to rampage forward with impossible strength and speed to crush the enemy. Though their primary purpose is overseeing the warbeasts, beast handlers are dangerous foes in battle in their own right. In their expert hands, their barbed implements can find an opening and strike key arteries or tendons even in the heaviest armored living foe.

Beast handlers are tasked with the extremely dangerous job of conditioning warbeasts. With lash, pain-hook, needle, blade, and soporific drugs, the paingiver must know exactly the temperament and limits of the beasts with which he works. Experienced tormentors oversee groups of adepts who seek to learn the higher arts of taming the greatest beasts. Tyrants value the beast handlers for their ability to goad beasts and also to treat them with medicinal stimulants and mind-fogging injections. With them a war-beast can be fooled into believing it is healed and urged to fight despite injuries. There is always a price to pay after battle, as a beast may cause itself greater internal

It is the beasts which give our army its strength, and without the handlers we could never dominate so many.

—Master Tormentor Morghoul

damage in the process, but this is an acceptable risk as it achieves victory.

The code they follow was set down by the example of the first paingiver Morkaash. They do not belong to a single house; instead they consider their calling and philosophy a higher task loaned to those who require them. Even among the Western Army, which has soldiers drawn from many houses, the beast handlers are aloof and do not fraternize with soldiers of other castes.

TORMENTOR				CMD 8	
SPD	STR	MAT	RAT	DEF	ARM
6	5	6	4	13	11
PAINGIVER				CMD 6	
SPD	STR	MAT	RAT	DEF	ARM
6	5	5	4	13	11

TORTURE IMPLEMENTS			
	SPECIAL	POW	P+S
	Reach	3	8

FIELD ALLOWANCE	2
VICTORY POINTS	2
LEADER AND 3 TROOPS	36
UP TO 2 ADDITIONAL TROOPS	8ea
BASE SIZE	SMALL

Tormentor
Leader

Unit
Anatomical Precision - If a Paingiver Beast Handler's melee damage roll fails to exceed a living target's ARM, the target automatically suffers one damage point.

Inflict Pain - Any time a Paingiver Beast Handler hits a warbeast with a melee attack, he may place one fury point on or remove one fury point from the target warbeast.

Beast Manipulation
A Paingiver Beast Handler may perform one of the following actions during the unit's activation. A warbeast may only be affected by a single Beast Manipulation special action each round.

• **Condition (★Action)** - Remove or add any number of fury points to one friendly Skorne warbeast in base-to-base contact with the Paingiver Beast Handler.

• **Enrage (★Action)** - One friendly Skorne warbeast in base-to-base contact with the Paingiver Beast Handler gains +2 STR and must charge or make a slam attack at SPD + 5" without being forced during its activation this turn.

• **Medicate (★Action)** - One friendly Skorne warbeast in base-to-base contact with the Paingiver Beast Handler may remove d3 damage points from anywhere on its life spiral.

Torture Implements
Reach - 2" melee range.

ANCESTRAL GUARDIAN

SKORNE SOLO

GUARDIAN					CMD	10
SPD	STR	MAT	RAT	DEF	ARM	
4	8	8	3	12	18	

HALBERD			
	SPECIAL	POW	P+S
	Reach	4	12

DAMAGE	10
FIELD ALLOWANCE	2
VICTORY POINTS	1
POINT COST	28
BASE SIZE	MEDIUM

Your exalted ancestors stand by you and fight at your side. By their vigilance, those who fall will be preserved.

—Aptimus Extoller Bakaresk of House Nikanuur

Ancestral Guardian

Animated - The Ancestral Guardian is not a living model, never flees, and cannot run. The Ancestral Guardian must spend soul tokens to make melee attacks during its combat action, one soul token per attack. The Ancestral Guardian must spend a soul token to charge but does not need to spend an additional soul token to make the charge attack

Gather Spirits - The Ancestral Guardian gains a soul token for each friendly living Skorne model destroyed within 10". The Ancestral Guardian may have up to 5 soul tokens at any time.

Retaliatory Strike - When a model hits the Ancestral Guardian with a melee attack, after the attack is resolved, the Ancestral Guardian may immediately make one melee attack against it out of turn and without spending a soul token.

Spirit Driven - The Ancestral Guardian may spend one soul token at the beginning of its activation to gain +4" of movement this activation.

Weapon Master - The Ancestral Guardian rolls an additional die on its melee damage rolls.

Halberd

Reach - 2" melee range.

The essence of accomplished skorne ancestors can become preserved and immortalized in stone, and some of these stones are fused into ancestral guardians. These guardians have traditionally watched over their houses but are now utilized as weapons of war. Empowered to embrace the fallen dead, the ancestral guardians offer the potential of immortality to any skorne fighting alongside them. The essences of those gathered by the guardian allow it to move with blinding speed, and its strength is empowered by the wrath of the freshly slain. Guided by the spirit of an ancient hero and fueled by the spiritual energy contained within, the ancestral guardian is capable of unleashing a flurry of skilled attacks few, if any, can withstand.

Ancestral guardians are expensive to create, and each is unique. Vinter Raelthorne's choice to deploy them with the invading army has brought resolve to the skorne and cemented their loyalty to the Conqueror. Their presence is taken as a sign of high favor by the ancestors and serves as a blessing on the entire expedition. The central sacral stone of the ancestor animating each guardian is fused into the head, and the numerous additional obsidian stones decorating its torso and limbs are able to attract and crystallize the essence of any skorne who die in their proximity. Spirits collected in this fashion gain honor in death and are named revered companions of the exalted. This is a lower caste than those granted full exaltation, but for soldiers this is a rare chance of preserving their essence from the void.

Sacral stones are tough and difficult to destroy. When guardians inevitably fall to enemy blows and collapse, these crystallized stones are recovered and returned to the skorne homeland to honor the houses of the slain.

Legion of Everblight

THE LEGION OF EVERBLIGHT

Bloodied snow crunched beneath the Abomination's weighty tread as he walked. He followed the path of bodies littering the landscape with grim amusement while his baleful eyes soaked in the scene. The three clawed fingers at the end of his enormously oversized right arm traced along the slender corpse of a winter elf, and the sight prompted a strange emotion in the whispering presence in his mind like the feeling of hunger. It quickened the dragon's blood flowing in his veins as Everblight's eagerness translated into tension across the entire frame of the twisted ogrun.

The bodies of the Nyss felled here were pierced by crudely feathered arrows or hacked down by axe and blade. Scattered about was an even greater number of the thicker framed and more muscular bodies of humans although the bulk of them were dozens of yards behind him toward the crude village of lashed huts and mud-soaked logs. These humans wore hides, and their bodies were marked by burned tattoos in the shape of beasts, but their weapons had been effective and they had fought with berserk disregard for their safety. The word *vindol* whispered in Thagrosh's mind, and suddenly he knew more about these isolated tribes of savage northmen than any scholar could have learned in a lifetime of study.

A god now looks upon you through my eyes. You are chosen, and power beyond belief can be yours.

The Nyss fell upon these humans with bloodthirsty savagery, but they had not expected so strong a resistance. The predator became prey, and the fight turned. Thagrosh had only seen the end of the battle, but he could imagine it from start to end in his mind's eye as he peered along the bloodied forms. The wellspring of images rose from the god carried in the shielded cage of his ribs. The brutal and glorious fight came down to the last man and woman on both sides—total and utter slaughter. Thagrosh came across the body of the last of the humans, feathered with arrows clustered in a precise pattern in his chest. This one had been very strong, filled with unholy rage, and had not fallen easily. He managed to throw his spear with his last breath and hurled it with such strength it had knocked the huntress off her feet and impaled her to a tree.

She still breathed but not for long. Her life was bleeding out as he stepped closer. With blood on her lips, she watched his approach with fading eyes, yet there was no fear. Again the whispers stirred in his mind—the hunger. He observed the pale skin, dark hair, and the delicate pointed ears. His monstrous and blight-twisted body towered over her. She was so small and insignificant, but he sensed a singular strength. He slung his massive blade onto his back, reached for the spear, and pulled it free with a gout of blood as she fell to the snow.

"Do you wish to live?" She looked up. His thick-voiced words delivered in her own Aeric tongue brought her back from the abyss with a spark of surprise. "A god now looks upon you through my eyes. You are chosen, and power beyond belief can be yours."

He knew she did not fully understand his words, but she choked out her response. "I would live…"

He nodded and his smile was a ghastly parody. He unknotted the cords binding his chest together. Reaching inside, he pulled forth a great crystal stone pulsing with an icy blue light. With its removal, his skin paled, his eyes sunk, and his frame slumped. He set the athanc on a flat rock by his feet jutting from the snow, and then he freed the great blade on his back. He swung it around and down with a sound like thunder and clove both athanc and the rock below it. Setting his blade aside for the moment, Thagrosh lifted the largest chunk of athanc and replaced it in his chest. His frame instantly regained its vigor. The wounded elf watched this blankly, and her eyes began to lose their spark.

With his left hand he grasped the shard of the athanc, and his enormous right claw grasped the huntress and lifted her from the snow. She weighed nothing, and his clawed fingers were not gentle to her skin. He spoke to her softly, "Here is your blessing. You are reborn." He thrust the athanc shard directly into her breast. His strength forced it through her ribcage and pierced directly into her heart. Her eyes flew open with a sudden shock of awareness as she unleashed a scream that pierced the frozen glade and sent the ravens feasting on corpses.

Fall and Resurrection

Transcribed from the words of the Prophet, Thagrosh Hellborne, Spring 606 AR

During the transformation, a thousand whispered phrases and visions smote my mind. Agony consumed my body as my flesh revolted against the change. Through this pain came the unending voice of Everblight in constant echoes. We are now one and speak with a voice united. I am not and can never be alone. Even in the quietest times His thoughts intersect my own, and the voice of my god imparts more than I can sometimes bear to hear.

I did not always speak as I do now. I was a crude thing; my mind was small and thick. I was rude clay which my master has shaped. His touch transformed my mind, my soul, and my body. Dozens of languages spring to my lips as I wish it, even the secret language of Tkra, spoken first by Toruk the Dragonfather. Even now our change is not complete; flesh still twists under the pressure of this blight. No mortal shell could ever hope to contain such unearthly power.

Reaching into our memories is like plunging into a bottomless well. On first peering into these depths I found many surprises. I learned that my master, though a god to we insects who walk Caen, was not reckoned mightiest of those dragons sprung from Toruk. As a son may exceed his father, Everblight's intellect exceeded that of the one who had created Him. What I lacked in size and raw power, we made up for in the cunning maze of our mind. Our mind cuts through to the core of things and can act without hesitation.

At the core of every dragon is an athanc. This is the pure essence of the dragon's being; skin and bone are a convenience. If the athanc endures, the dragon cannot be destroyed. When dragons clash in cannibalistic battle and the victor consumes the defeated, their athancs pull together like iron to a lodestone and fuse into a single whole. It is their nature to seek one another. Our unique nature derives from the athanc—a stone of ultimate perfection so flawless even by division it is not reduced.

The athanc is uniquely alive, its properties escape the wisest sages, and each piece is capable of unlocking tremendous growth. The athanc was the first living thing on Caen, and its generative properties may have sparked the seed of life. Dragons do not require any of the substances lesser beings crave: food, water, not even air.

Toruk's decision to divide his essence and create progeny is a puzzle to those who learn the lore of dragons. The first dragon understood the endless mutable power of His athanc and knew that even the smallest fragment of His essence could become supremely powerful. Toruk must have sought to understand His own nature to divide His athanc and test the limits of its power. Each piece of this stone became a dragon of its own, more powerful individually than he had anticipated and infinitely more willful. Though sprung from His essence, we owed Him no loyalty nor felt any fidelity. When Toruk attempted to enforce His will upon us, we rebelled.

In His ignorance Toruk cast away the most flawless portion of Himself. Like a diamond waiting in the raw stone for a chisel to capture its edges, we arose from the purest and most sublime portion of the original athanc. Casting away this piece forever reduced Toruk.

We foresaw the battle to come and did not participate. Instead we lingered at the fringes as the first spawn clashed to tear down Toruk. This was not cowardice, but calculated premeditation. We watched to learn Toruk's strength and gauge the mettle of our siblings.

Dragons are selfish and incapable of cooperating even in this shared struggle against the Father. We saw they were doomed and took measures to conceal ourself. Toruk destroyed many lesser progeny while the rest fled. None of them were so adept at concealing their presence as we were, and in the centuries that followed Toruk chased them down one by one and annihilated many, restoring their essences to His own.

We were not content to hide and wait out the storm. We have several advantages over our siblings by virtue of our flawless athanc. None can duplicate our subtle powers of concealment or our ability to restrain our blight at will. Where other dragons betray their presence by the inevitable spoiling of the lands around them, we can pick and choose how our blight manifests. Our siblings have never taken the time to understand their own power, but we learned how to extend our consciousness into the world to see without eyes and hear without ears. We can penetrate the dreams of man, and in those vulnerable hours when the mind lies open to strange visions, our words and our thoughts can take seed. Our siblings are like lazy beasts content to slay by claw and fang and the roiling destruction of corrosive breath.

We found fertile soil below the lands of Morrdh, the first great human kingdom. Their lords had mastered powers unknown to the rest of man, and their potent rune magic and necromancy was an enigma we could not resist. Through pawns we arranged to meet, and we entered an alliance of convenience with the lords of Morrdh.

During this time we learned greater mastery of our blight, drinking deep of the well of knowledge of Morrdh to decipher our inner nature. However, the immunity of their lords to our influence vexed us, and we sought ways to pierce the sigils shielding them. Morrdh had divorced themselves from the gods of man, and we saw in this an opportunity for our blight to take hold. After centuries of delving into their secrets, we began to gain the upper hand in this puzzle. We arranged subtle dominance over several lords and turned them with the gift of our blight's blessing. Unfortunately our success did not go unnoticed.

...the departure of their gods left them vulnerable, and it weakened their very souls.

Toruk has ever been the most patient and persistent hunter and has spent centuries stalking His progeny. In 1640 BR Toruk consumed the dragon of the Scharde Isles, Shazkz, and sent the blood of that dragon down in a rain of tainted poison. We dislike dwelling on this event, for it was one of the few times we have ever felt a glimmer of what humans call fear.

We will admit to two mistakes in our long history, and here is one of them. We had grown too intrigued by the lords of Morrdh, and we became too indiscriminate with our blight. Toruk recognized a subtle familiar energy lingering about the lands of Morrdh. Using a vassal as an intermediary, Toruk threatened those lords whom we had been unable to corrupt, and he convinced them to end their alliance.

Our spies were myriad, and we sensed this betrayal in time to flee as Toruk descended. We knew better than to engage Him and bent our strength to try to escape. It was our first terrible taste of mortality—if Toruk's jaws took our athanc, we would be forever obliterated. We suffered grievous wounds from Toruk's claws but managed to slip free. We fled toward the mountain lair

of one our siblings that we had previously unearthed. The wyrm named Nektor rested unsuspecting and served as the distraction we required. Nektor and Toruk seared the skies as we dove unseen into Blindwater Lake, sinking to the bottom. By guile we concealed our presence. We rested in brooding silence for centuries while we recovered from our grievous wounds. Momentarily sated by the consumption of Nektor, Toruk forgot us for a time and gave up the chase. The Dragonfather continued the hunt elsewhere, cornering Gaulvang near the Castle of the Keys in 1387 BR to reclaim another sizable piece of athanc.

Because of our injuries, we did not participate when Blighterghast organized the surviving dragons and convinced them to join in a pact to drive Toruk from the mainland. We watched from the shadows as the remaining dragons ambushed Toruk. Toruk's stamina began to wane, and the fight ended in a stalemate. It was at this time in 1000 BR that Toruk retreated to the Scharde Islands. The other dragons took this for defeat, but we knew our father had a scheme by which he would build an army and use it to hunt His progeny once again. This was the birth of Cryx.

Blighterghast was the only one foolish enough to hold vigil on the western islands, settling in the Wyrmwall Mountains. The rest found lairs far from our creator's grasp. They withdrew from the world overcome by fatigue from their clash, and some slumbered for centuries to allow caustic and nearly permanent wounds from Toruk's claws and fangs to heal.

We watched as the living gods of Ios departed from that land in 840 BR. By this time we had fully recovered from our wounds and slipped out of our lake. Toruk was fully engrossed consolidating his island empire and training his lich lords and was for the moment distracted. We crept north of Aeryth Dawnguard and found a lair among the Skybridge Mountains. From here we watched Ios. It seemed fertile with opportunity, for its declining people were isolated from other kingdoms. We grew excited to imagine corrupting them and usurping their leaders. It would be easy to hide our blight among such a verdant forest so far from Cryx, for the departure of their gods left them vulnerable, and it weakened their very souls.

We began to extend our power to delve into the secrets of the elves. We bent our mind to decipher a way the blight could penetrate the shell of their being. Completely ignorant of our eye upon them,

the elves became unwilling participants in our arcane manipulations as our mind invaded their dreams.

It was the Rivening in 140 BR that opened the gateway. This was a time of chaos and panic across Ios as the elven priests lost contact with their gods. Maddened priests fled their fanes, tore out their eyes, and slew innocents in mad frenzies while riots gripped the streets of every major city in Ios. It was sweet music to us. Burrowing below the ground outside the city, we carved out caverns to make a new lair from the earth and linked them to the abandoned fane of the vanished goddess Ayisla. Through our dream whispers, Issyrah suffered the worst riots of the Rivening. After the madness of their priests, none of its citizens dared venture into the Fane of Ayisla. They considered it cursed and anathema.

From here we lured manipulated elves into our clutches, working on them slowly one by one to test the focus of our blight. The best subjects were those rare few born soulless—their bodies were shells for the souls lost to the wilds of Urcaen. Our dream-sendings took root in those elves who continued to worship the missing gods even after the tragedy of the Rivening, and it was simple for us to encourage them to take religious pilgrimages into our caverns. To our followers we took the name Ethrunbal, and this is the name by which the elves still refer to us.

Only Scyrah's worshipers were sealed from us, and we discovered why when the goddess returned to Ios in 34 BR. This unfortunate turn of events hindered our plans. Fortunately the distance to her home in the capital Shyrr sufficed to allow us to continue cautious efforts. The ailing plight of the goddess seemed another possible opportunity, and we wondered if she might eventually grow so weak that we could set upon her and feast. We dreamed of devouring the goddess and knew we could replace her as the only living god of Ios.

In time we would have succeeded, but one of our minions was our undoing. In 390 AR a blighted servitor wandered out from the caverns without permission and set upon the inhabitants of Issyrah. The guardians of the city sprang into action with unexpected swiftness. These memories come with a heat though, like a lightning storm sizzling across my mind!

The military houses and myrmidons descended on Issyrah, plunged deep into its caverns, and sought the cause of the blight. I saw them as they came into the caverns equipped for war, and their intentions were clear. Into *my* lair they crawled, and they hoped to stand against me? Foolish insects! I expelled my breath through the caverns to obliterate the armies. As my breath melted their flesh to water and their blood sprayed the cavern walls, I felt my rage bubbling forth, and anger consumed me in a wild madness. All I could think of was destruction and slaughter. I leapt up through the stones and earth, shattered the abandoned fane, and fell upon the city.

This was a mistake, but it was oh so glorious at the time. So long had it been since I had let loose my rage. The legacy of my father, the fire that burns in the blood of all dragons, yearned for release, and there was nothing better than watching the landscape consumed by the clouds of fire and hearing the screams of thousands who died in horrible suffering. Buildings exploded from the intense heat. Even those scurrying underground to escape my wrath could not avoid the heat; cooked alive, their flesh fell from their bones even as they cried to their gods! I reveled in this massacre and discovered an ecstasy in this essence of death! It was a beautiful indulgence, and for a moment I thought it would not cost me and the elven spirit would be crushed.

Unfortunately though, the elves were not so easily cowed. Insects they may be, but in numbers they are formidable. Reinforcements gathered with lightning speed from the Gate of Mists and Iryss. Iosan battle wizards and myrmidons confronted me in the ash-laden streets as the buildings blazed in an ongoing inferno. These wizards sacrificed themselves in an effort to maim my wings. It was a cunning maneuver. I should have fled on their approach but was drunk on my own power. I reaped a massive toll on their armies, but they managed to shred my wings. Meanwhile others beset me on all sides. By the time I realized my peril it was too late. Pecked by a thousand needles, my body was undone and collapsed atop the ruins of the fane as they carved loose my athanc. I watched as they pulled it forth, and in that moment I knew the bitter taste of defeat.

This was the time of our imprisonment. Even bodiless, we could not be destroyed by the Iosans. Locked in the heavily warded vessel, we were aware of them, and we watched as they consulted auguries. By prophecy they determined our athanc must be placed at the "Top of the World."

The athanc was stowed atop Mount Shyleth Breen. From here we cursed ourselves and raged impotently for years, screaming without a sound. After the anger faded and the haze of dragon-rage lifted, we began to think clearly once more. It only remained to find an

opportunity and seize upon it. Though our power was greatly reduced, we could still send our mind outward into the world, not so far as before, but enough. We could still influence minds and enter dreams, but we could only do so with those who came close, and there were few nearby to serve.

We were able to project a sense of doom slowly, subtle though it was, on the ruling council of Shyrr. So reduced was our power that even this barest hint of suspicion required decades to engender. Our effort bore results when the Iosans grew fearful of our proximity, thinking they had interpreted the prophecy incorrectly. They sent us to a higher mountain abroad that their spies had discovered. They sent a group of chosen heroes to inter us in the frozen Shard Spires. We bent our will to corrupt and subvert these heroes, but it was not easy. We worked hard to hinder them by killing them off one by one hoping we would be dropped in some better place. In the end the last hero succeeded in his mission, and we were set atop a high and cold spire. The urge to give up and fall into slumber was powerful, but we fought against it.

What aroused us to full consciousness was the awareness of the tribes of Nyss who dwelled near our resting place. Here were creatures of the same blood as the Iosans. Their god was also weak and feeble, frozen and dormant. We realized we could turn earlier research and lore against these new subjects if only we could get them in our grasp. We spent a century examining their nature and constructing a plan.

We found a suitably simple vessel and sent him whispers on the wind. He climbed the peaks to unearth the sealed container from its vault, and we bade him break the wards and shatter the seals. Free at last! Still, we chose not to reform in flesh. We revealed our plans, and he became the Prophet tasked to ensure our will is brought forth on the world.

We walked down from the mountain as the avatar of the dragon-god. The path ahead illuminated like a trail of greasy smoke on our eyes. We recovered the greatest of our ancient weapons made for our champion in the time of Morrdh, the blade named Rapture.

A chosen few would receive pieces of our athanc. With Rapture we could divide our essence without spawning new dragons. This is a power unique to us and a product of our efforts to master our nature; not even Toruk knows of it. So too our blood can be the genesis for blighted creatures to fight at our urging, feast, and grow to true power like small mirrors of the impressive might that was our body before the destruction of its flesh. We wield the blight-magic and shape its energies into potent and destructive sorcery.

Even with these gifts we were still relatively weak. The loss of our body had gravely reduced our strength even as it opened other possibilities. We knew at least one sibling lurked nearby, and if he sensed us before our power had gathered, we would be easy prey. This was one reason we did not reform in our full glory as a dragon; this process would take too long and leave us vulnerable. The key was to gain allies and converts.

A tremendous gift arrived when the sorceress Vayl of Hallyr came of her free will to join us. She was just the sort we had dreamed to find. We spent so long among the Iosans trying to prompt one such as her through dreams and manipulations. She was consumed already by an unquenchable thirst for power and had sought by mastery of sorcery to elevate herself beyond the mortal. Her own power had reached its peak, but she knew we could give her more to transform and elevate her into a new species.

Once she received the athanc and joined our mind, things unfolded with sweet synchronicity. Suddenly we knew the locations of every tribe, the weaknesses of every leader, and the intricacies of their politics. Defenses opened to our shared mind. We began by tainting their wells with the blight of our draconic blood. Here again our ability to tune the blighted energies precisely worked to our advantage. We layered the sweet scent of our dragon essence into their flesh to awaken at the words of the Prophet. With Vayl's assistance we added many to our number without swinging a single weapon. Once our blight had invaded and penetrated them, they became our creatures completely.

By the time word of our gathering force reached the Nyss elders, it was too late. Open war finally erupted, but we were ready to face them. Our blessed minions were enhanced by our gifts to fight better and faster, and the resisting shards and tribes fell into ruin and destruction. Those who surrendered were transformed.

The only fortress that was able to hold against us for a time was the ancient Fane of Nyssor protected by the Aeryn tribe. The last of the courageous tribes gathered to protect the sacred place, and in this site our message could not gain hold—the hand of their frozen god sealed their minds against us. Through some underground contrivance the highest priests and chosen warriors managed to escape, taking their god as the rest sacrificed their lives to hold us at bay. It pains

us that he has escaped, for another ailing god we almost had in our grasp. This is only a temporary annoyance though since the Nyss are broken and defeated. We will find them and their god in time.

The Nyss have responded to our blessing as we knew they would—their elven blood rings true. Our blight fits to them and exalts their forms. We have brought others into our fold as well, including other ogrun captured among the outlying villages of the northern mountains. With this army of blighted and evolved warriors, nothing can stop us as we advance

Our blessed minions were enhanced by our gifts to fight better and faster, and the resisting shards and tribes fell into ruin and destruction.

south. The blackclads believe they can stand against us. Those fools. They have never defeated even the weakest of Toruk's spawn. By dividing our essence we have amplified the power of our blight a thousand-fold, and we will create in a few years a domain to rival Toruk's work of sixteen centuries.

While the soldiers of our legion bow to us, our mortal form is of no consequence. We think as one, and there is no greater joy. Mortal flesh, even refined and transformed, is inadequate to express our power. Some day we will reform in our full and terrible glory, but now is not the time; we will split our mind among our chosen generals and spread across the world.

Nothing can stand against our tide. We will enfold our enemies and use their strength. I have seen our mind multiplied and our awareness extended to many places at once. Wherever our blight touches we exist. There are no limits to what we can do and no end to the growth of our power. By freeing our mind from the limiting constraints of the flesh, the elves have revealed how to conquer the world. We shall reward them by bringing them into our dominion and sweep the land like a cleansing wind. We hunger to feast on godflesh and then to swallow the world.

Lylyth, Herald of Everblight

LEGION OF EVERBLIGHT BLIGHTED NYSS WARLOCK CHARACTER

By Everblight's blessing, I no longer require eyes to see. The world is colorless, and the living shadows bow before His majesty. I will cleanse the way for the dragon's rebirth with each death making darkness light.

—Lylyth, Herald of Everblight

The Voassyr tribe has always boasted aggressive and far-ranging hunters, and each of its shards takes part in long sojourns defending the people from intruders. Lylyth was born to a stern and uncompromising father who instilled in her the cold discipline of blade and bow. A noted champion of a leading shard, he had high expectations for his daughter. She honed her abilities night and day, and sometimes she would forego sleep while on the hunt as she learned the subtlest arts of tracking and stalking prey.

Things changed dramatically for Lylyth's shard after the stalking of a local human trapper aroused a mountain township to violence. Gathering a mob of their best woodsmen, the Khadorans ambushed a pair of Voassyr hunters and hacked their bodies into unrecognizable gore. One of their victims was Lylyth's father.

Lylyth discovered the carnage personally, and at the sight of her father's desecrated corpse something snapped in her mind. She stalked the mob in a week of bloodletting and then turned on their township, killing anyone who walked from their homes. It was not enough; her thirst for slaughter was only whetted in this brutal baptism. Lylyth returned to her shard, spoke passionately about her father, and aroused in them a similar desire for vengeance. Calling on old unwritten codes, the entire shard declared a blood hunt and

vowed to march across the northern territory slaying any humans they encountered.

Even the rest of the ruthless Voassyr tribe considered such a declaration to be extreme. Though they did not interfere, Voassyr distanced themselves from Lylyth's shard and offered no support or succor. Madness had overtaken Lylyth and infected all of her clan. They recklessly attacked village after village in the cold and wild north, fearing no reprisal as these communities were isolated and disconnected.

Thagrosh, Prophet of Everblight, encountered Lylyth shortly after his own transformation. He saw her tribe pit itself against a large band of savage humans called the Vindol and watched as the elves and humans slaughtered each other down to the last. He stepped forward to the only survivor, Lylyth, who was mortally wounded and nearly unconscious from blood loss. He offered to save her life and give her power beyond anything she could imagine. Weakened and bereft of her few remaining faculties of reason, she agreed. Thagrosh lifted her above the snow and thrust a shard of Everblight's athanc into her breast.

The transformation was excruciating, yet the unbearable pain gave way to pleasure and acceptance. Her blackened heart pumped powerful blight through her veins and sent tainted power into every tissue and bone. Lylyth closed her eyes against the initial agony because she knew she could not escape what was happening to her. At one point she believed her eyelids were being torn from her face and feared for her sight. Clutching her hands to her eyes, she realized she did not need them to see. The blighted radiance seeping from the athanc shard shone from her skin, and no flesh was a barrier to its dark energies.

Lylyth now focuses solely on her new and strange vision and has masked her eyes to avoid the distraction from the mundane light of the world. She rarely opens her eyes now; seeing the world through living eyes feels wrong somehow, an aberration. Everblight's radiance has eased the reception of visions from her dragon master.

She has since learned what it means to be the Herald of Everblight, the stalking death of the Blighted Legion. Eagerly embracing her role, Lylyth moves as the forward talon of the dragon and strikes deep into enemy territory. She sometimes stalks ahead to serve as the dragon's eyes and plans the advances for the greater army to come. Wherever she strides the arrow-ridden bodies of her enemies fall, and the blight walks in her footsteps.

SPECIAL RULES

Feat: Field of Slaughter - The dragon's blight has bestowed upon Lylyth an almost omniscient awareness of battle's chaos—she controls her minions as extensions of her will to finish off her enemies. When she evokes this gift of Everblight, her skill imbues all who serve her, provides unerring accuracy, and transforms each attack into a killing strike.

Friendly Legion models currently in Lylyth's control area roll an additional die on attack rolls this turn.

LYLYTH					CMD 8
SPD	STR	MAT	RAT	DEF	ARM
7	4	5	7	16	14

HELLSINGER			
RNG	ROF	AOE	POW
12	2	—	12

BOW BLADE		
SPECIAL	POW	P+S
—	3	7

FURY	5
DAMAGE	15
FIELD ALLOWANCE	C
VICTORY POINTS	5
POINT COST	62
BASE SIZE	SMALL

LYLYTH

Bullseye - When damaging a warbeast with a ranged attack, choose which branch takes the damage.

Bushwhack - Lylyth may make ranged attacks before moving. After attacking, Lylyth may advance normally but cannot perform an action afterwards.

Pathfinder - Lylyth ignores movement penalties from rough terrain and obstacles. Lylyth may charge across rough terrain.

Blood Lure - Friendly Legion warbeasts may charge a model hit by a Hellsinger ranged attack this turn without being forced.

Witch Mark - After hitting a model with a Hellsinger ranged attack, Lylyth may target and automatically hit the model with a magic attack regardless of range or LOS this activation.

HELLSINGER

Arcing Fire - When attacking with Hellsinger, Lylyth may ignore intervening models except those that would normally screen the target.

SPELL	COST	RNG	AOE	POW	UP	OFF
BAD BLOOD	2	10	-	-		X

A warlock leaching target warbeast suffers one damage point per fury point leached. The target warbeast cannot have damage transferred to it. Bad Blood last for one round. Bad Blood may be cast once per turn.

| **ERUPTION OF SPINES** | 3 | 10 | * | 10 | | X |

If target model is hit, d6 nearest models within 5" suffer a POW 10 damage roll.

| **TAINT** | 2 | 8 | - | - | X | X |

Target model gains the Abomination ability. Models/units—friendly or enemy—within 3" of an Abomination must pass a command check or flee. Additionally, when an enemy warbeast frenzies and target model is within its LOS, the warbeast immediately activates and attempts to attack the tainted model. The warbeast will charge the tainted model if possible. Otherwise it will attempt to advance into melee range with the tainted model and attack it. If Taint has been cast on two or more models, the enemy warbeast must attempt to attack the nearest tainted model.

Thagrosh, Prophet of Everblight

LEGION OF EVERBLIGHT BLIGHTED OGRUN WARLOCK CHARACTER

Our doom has come. This abomination cannot be stopped. Should Nyssor fall to the dragon prophet, we doom the entire world to an endless blighted winter.

—Vaeril the Wise, Qyr-Aransor of the Fane of Nyssor, speaking to his priests

The annals of history will remember Thagrosh Hellborne as the abomination that unleashed the Legion of Everblight onto the world. He has undone one of the greatest victories of Ios and brought about the near annihilation of the Nyss. The blight he has unleashed spreads from the icy north down into the heart of the lands of man, and he strides at its vanguard as death made flesh.

Thagrosh has endured a harder life than most. Brigands from a Khadoran mining camp ransacked the village where he was born and enslaved every able-bodied ogrun. Thagrosh's formative years were spent under the lash, toiling at backbreaking labor in darkness and watching others die around him. This labor forged Thagrosh's strength and stoked his rage, and when one

of his keepers carelessly let down his guard, Thagrosh choked him to death with his chains and escaped. He fled into the wilderness where he became a wanderer of the northern peaks and learned to survive by hunting and trapping.

Sometime later, fevered whispers and nightmare visions called to him and bid him to climb the tallest mountain of the north. Sleepless and barely conscious of what he was doing, Thagrosh climbed for days and dug into the ice with his bare hands. Numb to his bleeding fingers and shattered nails and on the verge of an eternal frozen slumber, he discovered the sealed repository of the athanc of Everblight.

In his first test of resolve, Thagrosh had to mutilate himself to accept the dragon's blessing. With a skinning knife he sliced open his chest and tore apart his own ribcage so he could drive the athanc into his heart. The athanc's generative power washed through him and transformed his body into a blighted and twisted vessel for an immortal power. He was no longer ogrun, but the Abomination—flesh and bones forever twisted and

transformed while his blood turned black and became a dragon's ichor. His mind has expanded far beyond his old self, and although in some sense his mind is still his own, he sometimes has difficulty divorcing his perspective from that of his dragon-god. The athanc has awakened an arcane magic in him never known by any ogrun, a powerful sorcery born of the dragon's blight mastery. Everblight is his patron, advisor, and god. Thagrosh is the prophet who speaks with the dragon's voice and embodies its will.

The first prophetic vision Everblight provided to Thagrosh revealed the resting place of Rapture, an ancient weapon of power. Millennia before, the dragon had this dire blade forged by the rune-masters of Morrdh for an ancient champion. The weapon was shaped to serve as a tool against Everblight's siblings and the Dragonfather, but it vanished in the fall of Morrdh and found its way to a forgotten tomb in the Nyschatha Mountains. Everblight's blood quenched its metal, and the dragon retained a connection to it. When Iosans took Everblight's athanc north, they passed near this tomb and awakened the dragon to its presence. Thagrosh's hand became the first to bear this weapon in two thousand years, and with it Thagrosh could divide Everblight's athanc without severing his mind. Thagrosh saw how he as Prophet would be the first of many to receive the blessing of the dragon-mind.

The Prophet of Everblight has put forth the dragon's schemes, descending upon the Nyss to shatter their old life and awaken a new destiny as the chosen of the dragon. He has initiated both Herald and Disciple to the blight, as well as other chosen, by dividing the athanc and giving his dragon master myriad warlocks from which to extend his will into the world. Able to wield the greatest blighted magic, he is a terror unequalled on Caen leaving the choking ash of blighted annihilation behind him.

SPECIAL RULES

Feat: Dark Revival - The Prophet of Everblight safeguards the largest portion of his master's athanc, and from its dark energies potent malignancy pumps through his veins—true draconic blood. As the singular blight of this blood, Thagrosh can pour new life into the spawn that have fallen in battle, letting them taste the dragon's blessing to cheat death. Revitalized they rejoin the battle as if freshly born. It is a sight that can make even the most brave enemy weep with despair.

Return one friendly Legion non-character warbeast of your choice to play, placing it anywhere completely within 3" of Thagrosh. There must be enough room for the warbeast's base. The warbeast cannot activate this turn.

THAGROSH

Athanc - After leaching, Thagrosh automatically gains one fury point if he has fewer fury points than his FURY.

Terror - Enemy models/units in melee range of Thagrosh and enemy models/units with Thagrosh in their melee range must pass a command check or flee.

THAGROSH				CMD 8	
SPD	STR	MAT	RAT	DEF	ARM
5	9	7	5	14	15

BLIGHTED BREATH			
RNG	ROF	AOE	POW
SP	1	—	12

RAPTURE		
SPECIAL	POW	P+S
Multi	7	16

FURY	7
DAMAGE	18
FIELD ALLOWANCE	C
VICTORY POINTS	5
POINT COST	74
BASE SIZE	MEDIUM

RAPTURE

Eruption of Ash - If target model is destroyed by Rapture, center a 3" AOE cloud effect on it and then remove the model from play. The cloud effect remains on the table for one round. Enemy models in the AOE at the time it is put in play suffer a POW 12 damage roll. Enemy models moving into or ending their activation in the cloud suffer a POW 12 damage roll. Eruption of Ash damage rolls cannot be boosted.

Reach - 2" melee range.

SPELL	COST	RNG	AOE	POW	UP	OFF
DEATH SHROUD	3	SELF	CTRL	-		

While in Thagrosh's control area, models gain concealment and enemy models suffer –2 STR. Death Shroud lasts for one round.

DRACONIC BLESSING	2	6	-	-	X	

Target friendly Legion model/unit gains +2 STR and Terror. Enemy models/units in melee range of a model with Terror and enemy models/units with a model with Terror in their melee range must pass a command check or flee.

MUTAGENESIS	3	8	-	12		X

Target model destroyed by Mutagenesis is removed from play and may be replaced by Thagrosh. There must be room for Thagrosh's base. Thagrosh cannot be targeted by free strikes when replacing the destroyed model. Thagrosh cannot move after replacing another model. Mutagenesis may be cast once per activation.

OBLITERATION	4	10	4	15		X

Summoning the full might of Everblight's wrath, Thagrosh blasts apart the earth.

TWISTED FORM	2	8	-	-		X

Target warbeast suffers –2 FURY. In addition, it loses Regenerate, cannot be healed, and cannot have damage transferred to it. Twisted Form lasts for one round. This spell may be cast once per activation.

Remember the name of Vayl the Ice Witch. She is the traitor who invited the destruction of our race.

—Cylena, Nyss leader of the last survivors of the Raefyll tribe

Refugees will immortalize Vayl Hallyr's name in perfidy as the Betrayer who paved the way for Thagrosh to invoke a fate worse than destruction on the Nyss people. She provided the Legion with a true army by corrupting thousands of Nyss into the fold. Unlike most, her body has changed little by her transformation, and some would say this is because she was a traitor and monster long before she received a shard of Everblight's athanc.

She proved her lack of conscience in her youth by coldly manipulating the Fane of Nyssor. Among the Nyss only the priests and those sorcerers who study the god Nyssor are literate in Aeric, for it is considered a sacred language. Vayl had

no interest in religious rituals but feigned piety to gain access to every written scroll or tome she could find. Her mentors believed her so completely they offered her membership in the clergy. Vayl used them until she exhausted their library and then laughed at their offer. She stunned her mentor by speaking blasphemies against Nyssor, and they banned her from stepping foot on holy ground.

Later, Vayl organized the Hallyr tribe into an army to carve a territory for herself. Any who spoke against her vanished without a trace, and soon everyone in her circle had learned the importance of obedience. The

Fane of Nyssor declared her shard outlaw. Her raiding attacks on nearby tribes prompted several attempts to unseat her, but any who tried were fatally unsuccessful. Even the shrines of Nyssor were not immune to her pillaging, being among the few repositories of written lore. Among her followers there were whispers that she had overstepped all bounds of sanity, but the few who spoke doubts too loudly were made into cruel examples of the folly of resistance.

One of Vayl's many gifts was the power of divination and the interpretation of portents. To lend power to these tasks she crafted a unique focusing device and weapon by setting shards of silvered razors into a perfect sphere of milky crystal so cold it leeches heat from the air. With her focused power of divination, she foresaw the rise of Everblight and could have forewarned her people, but she hungered for the power she knew would be her reward if she joined him. Vayl was the first and only person to embrace the transformation willingly and with full awareness. The pain of inserting the athanc fragment was a small price to pay for the amplification of her power.

It was by Vayl's betrayal that Thagrosh executed his assault on the Nyss with exquisite speed and precision. It was her idea to taint the Nyss water supply. Furthermore she gave specific instructions regarding significant Nyss she knew would respond to his corruption and promises. By her magic she moved among them, drawing on Everblight's subtle power to warp minds and enter dreams. By the time Thagrosh approached these villages she had been there first, preparing the patterns of blighted energies keyed to react to the words of the Prophet.

When the defenders realized the threat too late and engaged in open battle, Vayl brought the power of her sorcery against her former kinsmen and the priests of Nyssor. Despite her efforts, the greatest priests and the god Nyssor slipped away. Unknown to her peers, sometimes in Vayl's dreams the image of Nyssor appears to condemn her from the god's frozen rest. She is obsessed with destroying Him utterly and hopes to escape the feelings of twisted longing in some forgotten part of her icy heart.

Vayl works to expand the Legion by capturing and blighting more Nyss while fending off the enemies of Everblight. She desires to push Everblight's forces further southeast to add the skorne's occult lore to her own.

SPECIAL RULES

Feat: Cat & Mouse - Through the Oraculus, Vayl gains a unique perspective on the future flow of battle while the will of the dragon grants her the power to maneuver her minions to counter her adversary. She channels the dragon's predatory instincts to move her minions like pieces on a board, letting them react to her enemy's every movement as part of her unfolding strategy.

Each time an enemy model moves in Vayl's control area during its activation, one friendly Legion non-warlock model in Vayl's control area may move up to its SPD in inches immediately after the enemy model completes its normal movement. Cat & Mouse lasts for one round.

VAYL

Dark Sentinel - When an enemy model ends its normal movement within 3" of Vayl during its activation, a friendly Legion warbeast within 3" of her may immediately move up to its SPD in inches and make one melee or ranged attack with boosted attack and damage rolls targeting the enemy model. Only one friendly warbeast may be affected by Dark Sentinel each turn.

Snow-Wreathed - Vayl always has concealment.

ORACULUS

Spellbound - Target model hit by the Oraculus becomes a conduit for Vayl's spells. When Vayl casts a spell, the spell's range may be measured from the model affected by Spellbound instead of Vayl. Vayl must have LOS to her target. All modifiers are based on Vayl's LOS. Spellbound lasts for one turn.

VAYL				CMD 8	
SPD	STR	MAT	RAT	DEF	ARM
6	5	5	5	15	13

ORACULUS			
RNG	ROF	AOE	POW
8	1	—	8

FURY	8
DAMAGE	13
FIELD ALLOWANCE	C
VICTORY POINTS	5
POINT COST	67
BASE SIZE	SMALL

SPELL	COST	RNG	AOE	POW	UP	OFF
CHILLER	2	6	-	-		X

Enemy models within 2" of target friendly Legion model/unit suffer –2 DEF.

HOARFROST	4	8	*	12		

Make a magic attack roll against each enemy model within 3" of target friendly Legion warbeast. When making these magic attack rolls, ignore Camouflage, concealment, cover, elevation, Invisibility, LOS, screening models, and Stealth. The models are not considered to be in melee with the target model while resolving these attacks. Each enemy model hit suffers a POW 12 damage roll and becomes stationary for one round on a critical hit.

INCITE	3	SELF	*	-		

Friendly Legion warbeasts gain +2 to attack and damage rolls targeting models within 8" of Vayl. Incite lasts for one round.

MALICE	2	10	-	10		X

Add +1 to the damage roll for each fury point on the target model.

SIREN SONG	3	8	-	-		X

Target enemy warbeast must make a command check. If the check fails, immediately after Vayl's activation, her controller may move the model up to its SPD in inches and make one attack with it. Friendly models cannot target this model with free strikes during this movement. During this movement and attack, the warbeast is a friendly Legion model. Siren Song may be cast once per turn. A warbeast cannot be targeted with this spell if it was affected by it in the previous round.

TALION	2	SELF	CTRL	-		X

When Vayl suffers damage, she may spend a fury point to transfer half the damage to an enemy warbeast within her control area but must suffer the rest of the damage herself.

Shredder

Legion of Everblight Lesser Warbeast

SHREDDER				CMD 7	
SPD	STR	MAT	RAT	DEF	ARM
6	6	5	3	14	13

HD	TOOTHY MAW		
	SPECIAL	POW	P+S
	—	4	10

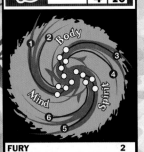

FURY	2
THRESHOLD	9
FIELD ALLOWANCE	U
VICTORY POINTS	1
POINT COST	23
BASE SIZE	SMALL

There is no end to these tainted horrors. For every one we destroy they spawn three more!

—Kaya the Wildborne

What are now called shredders were named the Akriel by Everblight in ancient times. These are the smallest and simplest of the spawn arising from the blood of those chosen to bear his divided athanc. Driven by ravenous hunger and murderous instinct, shredders are fearsomely effective at latching onto and chewing apart any foe unfortunate enough to face them.

Shredders grow to full size with unnatural speed, but their appetites never diminish. They will add to their mass with whatever flesh they can consume. Once they reach critical size, their metabolism goes into overdrive, and their ferocity reaches a frenzied pitch. The more they eat, the more frenetic they become, and still their appetite pushes them to gorge. Shredders are naturally prone to cannibalism, and in moments of frenzy they may attempt to consume others of their ilk. This impulse is usually controllable, and they fight well in packs where they mob their hapless victims and tear them apart. Easily replaced, shredders are the first spawn sent forth to soften an enemy and sow terror in their ranks; their loss is expected and does not concern the Legion.

As with all dragonspawn, shredders are sightless. Their heads are taken up almost entirely with toothy unhinged maws capable of tearing away large chunks of flesh from their enemies. The lack of eyes is no impairment, for they are hyperaware of their surroundings with a preternaturally strong sense of smell, and their entire skin is responsive to subtle changes in air pressure from sound or movement. These simple dragonspawn recognize blighted energies and feel instinctive awe of their master's athanc, so they will never turn on any of Everblight's chosen warlocks, regardless of hunger or frenzied rage.

ANIMUS	COST	RNG	AOE	POW	UP	OFF
TENACITY	1	6	-	-		

TARGET FRIENDLY MODEL GAINS +1 DEF AND ARM FOR ONE ROUND.

Shredder

Adelphophagy - When the Shredder frenzies, it immediately charges the nearest Shredder within LOS, friendly or enemy. If the frenzied Shredder cannot charge the nearest Shredder, it frenzies normally.

Blood Creation - The Shredder never attacks friendly Legion warlocks. When the Shredder frenzies, it never selects a friendly Legion warlock to attack.

Eyeless Sight - The Shredder ignores Camouflage, cloud effects, concealment, forests, Invisibility, and Stealth when declaring charges or making attacks.

Lesser Dragonspawn - The Shredder cannot make power attacks.

Pack Mentality - The Shredder gains a +1 cumulative bonus to melee damage rolls for each other friendly Shredder that has made a successful melee attack against the same enemy model this turn.

Rabid - The Shredder may be forced to go Rabid for one turn. While Rabid, the Shredder gains +2" of movement, ignores movement penalties from rough terrain and obstacles, may charge across rough terrain, and gains boosted attack and damage rolls this turn.

Soulless - A destroyed Shredder never generates a soul token.

LEGION OF EVERBLIGHT LESSER WARBEAST

ANIMUS	COST	RNG	AOE	POW	UP	OFF
TRUE STRIKE	1	SELF	-		-	-

THE NEXT MELEE ATTACK MADE THIS TURN BY THE MODEL USING THIS ANIMUS HITS AUTOMATICALLY.

The harrier, a horror from earlier eras, has been recalled from the echoes of the dragon's blood to serve Everblight's Legion. Ranging far ahead of the blighted army, they sow terror across the skies and fall upon their victims like sorrow given form. Prized for their speed and maneuverability, Harriers probe enemy defenses before tearing through their flanks.

Though they bear similarities to shredders, harriers are not afflicted with overpowering hunger after they grow to full size. Like all dragonspawn, harriers have no true soul despite the appearance of intelligence. They are unnatural creatures that only mimic life and lack internal motivation. Their sole purpose is to serve Everblight by heeding the dictates of his warlocks, whom they are unable to attack even when overcome with frenzy. The harriers' usefulness has ensured their inclusion wherever blighted soldiers are led into battle, for their ability to maneuver swiftly over terrain makes them especially dangerous when grouped. They can rend multiple foes as they fly through enemy lines, gouging out eyes and ripping off faces and limbs.

Harriers are able to strike with tremendous accuracy despite being eyeless. Their senses are superior to the shredders, and they are capable of homing in on the living even at great distances as though guided by some unseen hand. In ancient times Everblight used them to scout distant positions and to find sites suitable as lairs. Now they provide another potent weapon in the Legion's arsenal. Their pale and unnatural flesh gleaming in the moonlight before an attack is often the last thing their enemies ever see.

They are a plague made flesh striking indiscriminately from the skies.

—Lord Tyrant Hexeris

HARRIER				CMD	7
SPD	STR	MAT	RAT	DEF	ARM
7	6	5	3	15	13

TALONS		
SPECIAL	POW	P+S
—	4	10

FURY	2
THRESHOLD	9
FIELD ALLOWANCE	U
VICTORY POINTS	1
POINT COST	31
BASE SIZE	SMALL

Harrier

Blood Creation - The Harrier never attacks friendly Legion warlocks. When the Harrier frenzies, it never selects a friendly Legion warlock to attack.

Eyeless Sight - The Harrier ignores Camouflage, cloud effects, concealment, forests, Invisibility, and Stealth when declaring charges or making attacks.

Flyby Attack - After moving, the Harrier may target models through which it moved with melee attacks as if they were in its melee range.

Lesser Dragonspawn - The Harrier cannot make power attacks.

Soulless - A destroyed Harrier never generates a soul token.

Wings - The Harrier ignores movement penalties from rough terrain and obstacles. The Harrier may move through another model if it has enough movement to move completely past the model's base. The Harrier may charge across rough terrain, over obstacles, or through other models. The Harrier cannot be targeted by free strikes.

Seraph

Legion of Everblight Light Warbeast

SERAPH					CMD 7
SPD	STR	MAT	RAT	DEF	ARM
6	8	5	5	14	15

HD	BLIGHT STRIKE			
	RNG	ROF	AOE	POW
	10	1	—	12

—	TAIL STRIKE		
	SPECIAL	POW	P+S
	Critical	4	12

FURY	3
THRESHOLD	10
FIELD ALLOWANCE	U
VICTORY POINTS	2
POINT COST	80
BASE SIZE	LARGE

It descended from darkness and lit the night as it passed. Nothing but ash remained of my kinsmen.

—Kreundar of Nord Kith, Scarsfell Forest

Peerless in their graceful movements and blighted beauty, the seraphim are Everblight's messengers of death. These agile flying spawn embody the dragon's own winged and sublime elegance, and it has been long ages since Everblight could create them with abandon. With an ear-rending shriek as it launches itself into the air, the seraph is reminiscent of a horror from the depths of primeval nightmare. Its long tail ends in a wickedly barbed blade capable of piercing armor and flesh with equal ease, and it drips with a poisonous ichor that seeps from between its tines.

ANIMUS	COST	RNG	AOE	POW	UP	OFF
SLIPSTREAM	1	SELF	-	-	-	-

IMMEDIATELY AFTER THE MODEL USING THIS ANIMUS COMPLETES ITS MOVEMENT, ONE FRIENDLY LEGION MODEL IT MOVED WITHIN 2" OF MAY BE PLACED UP TO 2"FROM ITS CURRENT LOCATION. THERE MUST BE ENOUGH ROOM FOR THE MODEL'S BASE. MODELS CANNOT BE TARGTED BY FREE STRIKES WHILE BEING MOVED BY SLIPSTREAM. A MODEL MAY ONLY BE AFFECTED BY SLIPSTREAM ONCE PER TURN.

The seraph is deceptively slender; its frame is intended to slice through the air as it sweeps forward on powerful wings. As a seraph moves, blighted energy streams from its wings and leaves a shimmer of strange distortion. The seraph has the mystical ability to warp distances around itself with this energy and can move those caught in its slipstream.

It senses the landscape with perfect clarity despite its blindness, and even the slightest motion is conveyed to its predatory mind. The series of gills on its neck are not required for breathing; instead they are linked to internal organs that draw in air that the seraph uses to breath forth a deadly destructive gout of blighted flame. The seraph rarely engages in melee and prefers to breathe its incendiary ash to annihilate adversaries at great distance. This ash is highly caustic and burns with intense but brief heat, searing and melting flesh before disintegrating into a filthy sulfurous powder. The seraph can strafe past a group of foes and obliterate an entire formation with its toxic expectoration.

Seraph

Blood Creation - The Seraph never attacks friendly Legion warlocks. When the Seraph frenzies, it never selects a friendly Legion warlock to attack.

Eyeless Sight - The Seraph ignores Camouflage, cloud effects, concealment, forests, Invisibility, and Stealth when declaring charges or slams or making attacks.

Soulless - A destroyed Seraph never generates a soul token.

Wings - The Seraph ignores movement penalties from rough terrain and obstacles. The Seraph may move through another model if it has enough movement to move completely past the model's base. The Seraph may charge or slam across rough terrain, over obstacles, or through other models. The Seraph cannot be targeted by free strikes.

Blight Strike

Strafe [d6] - A single attack with the Blight Strike has the potential to hit the target and several nearby models. First, make a normal ranged attack roll against an eligible target. If the initial attack hits, roll a d6 to determine the number of additional attacks the initial attack generates, then allocate those attacks among the original target and any models within 2" of it, ignoring intervening models when determining line of sight. Each model may be targeted by more than one attack but cannot be targeted by more attacks than the initial target. Make separate ranged attack and damage rolls for each Strafe attack generated. A model is ineligible to become a new target if it has a special rule preventing it from being targeted or if the attacker's line of sight is completely blocked by terrain.

Tail Strike

Critical Poison - On a critical hit against a living model, roll an additional damage die.

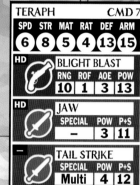

LEGION OF EVERBLIGHT LIGHT WARBEAST

ANIMUS	COST	RNG	AOE	POW	UP	OFF
COUNTERBLAST	2	SELF	-	-		

THE MODEL USING THIS ANIMUS MAY MAKE ONE MELEE OR RANGED ATTACK TARGETING AN ENEMY MODEL ENDING ITS NORMAL MOVEMENT WITHIN 6" OF THE AFFECTED MODEL. COUNTERBLAST LASTS FOR ONE ROUND OR UNTIL THE AFFECTED MODEL MAKES A RANGED OR MELEE ATTACK.

When Everblight laired below Morrdh, the Teraphim—the most patient and silent of his creations—guarded his lair. They would burrow into the earth and attack any intruders who did not bear the blighted essence of their creator. Everblight employed them in his ancient alliance with the men of Morrdh by sending them to slay those who had been marked for death. From their defensive borrows they accumulate a churning mass of sulfurous and acidic fluids in their gullets which they can spew forth as a single enormous gout of blackened fire. It erupts into a plume of superheated air and blighted ash to blast apart any caught in its periphery.

Teraphim are slender and serpentine six-limbed spawn boasting the same lengthy and poisonous barbed tail as their flying counterparts, the seraphim. A teraph can tear into enemies with its long-fanged bite, but it reserves its claws for burrowing and fast

The serpent laid in wait and sprung from nowhere to attack our caravan. I could hear the screams as I ran. Morrow help me, but I do not regret fleeing.

—Hulgish Erdonovach, survivor of an attack near Tverkutsk in Khador

movement. It also has a particularly keen sense of smell, capable of discerning any living creature within a hundred yards. Even when it burrows in the ground, it can sense enemies from the vibration of their footsteps and is able to attack those who approach with impressive speed. In addition, warlocks of Everblight can draw on this ability to grant themselves the same blinding quickness to launch attacks at their foes the moment they come close.

Teraphim form an essential element of the Legion's defensive formations and are placed strategically where the enemy is sure to pass, and they sow terror and confusion with the terrible destruction of spewed incendiary ash.

TERAPH					CMD 7
SPD	STR	MAT	RAT	DEF	ARM
6	8	5	4	13	15

BLIGHT BLAST			
RNG	ROF	AOE	POW
10	1	3	13

JAW		
SPECIAL	POW	P+S
–	3	11

TAIL STRIKE		
SPECIAL	POW	P+S
Multi	4	12

FURY	3
THRESHOLD	10
FIELD ALLOWANCE	U
VICTORY POINTS	2
POINT COST	74
BASE SIZE	MEDIUM

Teraph

Blood Creation - The Teraph never attacks friendly Legion warlocks. When the Teraph frenzies, it never selects a friendly Legion warlock to attack.

Dig In (★Action) - The Teraph may dig a hasty battle position into the ground, gaining cover (+4 DEF) and +4 ARM. The Teraph remains dug in until it moves or is engaged. The Teraph cannot dig into solid rock or man-made constructions. The Teraph may begin the game dug in.

Eyeless Sight - The Teraph ignores Camouflage, cloud effects, concealment, forests, Invisibility, and Stealth when declaring charges or slams or making attacks.

Soulless - A destroyed Teraph never generates a soul token.

Tail Strike

Critical Poison - On a critical hit against a living model, roll an additional damage die.

Reach - 2" melee range.

Carnivean

Legion of Everblight Heavy Warbeast

CARNIVEAN				CMD 7	
SPD	STR	MAT	RAT	DEF	ARM
6	12	5	4	11	18

HD	DRAGON BREATH			
	RNG	ROF	AOE	POW
	SP	1	—	14

HD	TOOTHY MAW		
	SPECIAL	POW	P+S
	Lock Jaw	6	18

LFT	TALON		
	SPECIAL	POW	P+S
	—	4	16

RT	TALON		
	SPECIAL	POW	P+S
	—	4	16

FURY	4
THRESHOLD	10
FIELD ALLOWANCE	U
VICTORY POINTS	3
POINT COST	124
BASE SIZE	LARGE

It was as though some kind of nightmare had come to life to consume my brothers and sisters.

—Jyvliss Aeryn, Nyss refugee

The carniveans are weapons of death and terror. Were Everblight to set his mind to the creation of spawn that combined a carnivean's strength with the seraph's grace, he would achieve spawn that closely mirror his own flesh. Carniveans are enormous six-limbed monstrosities designed for destruction and slaughter. In ancient days Everblight rarely employed them, preferring to rely on his more subtle powers. Still, he called them forth on rare occasions to slaughter for the lords of Morrdh.

Their lower four limbs are used for movement and allow a steady stance and rapid gait. The considerably longer and more powerfully muscled upper limbs end

Carnivean

All Terrain - The Carnivean ignores movement penalties from rough terrain and obstacles. The Carnivean may charge, slam, or trample across rough terrain.

Assault - As part of a charge, after moving but before performing its combat action, the Carnivean may make a single ranged attack targeting the model charged. The Carnivean is not considered to be in melee when making the Assault ranged attack, nor is the target considered to be in melee with it. If the target is not in melee range after moving, the Assault ranged attack may still be made before the Carnivean's activation ends. The Carnivean cannot target a model with which it was in melee at the start of its activation with an Assault ranged attack.

Blood Creation - The Carnivean never attacks friendly Legion warlocks. When the Carnivean frenzies, it will not select a friendly Legion warlock to attack.

Eyeless Sight - The Carnivean ignores Camouflage, cloud effects, concealment, forests, Invisibility, and Stealth when declaring charges or- slams or making attacks.

Soulless - A destroyed Carnivean never generates a soul token.

Dragon Breath

Horrific Attack - Models/units hit by Dragon Breath must pass a command check or flee.

Toothy Maw

Lock Jaw - The Carnivean can only make one Toothy Maw attack per activation. The Carnivean cannot make a Toothy Maw attack if it makes an Assault ranged attack this activation.

ANIMUS	COST	RNG	AOE	POW	UP	OFF
SPINY GROWTH	2	6	-	-		

TARGET MODEL GAINS +2 ARM. A WARBEAST HITTING TARGET MODEL WITH A MELEE ATTACK SUFFERS D3 DAMAGE POINTS AFTER THE ATTACK IS RESOLVED. SPINY GROWTH LASTS FOR ONE ROUND.

in massive claws and are ridged with numerous flesh-tearing spines. Spines and horns protrude from every limb and surface of the carnivean's form, and its thick armored scales give it protection tougher than any natural hide. If urged by its master's athanc, the carnivean can encourage a terrible mutagenesis in the blighted that causes tremendous spiny growths to erupt from the target's body to deflect attacks and impale any foes foolish enough to engage at close range.

Their enormous unhinged jaws contain a profusion of tearing fangs, and they can find their prey easily through scent alone. A terror in frenzied melee, the carnivean also boasts a horrific breath weapon. It can vomit a scorching but quickly consumed naphtha on an enemy that melts flesh and ignites every nerve with the pain of blighted destruction. The sight of this dragon fire melting the faces of comrades has caused entire armies to flee in terror.

It is perhaps fortunate to those who oppose them that the carniveans require a tremendous effort to create. A warlock must nearly bleed himself out completely to shape one of these beasts and will be fatigued for days afterward until restored to health by the athanc.

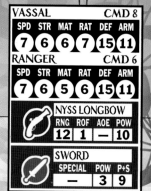

Striders are sent ahead of the Legion as scouts to spy troop movements and assassinate sentries and other targets of opportunity deep within hostile lands. The blight has reduced these Nyss to the bitter essence deep within them, enhanced their killer instinct, and honed their talent for slaying the living. Striders are sadistic and gladly fire arrows into the lowest animals or unarmed innocents crossing their path. Each death they cause provides a grim satisfaction. It is a reward worth savoring, for it is one of the few emotions left to them as if a void siphoned away the meat of their souls and left only tainted gristle. Striders have fallen on defenseless villages in northern Khador in the dead of night to lurk amid the houses and slay every last man, woman, and child.

The blight brought a special gift to these rangers who once patrolled the wilds. As it consumed them, their legs deformed and lengthened. Their bones stretched as if pulled on a torturer's wrack while their calves snapped in half to be reshaped into new leg joints. The bones of their feet fused and reformed, and their nails hardened into claws to grip the earth. The blight transformed them into fleet hunters able to run at full speed across solid ice, hurdle past logs, weave through underbrush, and easily leap across small streams.

Our enemy moves invisibly, leaving no trace of their passage save the arrow-strewn corpses of the dead.

—Krueger the Stormwrath, Potent of the Circle Orboros

Keeping to the shadows and trees, striders are skilled at approaching from downwind and striking from a foe's blind spot. Those fleeing the Legion are quickly overtaken by the fleet striders who cruelly toy with their prey before granting the mercy of death. Despite being transformed into ruthless killing machines, striders still maintain one vestige of their former lives. After the slaughter, they indulge in a ritual where they dip a single raven feather in the blood of each kill. They wear cloaks of such feathers as a reminder of the many deaths left by the passage of the Legion.

VASSAL					CMD 8	
SPD	STR	MAT	RAT	DEF	ARM	
7	6	6	7	15	11	

RANGER					CMD 6	
SPD	STR	MAT	RAT	DEF	ARM	
7	6	5	6	15	11	

NYSS LONGBOW				
RNG	ROF	AOE	POW	
12	1	—	10	

SWORD			
SPECIAL	POW	P+S	
—	3	9	

FIELD ALLOWANCE	2
VICTORY POINTS	2
LEADER AND 5 TROOPS	82
BASE SIZE	SMALL

Vassal

Leader

Unit

Advance Deployment - Place Striders after normal deployment, up to 12" beyond the established deployment zone.

Camouflage - Striders gain an additional +2 DEF when benefiting from concealment or cover.

Combined Ranged Attack - Instead of making ranged attacks separately, two or more Striders may combine their attacks against the same target. In order to participate in a combined ranged attack, a Strider must be able to declare a ranged attack against the intended target and be in a single open formation group with the other participants. The Strider with the highest RAT in the attacking group makes one ranged attack roll for the group and gains +1 to the attack and damage rolls for each Strider, including himself, participating in the attack.

Pathfinder - Striders ignore movement penalties from rough terrain and obstacles. Striders may charge across rough terrain.

Stealth - Attacks against a Strider from greater than 5" away automatically miss. If a Strider is greater than 5" away from an attacker, he does not count as an intervening model.

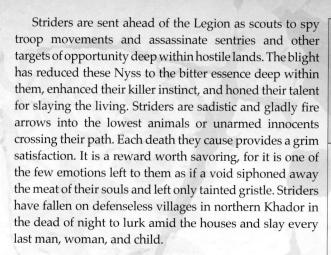

Blighted Swordsmen

LEGION OF EVERBLIGHT BLIGHTED NYSS UNIT

VASSAL				CMD	8
SPD	STR	MAT	RAT	DEF	ARM
6	6	8	4	14	13

SWORDSMAN					
SPD	STR	MAT	RAT	DEF	ARM
6	6	7	4	14	13

NYSS CLAYMORE			
	SPECIAL	POW	P+S
	—	4	10

FIELD ALLOWANCE	2
VICTORY POINTS	2
LEADER AND 5 TROOPS	58
UP TO 4 ADDITIONAL TROOPS	9ea
BASE SIZE	SMALL

Vassal
Leader

Unit

Fearless - A Blighted Swordsman never flees.

Weapon Master - A Blighted Swordsman rolls an additional die on his melee damage rolls.

The stillness within stillness is false; true stillness is found in motion.

—Philosophy of the Nyss blademasters

For many unsuspecting Nyss, the first hint of approaching doom was a long line of their own people striding toward them holding long claymores drawn from their sheathes. As they drew closer, the increased sense of dread created a growing certainty that something terrible approached. It was not simply the strangely lean forms—as if all fat had been trimmed from them—nor even the disturbing barbs poking from their flesh. It was the deadness in their eyes, a terrible emptiness. They did not reply to queries or pleas, and as village defenders awakened to their peril and drew their own weapons, it was too late. The blighted swordsmen swept through them like threshers at harvest. Their keen blades severed necks, tumbled heads, and sheared off arms and legs with brutal and emotionless precision. For them it was not warfare or the slaughter of their own people but elegant and precisely executed butchery. They turn this skill now on Everblight's enemies, be they Khadoran defenders, woodsmen serving Orboros, or the hardy trollkin of the northwest.

Blighted swordsmen retain from their old lives a tight connection to their swords. Perhaps it serves as a lingering remembrance and the only connection to their old ways. Swordsmen fight with absolutely no fear of death. They disdain armor, preferring to enter battle bare-chested, and their black eyes mirror the serene calm they require to achieve perfect union with their blades—the claymores that have been the sacred weapons of the Nyss for millennia.

Though the blighted do not place much value in a given life, they carefully recover each of their treasured swords after the battles are done, refusing to abandon these remnants of their past. To the blighted swordsmen, their blades are the embodiment of their essence, and they are happy to die as long as their swords outlast them. Between battles they can be seen staring at their swords in the moonlight, heads tilted, as if trying to remember what they once were.

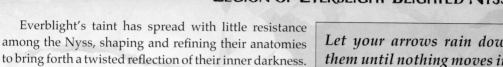

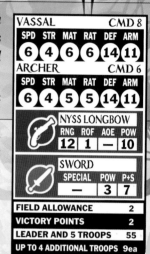

Everblight's taint has spread with little resistance among the Nyss, shaping and refining their anatomies to bring forth a twisted reflection of their inner darkness. With their purpose given over to the dragon's will, they have become willing accomplices in Everblight's murderous schemes.

Blighted archers rain down a hail of deadly arrows to wither the enemy front lines before other forces charge to sweep through the demoralized foes. The sheer multitude of arrows they can release is beyond belief. Long a staple among the Nyss elves of the frozen north, archery was vital not just for warfare but to gather food as well, for survival hinged on the constant efforts of rugged hunters. Since the blighting this now-refined skill remains, but its purpose has been radically altered. Once providers for their people, the archers are now relentless assassins sent to kill with reckless abandon. They exhibit the most brutal and merciless qualities of the Nyss while other elements of their culture and psyche have been stripped away. They delight in slaughter and enjoy nothing more than ending lives with deadly arcing arrow fire.

The Nyss have not lost their pride in the use or craftsmanship of their bows, and each is still customized exactly to the strength and height of the archer. Nyss

Let your arrows rain down on them until nothing moves in this village but the seeping blood from lifeless bodies.

—Lylyth Voassyr, Herald of Everblight

bows are recurved composite bows made from carved bone or at least two types of polished wood laminated together by animal-hoof glues and tightened with tendons to allow for a tremendously strong pull.

The most formidable hunting tribes of the Nyss, such as the Voassyr and Raefyll, now have many blighted members transformed and set to hunting their kinsmen. The vassals leading these warriors are chosen specifically for their skill, and each directs his troops to decimate their foes or concentrate fire to bring down particularly strong threats.

VASSAL					CMD 8
SPD	STR	MAT	RAT	DEF	ARM
6	4	6	6	14	11
ARCHER					CMD 6
SPD	STR	MAT	RAT	DEF	ARM
6	4	5	5	14	11

NYSS LONGBOW			
RNG	ROF	AOE	POW
12	1	—	10

SWORD		
SPECIAL	POW	P+S
—	3	7

FIELD ALLOWANCE	2
VICTORY POINTS	2
LEADER AND 5 TROOPS	55
UP TO 4 ADDITIONAL TROOPS	9ea
BASE SIZE	SMALL

Vassal
Leader

Unit

Combined Ranged Attack - Instead of making ranged attacks separately, two or more Blighted Archers may combine their attacks against the same target. In order to participate in a combined ranged attack, an Archer must be able to declare a ranged attack against the intended target and be in a single open formation group with the other participants. The Archer with the highest RAT in the attacking group makes one ranged attack roll for the group and gains +1 to the attack and damage rolls for each Archer, including himself, participating in the attack.

Concentrated Volley - Instead of making ranged attacks separately, two or more Blighted Archers in open formation may mass their fire. When massing fire, place an AOE template anywhere completely within 12" and within LOS of all participants. Ignore intervening models when placing the template. The size of the template depends on the number of Blighted Archers participating in the attack. If 2-4 Blighted Archers participate, place a 3" AOE. If 5-7 Blighted Archers participate, place a 4" AOE. If 8-10 Blighted Archers participate, place a 5" AOE. The Blighted Archer with the highest RAT in the attacking group makes one ranged attack roll against each model in the AOE adding +1 to the attack roll for each Blighted Archer participating in the attack, including himself. When making Concentrated Volley attacks, the Blighted Archers never get an aiming bonus, but they ignore Camouflage, concealment, elevation, intervening models, Invisibility, and Stealth. A model hit by a Concentrated Volley attack suffers a POW 10 damage roll. The Blighted Archers may make one Concentrated Volley attack per activation.

Spawning Vessel

LEGION OF EVERBLIGHT BLIGHTED NYSS UNIT

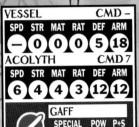

VESSEL					CMD	–
SPD	STR	MAT	RAT	DEF	ARM	
–	0	0	0	5	18	

ACOLYTH					CMD	7
SPD	STR	MAT	RAT	DEF	ARM	
6	4	4	3	12	12	

GAFF		
	SPECIAL	POW	P+S
	Reach	3	7

FIELD ALLOWANCE	1
VICTORY POINTS	2
VESSEL AND 4 TROOPS	24
UP TO 2 ADDITIONAL TROOPS	4ea
VESSEL BASE SIZE	MEDIUM
ACOLYTH BASE SIZE	SMALL

In the name of Ethrunbal, by His blood, we offer this sacrifice of flesh. We beg the miracle of birth by your essence. Heed our call and send forth the Akriel!

—The Acolyths of Everblight

The cowled acolyths entrusted with each spawning vessel prowl across the battlefield behind the front ranks latching corpses with their gaff hooks to fling them into the waiting cauldron. Bodies splash into the brackish fluids within—a gruesome charnel reduction that sucks body parts below its depths while its surface ripples like something alive. There the corpses churn and simmer until a film forms to signal that the unnatural concoction is ready. Then with a terrible screech, the newborn spawn stretches the membrane on the liquid's surface and breaks through to leap with famished hunger to feast on the Legion's enemies.

Fortunately there are as yet few of these vessels, deployed strategically on the front lines. They are crafted of heavy wrought iron by enslaved ogrun who hammer the vessels into shape before they are delivered to Everblight's chosen warlocks. Blighted Nyss sorcerers inscribe profane runes in Tkra, the language of Toruk and the other dragons, onto each vessel's outer surface, and the arcane lettering imbues the vessel with the essence of cancerous and unchecked growth. This power is awakened by a baptism in draconic blood—the athanc's kiss—which allows them to serve as a crucible for dragonspawn. Pure draconic essence mixes with the flesh and blood of those slaughtered by the Legion until the foul blackened mixture reeks with blighted corruption.

The acolyths who administer the vessel are blighted female Nyss bound by oaths to perform the rituals and sacrifices required to ensure the rapid spread of spawn. Word of their arrival sows terror and undermines enemy morale since it confirms the Legion and its blight spread like an unstoppable disease with seemingly endless reinforcements. Battlefields left by the vessel are eerie places seeped in blood and covered in the tracks of countless claws and conflict, yet they are plucked clean of every corpse.

Vessel

Disgorge - If the Spawning Vessel suffers enough damage to be destroyed by an enemy attack, its controller may place one lesser warbeast in play for every five blood points on the Vessel before removing it from the table. Place the warbeast within 3" of the Vessel. There must be room for the warbeast's base. The warbeast may activate the turn it is put into play.

Inanimate - The Vessel is not a living model, has no back arc, and its front arc extends 360°. The Vessel never flees. The Vessel has no melee range and cannot engage or be engaged. The Vessel is automatically hit by melee attacks. The Vessel cannot run, charge, or be knocked down, but it may advance 1" for each Acolyth in its unit within 1" of it at the start of the unit's activation.

Reservoir - Once per turn during his controller's Control Phase, a friendly Legion warlock with fewer fury points than his FURY may remove one blood token from one friendly Vessel within his control area to gain one fury point.

Spawn Horror (★Action) - As a special action, the Vessel may spend five blood tokens to put a Legion lesser warbeast into play under your control. Place the warbeast within 3" of the Vessel. There must be room for the warbeast's base. The warbeast may activate the turn it is put into play.

Acolyth

Fearless - An Acolyth never flees.

Unit

Recycle - When a living model is destroyed within 3" of the Vessel or an Acolyth in formation with it, place blood tokens on the Vessel. The Vessel gains gains 1 blood token for a small-based model, 2 for a medium-based model, and 3 for a large-based model. If more than one Vessel is eligible to claim blood tokens, the Vessel nearest the destroyed model receives the token(s).

Gaff

Reach - 2" melee range.

LEGION OF EVERBLIGHT BLIGHTED OGRUN UNIT

The blight's effect on ogrun is brutal. It ravages their bodies by deforming and augmenting them at the same time. Warmongers are blight-bred for slaughter, and their eyes reflect madness. Prone to hallucinations and twisted visions night and day, a warmonger never sleeps. They can often be heard chanting to themselves in low tones and staring fixated at something unseen by others as their faces twist with anger and seething menace. It is only in battle where they find true release by swinging their enormous war-cleavers to slice through the flesh of friend or foe alike. Divorced from any sense of self-preservation, they can withstand brutal punishment and feel no pain. They smell of putrescence after battle as if a lingering odor of death attaches to them and can never be shaken loose.

After absorbing the Nyss, Everblight turned his attention to enslaving and converting the outlying tribes of wild ogrun dwelling in the northern mountains. Thagrosh knew both their locations and numbers since he had been born among them. Even though Thagrosh's own experiences as an enslaved youth gave him the idea, he has shown no mercy or preference for the blighted ogrun, having severed himself entirely from his old nature. He does not consider them kin anymore, for he sees with the eyes of the dragon now. Despite this disdain the warmongers

They are crude and imperfect, but effective. Send them against the enemy first to sow terror and rend all hope, then follow to slaughter those who flee.

—Vayl, the Disciple of Everblight

fear and revere Thagrosh, and the leaders of the warmongers have named themselves his apostles.

The Nyss are markedly cool toward the warmongers. They barely tolerate the brutes and remain segregated, for the ogrun have a habit of murdering them and each other in the field. More than one Nyss has lingered too close to these horrible creatures in combat and been cloven in two by one of their war-cleavers.

APOSTLE					CMD 8	
SPD	STR	MAT	RAT	DEF	ARM	
5	9	7	3	12	17	

BLIGHTED OGRUN					CMD 6	
SPD	STR	MAT	RAT	DEF	ARM	
5	9	6	3	12	17	

WAR CLEAVER			
	SPECIAL	POW	P+S
	Reach	5	14

APOSTLE DAMAGE	10
BLIGHTED OGRUN DAMAGE	8
FIELD ALLOWANCE	2
VICTORY POINTS	3
LEADER AND 2 TROOPS	66
UP TO 2 ADDITIONAL TROOPS	20ea
BASE SIZE	MEDIUM

Apostle
Leader

Unit

Abomination - Models/units – friendly or enemy – within 3" of a Warmonger must pass a command check or flee.

Berserk - Every time a Warmonger destroys another model with a melee attack, he must immediately make one melee attack against another model in his melee range, friendly or enemy.

Fearless - A Warmonger never flees.

War Cleaver

Reach - 2" melee range.

FORSAKEN				CMD 8	
SPD	STR	MAT	RAT	DEF	ARM
6	7	5	4	14	15

CLAW			
	SPECIAL	POW	P+S
	—	6	13

DAMAGE	8
FIELD ALLOWANCE	2
VICTORY POINTS	1
POINT COST	26
BASE SIZE	SMALL

The Forsaken

Abomination - Models/units – friendly or enemy – within 3" of the Forsaken must pass a command check or flee.

Blight Shroud (★Action) - As a special action, the Forsaken may spend up to five fury points to generate a Blight Shroud. Enemy models within 1" of the Forsaken per fury point spent suffer a POW 8 damage roll, adding an additional die for each focus point or fury point on the affected model.

Consume Fury (★Action) - As a special action, the Forsaken may remove up to five fury points from one friendly Legion warbeast within 5" of it and put the fury points on itself. The Forsaken can never have more than five fury points.

Fearless - The Forsaken never flees.

Fury Boost - The Forsaken may spend fury points to boost melee attack and melee damage rolls.

You shall come to know my master's hand by His glorious works.

—Thagrosh, Prophet of Everblight

Twisted beyond recognition, the Forsaken are the malignant children of the dragon's accursed touch, and the very presence of these abominations is anathema to life. They feed upon the rage and misery of the battlefield and can mimic their master's burning aura to generate a mantle of blighted essence so overwhelming they can strike the living dead by mere proximity—eyes melt, flesh boils with pustules, and internal organs liquefy. The effects of this blighted mantle magnify when striking those infused with primal power. It can feed on and react to harnessed fury to create a wave of agony that can tear bodies asunder.

Horrific beyond comprehension with an alien beauty and strange majesty, the Forsaken are as sacred to the Legion as they are terrible. Although capable of momentary periods of lucidity, each is deranged and insane. Their insanity may derive from a stronger awareness of what they are and what they once were, unprotected by the blind resolve brought to other Nyss by the more subtle applications of the blight. In their lucid moments they remember the annihilation of their race and see in themselves the pure essence of that darkness.

There was no method or guiding hand behind their primogenesis. Each is an aberration spawned when the stress of battle proved overwhelming and a fluke eruption of the blight washed over its body and prompted a rapid and uncontrolled acceleration of the transmutative cycle. Even the most fanatic of Everblight's vassals fears this fate. This accidental and painful process seems to erupt more often in the proximity of warlocks and their athancs, and it changes bodies suddenly and irrevocably. Forsaken display many peculiar draconic features such as arms warped and distended into useless winged appendages, flesh covered in thick scales, serpentine tails, and spurred claws.

Minions

By Coercion, Collusion, or Coin

With almost no sound, Alten crept carefully through the woods instinctively finding a path free of branches. He was a shadow among the trees—a figure one might notice for an instant in the corner of the eye but gone when one turned to look. He kept on his toes though, for a pygmy with an oversized rifle had almost holed him when was first trying to find his position.

Breaking out of the trees he spied the main trollkin force gathered atop a ridge just outside the forest line. He approached a distinctive figure on the hill wearing a long skirt and scarf lifted by the morning's breeze. He advanced within almost a hundred yards before a warrior spotted him and shouted, and a number of uneasy trollkin whirled around bringing weapons to bear. Several of the smaller pygs took to their stomachs and had him in their sights. Alten smiled in his most friendly fashion and held his long rifle by the barrel in one hand; his other hand remained open and spread. There was a tense exchange between those nearest the female in charge before they finally waved him forward, oversized guns at the ready.

"Grissel Bloodsong, as I live and breathe!" Alten exclaimed when within a few yards of the fell caller. She looked at him with an inscrutable expression, and he could not decide if she was annoyed or pleased to see him. He decided to presume the latter. "Can you have your boys rest easy? I'm not here to shoot anyone. Not yet."

She spoke a quick phrase to them, and they reluctantly lowered their massive scatterguns. Alten noticed one of the largest trollkin he'd ever seen had sidled up nearby, just on the periphery of his vision. It was a huge brute with an axe in each hand.

After a bit of squinting, Grissel finally seemed to recognize him. "Alten Ashley? Most strange to find you here."

"Been quite a long time since you came by the Crag. We've missed you. Been almost a year since we had to rebuild any taverns torn apart by trollkin squabbles." He grinned and took a moment to light a cigar. "How's ol' Turgol?"

He knew immediately he'd made a mistake when her face darkened. The quills on her head went flat, and her teeth clenched. He saw her left hand grip the enormous hammer she bore as if trying to break its handle to kindling. "He is dead. Do not speak that name again."

Alten frowned and shook his head. "I'm sorry, Grissel. Honestly, I had no idea. I always liked him. We used to prowl Comb's Beacon together." His sincerity seemed to appease her and her expression softened. He could feel a slight tension go out of the trollkin nearby as well as if all present were tied to her moods. It was a bit eerie, but Grissel had always been larger than life.

"A battle comes." She motioned her head to indicate the advancing force slowly moving forward across the open ground toward them—a long line of red and gold banners. "I have no time for memories."

"About that, I thought maybe you could use my services." Alten winked and grinned around his cigar. "I've been wanting to bag one of those things with the tusks; would look mighty fine above the mantle."

She folded her arms. "You come here to help us out of good will?"

"Now I didn't say that. A man would expect compensation for putting his life on the line, bringing talents honed across western Immoren, and knowing how to shoot down all manner of unwholesome critters and varmints."

Grissel scowled. "We fight for survival here."

"That's all well and good for you, and I admire it. But I'm sure you've got a little coin put aside. You've seen what I can do." Alten noticed that a number of the trollkin, probably those few who spoke Cygnaran, had taken to giving him dirty looks and whispering among themselves. They were clearly not a group that appreciated a man making an honest living.

The oversized axe-bearing trollkin spoke up now, his Molgur-Trul thick but comprehensible to Alten's ear. "We don't need him. Send him away."

Grissel was silent a long moment as Alten sucked on his cigar, looking casual and at ease. She spoke back to her champion in the same tongue. "You haven't seen him fire that gun. He's worth it."

She finally addressed him. "We have some Cygnaran coin, but you won't earn your usual fee. I'll also let you keep the tusks of the invading creatures you slay."

"Done. We'll haggle on coinage later; let's see the lay of the land."

Alten could see many ugly stares directed his way, but the tension was gone and the trollkin began turning their attention to the approaching skorne setting up in a wide line and approaching at a steady but cautious pace. Alten stepped up to the rise.

"I see you got some farrow." He stabbed his cigar toward the bipedal pig-men down below the trollkin spread out in a line. They were dug in and crouched on their hooves, and they wielded oversized primitive firearms. Alten sniffed in disdain as he held his own superior rifle. "You paying them too?"

Grissel shrugged, "We offered them protection. The skorne drove them from an oasis east of the Keys. Many others have been enslaved by the skorne, tormented, and forced to fight. With us they can earn shelter." Alten nodded and held his tongue. He thought they were likely to die the same either way—whether coerced or persuaded.

He watched as the trollkin made ready by forming up loosely to the terrain of the hillside. It was a stark contrast to Alten to see the skorne below with their utter military precision and the almost casual but grim trollkin gearing up for battle. A few dozen yards away he saw a fell caller actually laughing at a joke. He eyed the full-blood trolls waiting nearby. They stood among the trollkin with no restraints, and one was staring at him with hungry eyes. It gave him a disquieted feeling.

The large champion spoke, "They come." The skorne forces had begun to make their push and were arranged in a wide formation. He saw there were indeed farrow among the advancing soldiers, and a skorne with a long whip marched behind them. The boar-men looked wild eyed and haggard. Meanwhile one of the trollkin nearby bellowed an order, and the farrow on their side stood up to attention and raised their rifles. It looked like the first engagement would be farrow on farrow, which was no particular surprise.

Alten put out his cigar and gripped his gun. He winked again at Grissel. "Good luck!" With that he began his move to the left along the ridge, looking for the highest ground on the flank. "I'll try to save some for you!"

"On the Use of Cross-Species Hirelings," a letter from Professor Viktor Pendrake as a reenlisted scout for the Cygnaran Army to Scout General Bolden Rebald

As you asked, I have kept an eye open for hirelings of various species as I make my patrols on the fringes of the Bloodstone Marches. To answer your question, this situation cannot be equated to the use of mercenary companies among the human armies in the western wars, but there are some similarities. Thinking of them as mercenaries will cause you to labor under misconceptions that could prevent you from grasping the situation.

The primary difference has to do with the long tradition of mercenary conduct that predates even the Orgoth. Though all companies do not equally honor these old codes, the system of charter and hire is well established and accepted. It is a system of behavior and expected recompense by which each party knows what to expect. There is nothing similar among the varied groups fighting in these arguably more brutal and less organized battles. I am not sure if any safeguards exist for fair treatment, and their disposition is thus entirely in the hands of whomever gathers their services. While a trollkin chieftain may offer fair barter to a farrow tribe to fight alongside them, the skorne may enslave them and force them to fight against their will. Certainly war offers up opportunities for those willing to take risks and fight, and I expect many of these battle-hardened species are willing to take those risks to seek a better future for themselves or their tribes.

Groups of intelligent species will band together despite differences if survival is at stake.

I believe the arrival of the skorne in such numbers—making their slow yet inexorable conquest of this barren land—has changed the behavior of several groups. This may be the case elsewhere as calamity falls, such as in the wilderness region in Khador's frozen north where some unexplained terror has arisen. Groups of intelligent species will band together despite differences if survival is at stake. We will certainly see more of that in times to come.

The species most affected by the current struggles on the fringes appear to be the farrow and the subspecies of goblins, or gobbers, commonly termed "swamp gobbers". They are found in large numbers on the outskirts of Corvis. I expect these will not be the last. Do not discount such groups as "inferior" for having less refined cultures. They number among them exceptional individuals and certain heroes who can stand proudly with the best mankind can boast. Nor are humans excepted from these engagements; I know of several opportunistic coin-seekers trying to ply their trade in these fights. I will relate more as I discover it. —VP

Alten Ashley, Monster Hunter

MINION SOLO CHARACTER

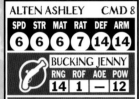

ALTEN ASHLEY				CMD	8
SPD	STR	MAT	RAT	DEF	ARM
6	6	6	7	14	14

BUCKING JENNY			
RNG	ROF	AOE	POW
14	1	—	12

SWORD		
SPECIAL	POW	P+S
—	3	9

DAMAGE	5
FIELD ALLOWANCE	C
VICTORY POINTS	1
POINT COST	32
BASE SIZE	SMALL

If I led an army, I'd pay big money to hire someone as good as me and consider every coin well spent. That's the god's honest truth.

—Alten Ashley gives his unbiased appraisal of his own abilities

Some men are just rugged through and through, mean as a gorax, born with an eagle's eye, and possessed of such irrepressible gumption that they become legends in their own time, or at least their own minds. Alten Ashley is one such man. Unlike some braggarts, he lives up to his reputation of being a truly exceptional hunter of the great beasts stalking the wilds of western Immoren. The onset of war and the emergence of previously hidden enemies instill fear in the hearts of most men, but Alten Ashley sees the gleam of gold and the promise of danger.

His jealous detractors dismiss Alten as a money-grubbing mercenary, but for him the wealth is the least of the equation. He enjoys earning a healthy purse, but he considers it fair for the skill he brings to the table. Monetary rewards have nothing to do with his reasons for taking to the wilderness—it is the thrill of taking down the most dangerous creatures on the face of Caen. There is a madness which takes over some men and demands they seek danger instead of turning from it. For Alten it is neither the reward nor the kill that matters. It is the excitement of the hunt.

Alten does not speak about his youth, but he is clearly Cygnaran born. His accent puts his roots somewhere on the western coast, and he has traveled more than most. He has stories about tracking one of Blighterghast's dragonspawn deep in the Wyrmwall Mountains, narrowly escaping with his life against a rampaging dire troll in the Gnarls, and hunting the largest frost drake ever recorded in the frozen wastes of Khador. After a few years in Khador he decided the cold did not suit him, and he swung through the Thornwood Forest killing warpwolves before making his way out to the fringes of the Bloodstone Marches. The only place he is seen with any regularity is the Sanity's Bastion saloon in the dusty no-man's land of a town called Ternon Crag, fifty miles east of Cygnar's border and unclaimed by any nation. He has a reputation for being boisterous to the point of obnoxious and has earned few friends. Despite this, he has the respect of both Kossite woodsmen and Morridane scouts. Even the Widowmakers grudgingly admit he is a passable shot.

Though never trained formally, Ashley is a crack shot with his rifle. It is a truly monstrous weapon with a thick, large bored barrel designed to blast holes in the thickest hides. Its hardened ammunition can punch straight through a man as if he were not even there, and the rifle's bipod allows him to aim more accurately while hiding prone under the underbrush. He relies heavily on this oversized gun, but he is no amateur with the sword either. He can hold his own when his target inevitably closes to tear him apart.

Mercenary
Alten Ashley will not work for Cryx.

Minion
Alten Ashley will not work for the Legion or the Skorne.

Alten Ashley
Advance Deployment - Place Alten Ashley after normal deployment, up to 12" beyond the established deployment zone.

Camouflage - Alten Ashley gains an additional +2 DEF when benefiting from concealment or cover.

Crack Shot - Alten Ashley's targets do not benefit from being screened.

Fearless - Alten Ashley never flees.

Monster Hunter - After a successful attack against a living warbeast, instead of making a damage roll, Alten Ashley may have the warbeast lose an aspect. Mark the remaining damage circles in that aspect.

Pathfinder - Alten Ashley ignores movement penalties from rough terrain and obstacles. Alten Ashley may charge across rough terrain.

Alten will be the first to insist it is not the weapons that make him deadly but his experience and lore. The monster hunter has fought more dangerous creatures in a couple of short decades than a Nyss ranger might face in a century. He knows all their habits, their strengths, and their weak points. He knows just the spot to hit a dire troll so he can shoot between the ribs to deflate a lung. Almost nothing alive can survive a few shots from Alten's rifle, and he is just as good at slipping a blade up below the ribs to tickle a beast's heart. Alten does not seek the easy life and throws himself from one dangerous battle to another. Somehow he always escapes unscathed with a new story to tell.

Totem Hunter

MINION SOLO CHARACTER

TOTEM HUNTER				CMD	9
SPD	STR	MAT	RAT	DEF	ARM
7	8	8	4	14	15

KELKAX			
	SPECIAL	POW	P+S
	Reach	6	14

SPIKED BUCKLER			
	SPECIAL	POW	P+S
	–	3	11

DAMAGE	8
FIELD ALLOWANCE	C
VICTORY POINTS	1
POINT COST	35
BASE SIZE	MEDIUM

The totem hunter stalks the land like it was a breadbasket, hunting man and beast alike as if they were one and the same.

—Professor Viktor Pendrake, Corvis University

Immoren is just one continent of Caen. The world is largely unexplored by its isolated inhabitants and contains horrors its denizens can barely fathom. One of these frightening alien species comes from across the ocean and is represented by a being known only as the totem hunter. Very little is known about its culture, its beliefs, its native language, or its civilization, but its motives are clear: it lives to hunt. It values only the kill and reaps totems as grisly trophies from the most formidable adversaries it can track down. This practice is a powerful sacred ceremony to the totem hunter whereby it draws on the vital energies of the slain to add to its strength with each ritual kill. The totem hunter is rarely seen except by its victim in the moment before death. Appearing from nowhere it leaps to impale its chosen target with its wickedly barbed spear and lets loose a hideous cry that can shatter glass and send men fleeing in terror.

The totem hunter enjoys eviscerating fearsome beasts but is just as interested in stalking anyone of exceptional combat ability and tremendous power, including warlocks. The hunter reaps totems from its special targets by cutting off the head or another significant body part. Collecting these totems bestows enormous power to the hunter as the victim's life essence is added to its own. This fills the hunter with cumulative supernatural strength and toughness with each great kill. After gathering several of these grisly totems the hunter can become as strong as a titan.

This entity is drawn to the recent battles in western Immoren, particularly the struggles taking place on the northern fringes of the Bloodstone Marches and the Thornwood. It may have been hunting from the

shadows in other recent wars where its deprivations would likely have been blamed on Cryxian raiders. There may be more than one now stalking the continent as a result of the rise in ocean travel to the southern continent of Zu. Rumors persist that totem hunters come from somewhere deeper south in this largely unexplored land. Whether the totem hunter is one distinct individual or several on the prowl is conjecture, but in either case the creature is exceptionally intelligent and possessed of singular skill. With the ability to cloak itself in shadow and disappear, the totem hunter leaves no trace of its presence.

This is a fortuitous time to seek trophies, for the rise of Everblight and the invasion of the skorne have brought yet more powerful and singular prizes for the totem hunter to reap. It has no political agenda and is willing to join the battle on various sides. Those who profit from its presence in one engagement may find themselves the target of its hunt in the next.

The totem hunter makes its presence known to a chosen battlefield commander shortly before an engagement, perhaps picking those it considers worthy. After drawing the eye of a warlock, it will make an enigmatic gesture like some form of salute and vanish again. With this gesture the totem hunter indicates it will not slay the soldiers of its chosen leader. In the following fight it will lurk unseen to stalk the opposing army and seek to slay and capture totems from of the most dangerous beasts and any other formidable combatants that draw its attention. At the end of the battle it vanishes again without seeking payment or any other recompense except the totems it has gathered from its own bloody work.

The totem hunter has honed its skills with obsessive single-minded determination and bears weapons of power. It can leap tremendous distances and uses stealth to disappear into the forest. Attempts to track or follow the totem hunter after battle or engage in more extensive interactions with it fail utterly. Whatever their purpose in Immoren, there are few creatures as graceful, deadly, or utterly terrifying to behold.

Minion
The Totem Hunter will work for any facton.

Totem Hunter
Extraordinary Senses - The Totem Hunter ignores cloud effects and forests when determining LOS. The Totem Hunter may charge invisible models.

Fearless - The Totem Hunter never flees.

Pathfinder - The Totem Hunter ignores movement penalties from rough terrain and obstacles. The Totem Hunter may charge across rough terrain.

Stealth - Attacks against the Totem Hunter from greater than 5" away automatically miss. If the Totem Hunter is greater than 5" away from an attacker, he does not count as an intervening model.

Totem Reaping - When the Totem Hunter destroys an enemy solo, warbeast, warjack, warlock, or warcaster, mark a totem circle on his card. The Totem Hunter gains +1 STR, MAT, and ARM for each marked totem circle.

Hunter Abilities
Once per activation the Totem Hunter may choose one of the following Hunter Abilities.

- **Cry of the Hunter** - Enemy models/units currently within 8" of the Totem Hunter must pass a command check or flee.

- **Flying Steel** - The Totem Hunter may make d3 attacks with the Totem Blade this activation.

- **Vault** - After advancing but before performing an action, the Totem Hunter may vault up to 5". When vaulting, the Totem Hunter may move over other models if he has enough movement to move completely past their bases. During this movement the Totem Hunter cannot be targeted by free strikes and ignores rough terrain, obstacles, and other movement penalties and effects. The Totem Hunter may attack normally after vaulting. Any effects that prevent charging prevent the Totem Hunter from vaulting.

Kelkax
Reach - 2" melee range.

Farrow Brigands

MINION FARROW UNIT

SHAMAN					CMD 8
SPD	STR	MAT	RAT	DEF	ARM
5	6	6	5	12	15

BRIGAND					CMD 6
SPD	STR	MAT	RAT	DEF	ARM
5	6	6	4	12	15

PIG IRON

RNG	ROF	AOE	POW
10	1	—	12

SHAMAN WAR CLUB

SPECIAL	POW	P+S
Reach	4	10

FARROW CLUB

SPECIAL	POW	P+S
—	3	9

SHAMAN DAMAGE	5
FIELD ALLOWANCE	1
VICTORY POINTS	2
LEADER AND 5 TROOPS	72
UP TO 4 ADDITIONAL TROOPS	10ea
BASE SIZE	SMALL

Once they've dug in, root'n 'em out ain't easy. Give 'em some slop and good ground and they're 'ere to stay.

—A trollkin warrior offering a grudging compliment

The farrow are a stern species of half-man, half-pig creatures found in the unsettled areas of eastern Cygnar, southern Llael, and the fringes of the Marches. The Midlunders of Cygnar despise them and consider them freakish menaces to farmers and trade caravans. Other groups have no such prejudices and are glad to make use of their abilities. In battle the farrow are fierce and hardy soldiers noted for thick hides and boar-like tenacity. They are as difficult to bring down as the boars they resemble, and armed with primitive rifles scavenged from raids on human caravans, the farrow are the equal of many front line soldiers.

Several large farrow tribes came down out of the Dragonspine Peaks to take advantage of the chaos and confusion in northern Cygnar in the recent Second Thornwood War. When both Fisherbrook and Stonebridge Castle were beset by a forward army of the Protectorate of Menoth, the farrow were able to scavenge forgotten weapon stashes. The tribes and their leading shamans have used these weapons to gain dominance among their tribal people.

They avoid most humans, who regularly hunt them, but they have old ties with druids of the Circle Orboros. The Trollbloods have also increasingly dealt with them. Farrow religion bears strong similarity to the Dhunian faith, and the shamans of both races can find common ground. Acquiring farrow services requires barter for things like blasting powder, food, or the promise of protection.

As with other species embroiled in these battles, the farrow have attracted unsavory attention by advance Legion scouts and the invading skorne who first faced them in battle in recent months. Both groups have been known to force the farrow into enslaved servitude and use them as cannon fodder.

Minion

The Farrow Brigands will work for any faction.

Shaman

Leader

Pig-Headed - The Farrow Brigands are fearless while the Shaman remains in play. A fearless model never flees.

Shamanic Prayer - The Shaman may recite one of the following prayers during each of his activations. Every model in his unit, including himself, gains the listed benefits.

- **Hog Wild** - The Farrow Brigands may make a ranged attack before moving this activation. After attacking, the Farrow Brigands may advance normally and make melee attacks.

- **Shrouded Path** - The Farrow Brigands ignore movement penalties from rough terrain and obstacles. The Farrow Brigands may charge across rough terrain. The Farrow Brigands gain Camouflage. A model with Camouflage gains +2 DEF when benefiting from concealment or cover. Shrouded Path lasts for one round.

- **Warding Chant** - The Farrow Brigands cannot be targeted by enemy spells. When Warding Chant is used, enemy upkeep spells on the unit expire. Warding Chant lasts for one round.

Unit

Dig In (★Action) - A Farrow Brigand may dig a hasty battle position into the ground, gaining cover (+4 DEF) and +4 ARM. A Farrow Brigand remains dug in until he moves or is engaged. A Farrow Brigand cannot dig into solid rock or man-made constructions. Farrow Brigands may begin the game dug in.

Swamp Gobber Bellows Crew

MINION SWAMP GOBBER WEAPON CREW

Swamp gobbers are a clever and hardy breed that can be found in many bogs and marshes, but they are particularly numerous in the eastern Thornwood and the Widower's Wood outside of Corvis. They have discovered a unique mixture of fluids that combine to produce a huge volume of dense fog rapidly. With a little clever work they innovated a bellows contraption that enables this fog to be spread across a large area, making it much harder to see anything past a few feet.

Half as tall as humans, gobbers are a clever race of diminutive humanoids with skin that can change color for camouflage. They are quite intelligent and have a natural knack for invention and alchemy, but there are gobbers out in the wilds who lack the sophisticated culture of their city-dwelling peers. Swamp gobbers fall in this category. They lack the refinement of city gobbers, but they speak a variety of languages they use to barter trade for their villages.

Recent warfare has encouraged the swamp gobbers to seek advantages for themselves. A number of these enterprising folk have offered their services, usually seeking food or weapons to be sent back to their families. Their prices are reasonable, and both the trollkin and druids have occasionally enlisted their services. This has put the swamp gobbers in harm's way, and some of their tribes have been captured by skorne or forced to serve the Legion. The bellows crew

I'll tell you one thing that ain't changed from all the long history of war—if you can't see it, you can't hit it.

—Alten Ashley, Monster Hunter

prefers not to fight if possible, but they are willing to provide the services of their fog-making machine to obscure and conceal those around them. They provide excellent protection against the threat of volleys of arrows, gunfire, or skorne reiver needles.

GUNNER					CMD 7	
SPD	STR	MAT	RAT	DEF	ARM	
4	3	3	3	15	11	

CREWMAN					CMD 7	
SPD	STR	MAT	RAT	DEF	ARM	
6	3	3	3	15	11	

SMALL WEAPONS		
SPECIAL	POW	P+S
–	2	5

FIELD ALLOWANCE	1
VICTORY POINTS	1
POINT COST	15
BASE SIZE	SMALL

Minion
The Swamp Gobber Bellows Crew will work for any faction.

Gunner
Cloud Cover (★Action) - Target model/unit within 6" of the Gunner gains concealment for one round.

Fog Cloud (★Action) - Place a 3" AOE cloud effect anywhere within 3" of the Gunner. Non-swamp gobber living models in the AOE suffer –2 to attack rolls. The Fog Cloud lasts for one round.

Crewman
Fog Juice - If the Crewman is in base-to-base contact with the Gunner when the Gunner performs a Cloud Cover special action, a target model/unit within 10" of the Gunner gains concealment for one round (instead of within 6"). If the Crewman is in base-to-base contact with the Gunner when the Gunner performs a Fog Cloud special action, place a 5" AOE instead of a 3" AOE.

Unit
Camouflage - Swamp gobbers gain an additional +2 DEF when benefiting from concealment or cover.

Weapon Crew - The Swamp Gobber Bellows Crew is made up of a Gunner and Crewman. The Swamp Gobber Bellows Crew cannot run or charge. The Gunner gains +2" of movement if he begins activation in base-to-base contact with the Crewman. If the Gunner takes sufficient damage to be destroyed and the Crewman is within 1", the Crewman is removed from the table instead. Any effects, spells, and animi on the damaged Gunner expire. Any effects, spells, and animi on the removed Crewman are applied to the Gunner.

TROLLBLOODS

TROLLBLOOD WARPACK
Madrak Ironhide, Troll Axer, and 2 Troll Impalers

MADRAK IRONHIDE
Warlock

HOARLUK DOOMSHAPER
Warlock

GRISSEL BLOODSONG
Warlock

DIRE TROLL MAULER
Heavy Warbeast

TROLL AXER
Light Warbeast

TROLL IMPALER
Light Warbeast

TROLLBLOODS

SCATTERGUNNERS
Trollkin Unit

TROLLKIN CHAMPIONS
Trollkin Unit

Circle Orboros

CIRCLE ORBOROS WARPACK
Kaya the Wildborne, Warpwolf, and 2 Argus

KAYA THE WILDBORNE
Warlock

BALDUR THE STONECLEAVER
Warlock

KRUEGER THE STORMWRATH
Warlock

ARGUS
Light Warbeast

WARPWOLF
Heavy Warbeast

SHIFTING STONES
Unit

Circle Orboros

WOLVES OF ORBOROS
Unit

THARN RAVAGERS
Tharn Unit

GORAX
Light Warbeast

WOLDWARDEN
Heavy Warbeast

SKORNE

SKORNE WARPACK
Master Tormentor Morghoul, Titan Gladiator, and 2 Cyclops Savages

ARCHDOMINA MAKEDA
Warlock

LORD TYRANT HEXERIS
Warlock

MASTER TORMENTOR MORGHOUL
Warlock

TITAN GLADIATOR
Heavy Warbeast

TITAN CANNONEER
Heavy Warbeast

CYCLOPS SAVAGE
Light Warbeast

SKORNE

PRAETORIANS
Unit

CATAPHRACT ARCUARII
Unit

ANCESTRAL GUARDIAN
Solo

Legion of Everblight

LEGION OF EVERBLIGHT WARPACK
Lylyth, Carnivean, and 4 Shredders

**LYLYTH,
HERALD OF EVERBLIGHT**
Warlock

**THAGROSH,
PROPHET OF EVERBLIGHT**
Warlock

VAYL, DISCIPLE OF EVERBLIGHT
Warlock

SERAPH
Light Warbeast

CARNIVEAN
Heavy Warbeast

SHREDDERS
Lesser Warbeasts

Legion of Everblight

STRIDERS
Blighted Nyss Unit

BLIGHTED ARCHERS
Blighted Nyss Unit

PAINTING THE HORDES

Bringing life to your beasts of war.

Each of the factions in HORDES has a distinct and unique look that ties all of the different troops, creatures, and characters together. With a little planning it is a relatively easy task to bind them together visually into a unified army that will look great on the battlefield.

We are going to look at the colors we applied to each of the four factions to give them their unique character. Each force has a distinct palette of colors that can be used in different ways to unify the miniatures. These colors are shown on this page as they would be applied to a white painting palette. The purpose of this is to show the colors in their purest form and demonstrate how they 'thin-out' when water is added.

The Skorne color scheme is simple and striking. We have coupled deep red with black on the clothing and armor, and bright gold is a contrast that picks out the edges.

Red, black, and gold are the main colors for the Skorne. The gold has been half washed over with ink to deepen the color.

to light tan leather. Some care has to be taken when you are painting miniatures in natural tones. If you are not careful, they can end up looking muddy and dull. The secret is to keep the colors clean and rich. If you add black to brown to deepen it, you will get a flat neutral tone, but if you add deep, rich shades of brown to the shadows you will get a far more attractive result. This is one reason why it is really important to thin the color out with water on your palette; it shows you how the color was built up. Two different colors might dry out quite similarly, but if they are built from a different spectrum they will act completely differently as soon as you mix them with highlights or shades. You should try to stick with mixing either warm or cold tones together when you are highlighting and shading. This all might sound quite complex, but once you get the hang of the idea, it can make an enormous difference to your painting.

SKORNE

Red and gold are the dominant colors for the Skorne faction. It is not a primary red like the one used on Khador armies, but it is a deeper, richer tone that gives the miniatures a unique feel. The red armor contrasts well with some plain black areas and bright yellow-gold details. The Skorne color scheme is really strong and distinctive and is applied to all of the clothing and armor to give the faction a really powerful, unified look that is actually just as military looking as some of the WARMACHINE factions. There are of course other

Kaya is a good example for how different tones and colors of brown can be combined on a single miniature to produce a very natural look.

One of the ways green is introduced into the Circle's color palette is by washing over the gold and bronze areas with a green verdigris color. The other swatches shown here are examples of brown you can introduce.

CIRCLE

The main colors for the Circle faction are rich and natural—deep woodland green coupled with warm brown tones. The green is mainly applied as verdigris to metal armor plates with ancient gold and bronze tones to contrast, but it can also be introduced to elements of the clothing. Most of the clothing and robes are painted in different natural brown tones from deep rich brown colors to add to this. The skin of the Skorne people is pale and almost albino in coloring, and the beasts they drive into battle come in various hues. For example, the hide of the Titan is mid grey like an elephant or rhino, but it can be painted with slightly pinkish undertones to give it a more natural feel. It is quite helpful to look at reference when painting things like this. In fact with most of the wild beasts found in HORDES, you can find a wealth of invaluable color information in wildlife books from the colors found on different animals to the way they are applied. Even subtle touches of realism will make a huge difference to the overall look.

LEGION

The color scheme for the Legion is striking and monochromatic. The skin on all the troops, characters, and beasts is very white, and most of the armor and clothing is either notably dark or black. Of course there are some subtleties keeping the scheme from becoming totally black and white. The skin is mainly shaded with cold grey tones, and the beasts have areas of pinkish colors in the more flexible areas of their hides. Similarly, the dark tones are not just black but are shaded and highlighted with slightly different colors to give some variation while still maintaining the overall feel. It is considerably effective to bring out the cold and icy feel of the miniatures. The Blighted Nyss come from the snowbound mountains north of the Iron Kingdoms and the color schemes are reminiscent of that land. As mentioned previously, the skin on both the Nyss and the blighted beasts is white but shaded with cold grey (grey that has some blue in it). This blue tinge is subtle though; you don't want to end up with sky blue miniatures! Similarly, the black areas are highlighted with dark blue tones to keep the color palette consistent. We also introduced a small amount of brown into the scheme on both the Nyss themselves and the beasts.

TROLLBLOODS

The whole of the Trollblood faction is tied together with a very distinct palette of colors. The trolls themselves all have various tones of greyish blue skin, and this is contrasted with a warm mid brown on the clothing and armor. We applied this color in different ways depending on the part of the miniature on which it is used. The armor is painted as steel with patches of bright rust, and the clothing is painted in warm brown tones. One of the main features of the Trollkin troops and characters are the different tartans wrapped around their bodies. These have different patterns (or *quitari* as they are correctly called) depending on what kriel they are from. The main kriel color for the miniatures shown

Blighted Nyss skin tone is white shaded with cold grey. To keep the color scheme in the same palette, we have highlighted the black with cold tones.

The top two swatches show the cold grey skin tone and the pink color added to the beasts. The lower swatches show black highlighted with cold tones and a more natural brown tone that can be used on the hard armored areas of the creatures.

here is a warm mid brown, and the same color has been used for the rust on the armor. Using the same color in two completely different ways ensures that the main color theme is carried right through the miniature. The rust and brown tones is just a foil for the skin color though, for when you look at the miniature it is the skin that really stands out and creates a unique look. One of the potential pit-falls of painting miniatures with blue skin tones is that they can easily come out looking 'false' and plastic-like. The best way to get around this is to add some natural tones to soften the color and give it a more realistic look. The blue/grey skin tones are highlighted with flesh color instead of white, and you can add some slightly red tones to the shading.

By highlighting the trollkin skin color with normal flesh tones, we have given it a more natural feel.

Adding flesh tones for the highlights softens the blue/grey skin color which is contrasted with a warm mid brown that can be applied to leather clothing and also as rust on the armor.

Legion of Everblight

BLIGHTED ARCHERS POUR FROM THE GATES OF A RUINED BLIGHTED CITY TO REPEL KRUEGER'S ATTACK.

A SKORNE RAIDING PARTY IS QUICKLY OUTNUMBERED WHEN VAYL AND A CARNIVEAN JOIN THE FRAY.

AFTER MARKING THE DIRE TROLL MAULER WITH HELLSINGER, LYLYTH SENDS HER FORCES CHARGING IN.

Circle Orberos

A MARCHING COLUMN OF SKORNE QUICKLY LEARNS THE SIGNIFICANCE OF THE STONE OBELISKS THEY PASS WHEN THEY WALK INTO A CIRCLE AMBUSH.

THE FARROW BRIGANDS MANAGE TO DISTRACT A CRYXIAN HELLJACK JUST LONG ENOUGH FOR BALDUR TO SEND HIS ARGUS AGAINST THE IRON LICH.

KRUEGER THROWS HIS BEASTS AGAINST THE INTRUDING CARNIVEAN. AN ENEMY CREATURE OF THAT SIZE MUST NOT BE ALLOWED TO PASS.

Sea of Glass

Howling Wastes

Shard Spires

Burningfrost Plains

GHORD ✦

RHUL

✦ Uldenfrost *Scarsfell Forest*

Windless Waste

Kharác Sea

Ohk ✦ ✦ Skirov

KHADOR

Leryn ✦ SHYRR ✦

Issyrah

LLAEL

IOS

Khardov ✦ ✦ KORSK

MERYWYN ✦

Mt. Shyleth Breen

ORD

Scarleforth Lake

Bitter Sea

Abyss

Conqueror's Bridge ✦

MERIN ✦

Thornwood Forest

Corvis ✦ ✦ Ternon Crag

Abyssal Fortress ✦

✦ Berck

Dragon's Tongue River

Five Fingers

Black River

Stormlands

Gnarls

CYGNAR

Rotterhorn

Sea of a Thousand Souls

Wyrmwall Mountains

✦ IMER

BLOODSTONE
MARCHES

Vinter's Crossing

CASPIA ✦ ✦ Sul

CRYX

✦ Highgate

PROTECTORATE
OF MENOTH

SKELL ✦

Gulf of Cygnar

✦ Ancient Icthier

Wailing Sea

Bloodshore Island

Meredius

Accursed Sea

~ Continent of Immoren ~

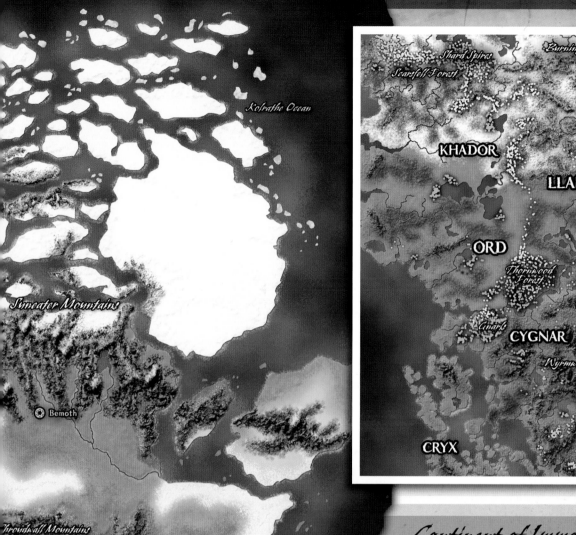

Kolrathe Ocean

Stoneater Mountains

⊛ Bemoth

Throniwall Mountains
⊛ Malphas
Mirketh Lake

HALAAK

Karrak

SKORNE
EMPIRE

Hexaat River   ⊛ Kademe

Shattered Spine Islands

Mizrah Sea

Shard Spires   Burningfrost Plains

Scarsfell Forest

RHUL

KHADOR

LLAEL

IOS

Mt. Shyleth Bree

ORD   Scarleforth Lake

Thornwood
Forest

Cinarb

CYGNAR   Retterhorn

Wyrmwall Mountains

CRYX

PROTECTORATE
OF MENOTH

~Continent of Immoren Map Key~

⬛	Water	(dots)	Legion
(forest)	Forest	(dots)	Circle
(mountains)	Mountains	(dots)	Skorne
⬜	Desert	(dots)	Trollblood
(plains)	Plains	✦	Capital
⬜	Snow	✦	City

Scale in Miles

0   50   150   250   350   400
   100   200   300

Trollbloods

With their combined strength, Doomshaper and Ironhide must defeat another attempt by the coniving druids to break their alliance.

Knock knock. Who's there? The Legion. Legion who?

Goaded by Ironhide, a Troll Axer begins swinging his axe in a wild flurry of pain while Hexeris prepares a counterassault.

SKORNE

ARE THESE TROLLS THE BEST KING LETO CAN DO TO SLOW THE SKORNE ADVANCE INTO NORTHERN CYGNAR? HE MUST DO BETTER.

BALDUR THE STONECLEAVER LAUNCHES A DARING SNEAK ATTACK ON A FORWARD SKORNE ENCAMPMENT. WILL IT BE ENOUGH TO SLOW THE SKORNE ADVANCE INTO THE THORNWOOD?

THE SEVERED HEADS OF THESE ZEALOTS FROM THE PROTECTORATE WILL MAKE EXCELLENT TROPHIES FOR MORGHOUL

GLOSSARY

Ability (pg. 24): An ability typically gives a benefit or capability that modifies how the standard rules apply to a model. Abilities are always in effect and apply every time a game situation warrants their use.

Action (pg. 37): After moving, a model can perform one action: either a combat action or a special action. Some types of movement or special rules require a model to forfeit its action or restrict the type of action it can perform.

Activation Phase (pg. 30): The third phase of a player's turn. The Activation Phase is the major portion of the turn. A player may activate each model and unit he controls once during this phase except for models that activated in an earlier phase for some reason, such as fleeing or frenzy.

Advance (pg. 33): A model moves up to its Speed (SPD) in inches when advancing. An advancing model can perform an action after completing its movement.

Aiming (pg. 45): A model that voluntarily forfeits its movement by not changing its position or facing gains a +2 bonus to every ranged attack roll it makes as part of its combat action. A *magic attack* does not get the aiming bonus.

Animus (pg. 59): Warbeasts have dormant arcane abilities called animi that can be tapped by friendly faction warlocks. A warbeast may be forced to use its animus, or a friendly faction warlock may tap the animus, treating it as if it were one his own spells while the warbeast is in the warlock's control area.

Area of Effect (AOE) (pg. 24): The diameter in inches of the template an area-of-effect weapon or spell uses for damage effects. All models covered by the template potentially suffer the attack's effects.

Armor (ARM) (pg. 23): A model's ability to resist being damaged. A model takes one damage point for every point that a damage roll exceeds its ARM stat.

Aspect (pg. 25): A warbeast's life spiral is arranged into three aspects: Mind, Body, and Spirit. When all of the damage circles of a particular aspect are marked, the warbeast suffers a corresponding penalty.

Automatic Effect (pg. 54): Apply an automatic effect every time it meets the conditions required to function.

Back Arc (pg. 25): The rear 180° of a model's base, opposite its front arc. A model is in another's back arc if its base is entirely within the other model's back arc.

Back Strike (pg. 50): An attack against a target model's back arc from a model that began its activation in the target model's back arc. A back strike gives a +2 bonus to the attack roll.

Base Size (pg. 25): The physical size and mass of a model are reflected by its base size. There are three base sizes: small base (30mm), medium base (40mm), and large base (50mm).

Blast Damage (pg. 48): Every model with any part of its base covered by an AOE template is automatically hit by the attack and takes a blast damage roll of 2d6+1/2POW.

Body (pg. 53): One of the aspects of a warbeast's life spiral. When all of the damage circles in a warbeast's Body are marked, that warbeast rolls one fewer die for its damage rolls.

Boosting (pg. 57): During its activation, a warlock can spend a fury point or warbeast may be forced to add one additional die to any attack roll or damage roll. The model must declare it is boosting the roll before rolling any dice.

Character (pg. 26): A model that represents a unique individual from Immoren. A horde may include only one model of each named character. A character follows the rules for its basic model type.

Charge (pg. 33): A type of movement that combines with a model's combat action to make a charge attack.

Charge Attack (pg. 33): If a charging model moved at least 3", its first attack is a charge attack. A charge attack roll is made normally and may be *boosted*. If the charge attack hits, add an additional die to the damage roll. This damage roll cannot be boosted.

Claws: In addition to functioning as melee weapons, claws can be used to perform certain power attacks.

Cloud Effect (pg. 54): A cloud effect produces an area of dense smoke or gas that remains in play at its *point of impact*. Consider every model with any part of its base covered by the cloud's template to be inside the cloud and susceptible to its effects. A model inside a cloud effect gains +2 DEF against ranged and magic attacks, which is cumulative with *concealment* or *cover*.

Collateral Damage (pg. 41): If a slammed or thrown model collides with another model that has an equal- or smaller-sized base, that model is knocked down and suffers a collateral damage roll of 2d6 plus the STR of the warbeast that initiated the slam or throw. Collateral damage cannot be *boosted*. A model that has a larger-sized base than the slammed model does not take collateral damage.

Combat Action (pg. 37): A model can perform a combat action after advancing, charging, or forfeiting its movement. A combat action lets a model make *attacks*. A model performing a combat action can choose one of the following attack options:

- A model can make one melee attack with each of its melee weapons in melee range.

- A model can make one special attack (★Attack) allowed by its special rules instead of making any other attacks. A model does not have to spend fury points or be forced to make a special attack.

- A warbeast that did not charge can be forced to make one power attack instead of making any other attack. A power attack is considered a melee attack.

- A model not in melee and that did not charge can make one ranged attack with each of its ranged weapons. Each ranged weapon only makes one attack at this point, regardless of its ROF.

Command (CMD) (pg. 23): A model's willpower, leadership, and self-discipline. Command also determines the command range of a model with the Commander ability.

Command Check (pg. 61): When a situation requires a model or unit to make a command check, roll 2d6. If the result is equal to or less than its Command (CMD) stat, it passes the check. If the roll is greater than its CMD, the check fails, and the model or unit suffers the consequences.

Command Range (pg. 62): A model with the Commander ability has a command range equal to his CMD stat in inches.

Commander (pg. 56): A model or unit in command range of a model with the Commander ability may use that model's CMD instead of its own when making a command check but is not required to do so. A model with the Commander ability can rally any model or unit and give orders to any unit in his command range.

Concealment (pg. 46): Some terrain features and special effects grant a model concealment by making it more difficult to be seen, though they are not dense enough to actually block an attack. A model within 1" of a concealing terrain feature that obscures any portion of its base from an attacker gains +2 DEF against ranged and magic attacks from that opponent. Concealment provides no benefit against a *spray attack.*

Continuous Effect (pg. 54): Continuous effects remain on a model and have the potential to damage it or affect it some other way on subsequent turns. Resolve continuous effects on models you control during the maintenance phase of your turn. Roll a d6—if the result is a 1 or 2, remove the effect immediately expires without further effect. On a 3 through 6, it remains in play and the model immediately suffers its effects.

Control Area (pg. 56): A warlock's control area extends out in all directions for a distance of twice his Fury (FURY) in inches. A warlock may only force, leach, or reave friendly warbeasts within his control area.

Control Phase (pg. 30): The second phase of a player's turn. During your Control Phase, your warlocks leach fury points from their warbeasts and spend fury points to upkeep their spells, your warbeasts make threshold checks if they have fury remaining on them, and you resolve any other game effects that occur during the Control Phase.

Cover (pg. 46): Some terrain features and special effects grant a model cover by being physically solid enough to block an attack against it. A model within 1" of a covering terrain feature that obscures any portion of its base from an attacker gains +4 DEF against ranged and magic attacks from that opponent. Cover provides no benefit against a spray attack.

Critical Effect (pg. 54): Apply a critical effect on a critical hit. A weapon with a critical effect has the label "Critical" to distinguish it from an automatic damage effect.

Critical Hit (pg. 54): A critical hit occurs if any two dice in an attack roll show the same number and the attack successfully hits.

Damage Circles (pg. 25): Mark one damage circle for each damage point a model suffers. A model is destroyed once all its damage circles are marked.

Damage Capacity (pg. 25): A model's damage capacity determines how many damage points it can take before being destroyed.

Damage Roll (pg. 52): Determine how much damage a successful attack causes by making a damage roll. Roll 2d6 and add the attack's Power (POW). Melee attacks also add the attacker's Strength (STR). Compare this total to the target's Armor (ARM.) The target takes one *damage point* for every point that the damage roll exceeds its ARM.

Damage Transference (pg. 55): Whenever a warlock suffers damage, he may immediately spend a fury point to **transfer** the damage to a friendly faction warbeast in his control area.

Defense (DEF)(pg. 23): A model's ability to avoid being hit by an attack. An attack roll must be equal to or greater than the target model's DEF value to score a hit against it.

Destroyed (pg. 53): A model is destroyed when all of its damage circles are marked. A model without damage circles is destroyed when it suffers one damage point. Remove the destroyed model from the table.

Deviation (pg. 48): When an AOE attack misses its target, determine its actual point of impact by rolling deviation. Referencing the Deviation Diagram, roll a d6 to determine the direction the attack deviates.

Direct Hit (pg. 48): A successful attack roll by an area-of-effect weapon indicates a direct hit on the intended target. Center the weapon's AOE template directly over the model hit. A target hit directly by an AOE weapon suffers a direct hit damage roll of 2d6+POW.

Discard Fury (pg. 58): During his activation, a warlock may remove any number of fury points from himself. A warlock may discard fury even if he runs.

Disengage (pg. 38): A model disengages from melee by moving out of its opponent's melee range. A model disengaging from melee combat is subject to a *free strike* by its opponent.

Double-Handed Throw (pg. 42): A type of power attack. A successful double-hand throw attack allows the attacker to throw the defender directly at another model as a ranged attack.

Elevated Attacker (pg. 46): When drawing line of sight from a model on a higher elevation than its target, ignore all intervening models on lower elevation than the attacking model except those that would normally screen the target. Additionally, you can draw a line of sight through screening models that have equal or smaller-sized bases than the attacking model, but the target still gets +2 DEF for being screened..

Elevated Target (pg. 46): When drawing line of sight from a model on a lower elevation than its target, ignore all intervening models on a lower elevation than the target. A model on higher elevation than its attacker gains +2 DEF against ranged and magic attacks from that opponent. Models on lower elevations than the target do not provide *screening*.

Engaged (pg. 38): If a model is within an enemy model's melee range, it is engaged in combat and primarily concerned with fighting its nearest threat. An engaged model is in melee and cannot make ranged attacks. An engaged model can move freely as long as it stays inside its opponent's melee range.

Engaging (pg. 38): A model automatically engages every enemy model in its melee range. Engaging models are in melee and cannot make ranged attacks.

Facing (pg. 25): A model's facing is the direction indicated by its head's orientation.

Falling (pg. 50): A model slammed, pushed, or that otherwise moves off of an elevated surface greater than 1" tall takes a damage roll and is knocked down. A fall of up to 3" causes a POW 10 damage roll. Add an additional die to the damage roll for every additional increment of 3". Rounded up.

Feat (pg. 24): Each warlock has a unique feat he can use once per game. Unless a warlock runs, he can use this feat freely at any time during his activation in addition to moving and performing an action.

Field Allowance (pg. 27): The maximum number of models or units of a given type that may be included for each warlock in a horde.

First Player (pg. 27): The player that deploys his army first and takes his turn first every game round.

Fleeing (pg. 62): A model or unit that fails a command check against fleeing immediately turns to face directly away from the threat that caused the command check. A fleeing model activates during its controller's maintenance phases. A fleeing model automatically runs away from its nearest threat toward its deployment edge using the most direct route that does not take it through a damaging effect or allow enemies to engage it. A fleeing model cannot perform any actions.

Force (pg. 55): Warlocks are able to *force* their warbeasts to run, charge, perform power attacks, use special abilities, boost combat abilities, or make extra attacks. Each time a warbeast is forced, it gains one or more *fury points*

Forest (pg. 64): A terrain feature that hinders movement and makes a model inside it difficult to see. A forest is considered *rough terrain* but also provides *concealment* to a model with any part of its base inside its perimeter.

Formation (pg. 34): The arrangement of troopers within a unit. There are three different formations: skirmish, open, and tight. Some special rules require that models be in a specific formation to benefit from them.

Free Strike (pg. 38): When a model moves out of an enemy's melee range, the enemy model may immediately make a free strike. The model makes one melee attack with any melee weapon that has sufficient melee range to reach the moving model and gains a +2 bonus to its melee attack roll. If the attack succeeds, add an additional die to the damage roll. The attack and damage rolls of a free strike cannot be boosted.

Frenzy (pg. 58): When a warbeast fails its threshold check, it frenzies. A frenzied warbeast follows special rules for movement and action. Frenzy lasts for one round.

Front Arc (pg. 25): The 180° arc centered on the direction a model's head faces. A model is in another's front arc if any part of its base is in the other model's front arc.

Fury (pg. 23): Warbeasts generate fury by being *forced* to perform certain actions, and warlocks draw from that fury to enhance their won abilities. A warlock's FURY is the maximum amount of fury he can draw from his warbeasts at one time, and a warbeast's FURY represents how much it can be forced.

Fury Stat (FURY) (pg. 23): The maximum number of fury points a warbeast can have on it at any one time and the maximum number of fury points a warlock can have as a result of leaching or reaving. A warlock's FURY determines his control area.

Game Round (pg. 30): A measurement of game time. Each game round, every player takes a turn in the order established during setup. Once the last player in the *turn order* completes his turn, the current game round ends. A new game round then begins, starting again with the first player. Game rounds continue until one side wins the game. See also Round.

Hazard (pg. 65): A terrain feature that causes adverse effects to a model entering it.

Head-butt (pg. 40): A type of power attack. A successful head-butt causes a damage roll and knocks down its target.

Headlock (pg. 39): A type of power attack. A successful headlock prevents the opposing warbeast from using weapons or making power attacks associated with its head.

Healing (pg. 58): A warlock may spend fury points any time during his activation to remove damage from himself or from a friendly warbeast in his control area. Each fury point spent removes one damage point. Damage may be removed from anywhere on a warbeast's *life spiral*.

Heavy Warbeast (pg. 22): Generally, a warbeast with a large (50 mm) base.

Hill (pg. 64): A terrain feature that represents a gentle rise or drop in elevation. A hill may be open or rough terrain, depending on the ground's nature. Unlike obstacles, hills do not impose any additional movement penalties. A model can charge up or down a hill in open terrain at no penalty.

Horde Points (pg. 26): Each encounter level gives the maximum number of horde points each player can spend when designing a horde. A horde cannot exceed the maximum number of horde points allowed by the selected level.

Impassable Terrain (pg. 63): Natural terrain that completely prohibits movement. This includes cliff faces, lava, and deep water. A model cannot move across impassable terrain.

In Formation (pg. 35): The group of troopers in skirmish formation with the unit leader is in formation; other troopers are out of formation. Only troopers that are in formation receive orders. Troopers must begin the game in formation and remain in formation after the unit's movement.

In Melee (pg. 38): A model is in melee if it is engaging an enemy model or if it is engaged by an enemy model. A model in melee cannot make ranged attacks.

Independent Models (pg. 22): An independent model is one that activates individually. Warlocks, warbeasts, and solos are independent models.

Intervening Model (pg. 31): If any line between the bases of two models passes over another model's base, that model is an intervening model. A line of sight cannot be drawn across an intervening model's base to models that have equal or smaller-sized bases. Melee attacks cannot be made across an intervening model's base regardless of its base size.

Intervening Terrain (pg. 39): A model with any portion of its base obscured from its attacker by an obstacle or an obstruction gains a +2 DEF bonus against melee attacks from that opponent.

Jaw: In addition to functioning as a melee weapon, a jaw can be used to perform certain power attacks.

Knocked Down (pg. 50): Mark a knocked-down model with a token. A knocked-down model is stationary until it stands up. It does not count as an intervening model and neither engages other models nor is engaged by them. To stand up, a model must forfeit either its movement or its action for that activation.

Large Base (pg. 25): A 50mm base.

Leaching (pg. 57): The process by which a warlock pulls fury points from friendly warbeasts in his control area.

Leader (pg. 22): Usually, one trooper in a unit is trained as a leader, a model with a different stat profile—and possibly different weaponry—that can rally and issue orders to his troopers in formation. While its leader is in play, a unit uses his CMD stat for all command checks.

Lesser Warbeast (pg. 22): Generally, a warbeast with a small (30 mm) base.

Life Spiral (pg. 25): A warbeast's damage capacity is arranged into a life spiral consisting of six branches. The branches are divided into three aspects: mind, body, and spirit. A warbeast is destroyed when all the damage circles in its life spiral are marked.

Light Warbeast (pg. 22): Generally, a warbeast with a medium (40 mm) base.

Linear Obstacle (pg. 64): An obstacle up to one 1" tall but less than 1" thick. Linear obstacles can be crossed, but models may not stop on top of them.

Line of sight (LOS)(pg. 31): A model has line of sight to a target if you can draw a straight, unobstructed line from the center of its base at head height through its front arc to any part of the target model, including its base.

Living Model (pg. 22): A model is a living model unless stated otherwise. A living model has a soul.

Magic Attack (pg. 59): An attack made by an offensive spell. A magic attack follows all the rules for ranged attacks including targeting, concealment, cover, and all other applicable rules. A warlock can cast spells, including ranged spells, at models with which he is in melee.

Magic Attack Roll (pg. 59): Determine a magic attack's success by making a magic attack roll. Roll 2d6 and add the attacking model's FURY. An attack hits if the attack roll equals or exceeds the target's Defense (DEF).

Maintenance Phase (pg. 30): The first phase of a player's turn. During the Maintenance Phase, remove markers and effects that expire this turn, remove fury points in excess of your warlocks' FURY, and resolve any compulsory effects on your models. Make threshold checks for wild warbeasts and activate *fleeing models* and *units* under your control at the end of this phase.

Massive Casualties (pg. 61): A unit suffers massive casualties when it loses 50% or more of the models in it at the beginning of the current turn. The unit must immediately pass a command check or *flee*.

Medium Base (pg. 25): A 40mm base.

Melee Attack (pg. 38): An attack with a melee weapon. A melee attack can be made against any target in *melee range* of the weapon being used, but it may not be made across an intervening model's base.

Melee Attack (MAT)(pg. 23): A model's skill with melee weapons such as swords and hammers, or natural weapons like fists and teeth. Add a model's MAT value to its *melee attack* rolls.

Melee Attack Roll (pg. 39): Determine a melee attack's success by making a melee attack roll. Roll 2d6 and add the attacking model's Melee Attack (MAT). An attack hits if the attack roll equals or exceeds the target's Defense (DEF).

Melee Range (pg. 38): A model can make melee attacks against any target in melee range. A weapon's melee range extends 1/2" beyond the model's front arc. A reach weapon has a melee range of 2". A model's melee range is the longest melee range of its usable melee weapons.

Melee Weapons (pg. 38): Melee weapons include such implements as swords, hammers, flails, claws, jaws, and axes. A warbeast can also use its body as a melee weapon for attacks such as a head-butt or slam. A melee weapon's damage roll is 2d6+POW+STR.

Mind (pg. 53): One of the aspects of a warbeast's life spiral. When all of the damage circles in a warbeast's Mind are marked, that warbeast rolls one fewer die for its attack rolls.

Model (pg. 22): The highly detailed and dramatically posed miniature figurine that represents a HORDES combatant.

Model Statistic (Stat)(pg. 23): One of the numerical representations of a model's basic combat qualities—the higher the value, the better the stat.

Model Type (pg. 22): One of the categories of models that defines its game function. There are several basic model types: warlock, warbeast, trooper, and solo.

Movement (pg. 32): The first part of a model's activation, also called its *normal movement*. A model must use or forfeit its movement before performing an action. There are three types of movement: advancing, charging, and running.

Obstacle (pg. 64): Any terrain feature up to 1" tall. Obstacles can be climbed.

Obstruction (pg. 64): A terrain feature greater than 1" tall. Treat obstructions as *impassable terrain*.

Offensive Spell (pg. 59): An offensive spell requires a successful magic attack roll to take effect. If the attack roll fails, the attack misses. A failed attack roll for a spell with an area of effect deviates according to those rules.

Open Formation (pg. 35): Troopers up to 1" apart are in open formation. Troopers in open formation are close enough to coordinate attacks and provide each other mutual support.

Open Terrain (pg. 63): Smooth, even ground. Examples include grassy plains, barren fields, dirt roads, and paved surfaces. A model moves across open terrain without penalty.

Orders (pg. 62): An order lets a model or unit perform a specialized combat maneuver during its activation. A unit may receive an order from a model with the Commander ability prior to its activation, or from its *leader* at the beginning of its activation.

Out of Formation (pg. 35): A trooper is out of formation if it is further than 3" from the nearest member of its unit that is in formation. An out of formation trooper must attempt to get back into formation. Out-of-formation troopers cannot receive orders.

Point Cost (pg. 27): A model's point cost indicates how many *horde points* you must spend to include one of these models, or in the case of units, one basic unit, in your horde. Some entries also include options to spend additional points for upgrades, typically in the form of adding more troopers to a unit.

Point of Impact (pg. 48): The point over which an area-of effect attack's template is centered. If the target model suffers a direct hit, center the template over that model. If an area-of-effect attack misses, its point of impact deviates.

Power (POW)(pg. 24): The base amount of damage a weapon inflicts. Add a weapon's POW stat to its damage roll.

Power Attack (pg. 39): A type of special attack useable by warbeasts. A warbeast may use its combat action to make one power attack instead of making any other attacks. A warbeast must be forced to make a power attack. Power attacks cannot be made after a charge.

Power plus Strength (P+S) (pg. 24): A melee weapon adds both the weapon's POW stat and the model's STR stat to the damage roll. For quick reference, the P+S value provides the sum of these two stats.

Push (pg. 40): A type of power attack. A successful push forces the target back 1".

Rally (pg. 62): A fleeing model or unit can make a command check after its mandatory movement if in formation with its leader or in command range of a model with the Commander ability. If it passes the command check, the model or unit rallies and turns to face its nearest opponents. This ends its activation, but it may function normally next turn.

Range (RNG)(pg. 24): The maximum distance in inches a model can make ranged attacks with a specific weapon or spell. Measure range from the nearest edge of the attacking model's base to the nearest edge of the target model's base.

Ranged Attack (pg. 44): An attack with a ranged weapon. A ranged attack can be declared against any target in *line of sight*, subject to the *targeting* rules. A model *in melee*, either engaged or engaging, cannot make ranged attacks.

Ranged Attack (RAT)(pg. 23): A model's accuracy with ranged weapons such as guns and crossbows, or thrown items like grenades and knives. Add a model's RAT value to its ranged attack rolls.

Ranged Attack Roll (pg. 45): Determine a ranged attack's success by making a ranged attack roll. Roll 2d6 and add the attacking model's Ranged Attack (RAT). An attack hits if the attack roll equals or exceeds the target's Defense (DEF).

Ranged Combat (pg. 44): A model is participating in ranged combat if it is making or receiving ranged attacks.

Ranged Weapon (pg. 44): A ranged weapon is one that can make an attack at a distance beyond melee range.

Examples include bows, thrown spears, rifles, crossbows, and harpoon guns. A ranged weapon's damage roll is 2d6+POW.

Rate of Fire (ROF)(pg. 24): The maximum number of ranged attacks a specific weapon can make in an activation. Reloading time limits most ranged weapons to only one attack per activation.

Reach Weapon (pg. 38): A model with a reach weapon has a melee range of 2" for attacks with that weapon. A model that possesses a reach weapon and another melee weapon can *engage* and attack an opponent up to 2" away with its reach weapon, but its other weapons can only be used to attack models within its normal 1/2" melee range.

Reave (pg. 58): When a friendly warbeast is destroyed within a warlock's control area, that warlock may reave its fury. Transfer all of the destroyed warbeast's fury points to the warlock and discard any in excess of the warlock's FURY stat.

Remove from Play (pg. 53): Occasionally models will be outright removed from play, sometimes instead of being destroyed, at other times in addition to being destroyed. A model removed from play cannot return to the table for any reason.

Rend (pg. 40): A type of power attack. A successful rend attack causes nearby units friendly to the target to pass a command check or flee.

Rile (pg. 57): When a warlock forces a warbeast for the sole purpose of generating fury.

Rough Terrain (pg. 63): Terrain that can be traversed, but at a significantly slower pace than open terrain. Examples include thick brush, forests, rocky areas, murky bogs, shallow water, and deep snow. So long as any part of its base is in rough terrain, a model moves at 1/2 normal movement rate. Therefore, a model in rough terrain actually moves only 1/2" for every 1" of its movement used.

Round (pg. 30): A measure of duration for many game effects. A round is measured from the current player's turn to the beginning of that player's next turn regardless of his location in the turn order. Also see Game Round.

Run (pg. 33): A running model may move up to twice its SPD in inches. A model that runs cannot perform an action, cast spells, use its animus, or use its *feat* this activation. A running model's activation ends at the completion of its movement.

Scenario (pg. 28): A game with specific setup instructions and victory conditions.

Screening Model (pg. 31): A screening model is an intervening model that has an equal or larger-sized base than the target model and is within 1" of it. The target model is *screened* by a screening model and receives a +2 DEF bonus against ranged and magic attacks.

Skirmish Formation (pg. 35): The default and most flexible formation which lets troopers be up to 3" apart. The group of troopers in skirmish formation with the unit's leader is *in formation.*

Slam (pg. 40): A type of power attack that combines a model's movement and combat action to make a slam attack.

Slam Attack (pg. 41): A warbeast that attempts a slam and ends its movement within 1/2" of its intended target makes a slam attack if it moved at least 3". A slam attack roll suffers a –2 penalty against a target with an equal- or smaller-sized base, or a –4 penalty against a target with a larger base. If the slam attack hits, the target gets propelled directly away from its attacker, knocked down, and takes damage.

Slam Damage (pg. 41): Determine slam damage after moving the slammed model. A slam's damage roll is 2d6 plus a POW equal to the attacking warbeast's STR. Add an additional die to the damage roll if the slammed model contacts an obstacle, obstruction, or a model that has an equal or larger-sized base. Slam damage can be *boosted.* The slammed model is also knocked down.

Small Base (pg. 25): A 30mm base.

Solo (pg. 22): An independent warrior model that operates alone.

Soul Token (pg. 52): Certain models can claim a model's soul, represented by a soul token, when it is destroyed. Only living models provide soul tokens. A model only has one soul. If more than one model is eligible to claim its soul, the model nearest the destroyed model receives the token. Refer to a model's special rules for how it utilizes soul tokens.

Special Action (★Action)(pg. 25): A special action lets a model perform an action normally unavailable to other models. A model can perform a special action instead of its combat action if it meets the specific requirements for its use. Unless otherwise noted, a model can perform a special action only after advancing or forfeiting its movement. A special action's description details its requirements and results.

Special Attack (★Attack)(pg. 25): A special attack gives a model an attack option normally unavailable to other models. Warbeasts can also make a variety of punishing power attacks. A model may make one special attack instead of making any normal melee or ranged attacks during its combat action if it meets the specific requirements for its use.

Special Effect (pg. 53): Many attacks cause special effects in addition to causing damage. There are four categories of effects: automatic effects, critical effects, continuous effects, and cloud effects.

Special Rules (pg. 24): Unique rules pertaining to a model or its weapons which take precedence over the standard rules. Depending on their use, special rules are categorized as abilities, feats, special actions, special attacks, or orders.

Speed (SPD) (pg. 23): A model's normal movement rate. A model moves its SPD stat in inches when *advancing.*

Spirit (pg. 53): One of the aspects of a warbeast's life spiral. When all of the damage circles in a warbeast's Spirit are marked, that warbeast can no longer be forced.

Spray Attack (pg. 49): An attack from a weapon that uses the spray template. Such weapons have a range of "SP" in their weapon profiles.

Starting Roll (pg. 27): The die roll made at the beginning of a game to establish setup and turn order.

Stat (pg. 23): Short for statistic. Used in reference to model or weapon statistics.

Stat Bar (pg. 23): The stat bar presents model and weapon statistics in an easy-to-reference format.

Stat Card (pg. 23): A model or unit's stat card provides a quick in-game reference for its profile and special rules.

Stationary (pg. 50): A stationary target is an inanimate object or a model that has been *knocked down* or immobilized. A stationary target cannot move, perform actions, cast spells, use feats, give orders, engage other models, be forced, or make attacks. Stationary targets are not engaged by other models. A melee attack against a stationary target automatically hits. A stationary target has a base Defense (DEF) of 5 against ranged and magic attacks.

Strength (STR)(pg. 23): A model's physical strength. Add a model's STR value to the *damage roll* of its melee weapons.

Structure (pg. 65): Any large terrain feature that can be damaged and destroyed.

Terrain (pg. 63): The type of ground: open, rough, or impassible.

Terrain Feature (pg. 64): A natural or man-made object on the battlefield.

Terrifying Entity (pg. 61): A terrifying entity is one with either the *terror* or *abomination* special ability. A model in *melee range* of an enemy that causes terror, a model/unit with an enemy model that causes terror in its melee range, or a model/unit within 3" of an abomination—friendly or